P9-CER-954

Social Dance

Steps to Success

Second Edition

Judy Patterson Wright, PhD

Human Kinetics

Library of Congress Cataloging-in-Publication Data

Wright, Judy Patterson, 1946-
    Social dance : steps to success, 2nd ed. / Judy Patterson Wright.--
        p. cm.
    ISBN 0-7360-4505-8 (soft cover)
    1.   Ballroom dancing--Study and teaching.   I. Wright, Judy Patterson,
1946- Social dance instruction. II. Title.
    GV1753.5 .W75 2003
    793.3'3--dc21

                                                                                        2002010840

ISBN: 0-7360-4505-8

Copyright © 2003 by Human Kinetics Publishers, Inc.
Copyright © 1992 by Leisure Press

All rights reserved. Except for use in a review, the reproduction or utilization of this work in any form or by any electronic, mechanical, or other means, now known or hereafter invented, including xerography, photocopying, and recording, and in any information storage and retrieval system, is forbidden without the written permission of the publisher.

Developmental Editor: Leigh LaHood; **Copyeditor:** Barbara Field; **Proofreader:** Coree Schutter; **Graphic Designer:** Keith Blomberg; **Graphic Artist:** Tara Welsch; **Cover Designer:** Keith Blomberg; **Photographer (cover):** Leslie A. Woodrum; **Art Manager:** Carl D. Johnson; **Line Drawings:** Dick Flood; **Mac Art:** Roberto Sabas; **Printer:** United Graphics

Human Kinetics books are available at special discounts for bulk purchase. Special editions or book excerpts can also be created to specification. For details, contact the Special Sales Manager at Human Kinetics.

Printed in the United States of America   10   9   8   7   6   5   4   3   2   1

Human Kinetics
Web site: www.HumanKinetics.com

United States: Human Kinetics
P.O. Box 5076
Champaign, IL 61825-5076
800-747-4457
e-mail: humank@hkusa.com

Canada: Human Kinetics
475 Devonshire Road Unit 100
Windsor, ON N8Y 2L5
800-465-7301 (in Canada only)
e-mail: orders@hkcanada.com

Europe: Human Kinetics
107 Bradford Road
Stanningley
Leeds LS28 6AT, United Kingdom
+44 (0) 113 255 5665
e-mail: hk@hkeurope.com

Australia: Human Kinetics
57A Price Avenue
Lower Mitcham, South Australia 5062
08 8277 1555
e-mail: liahka@senet.com.au

New Zealand: Human Kinetics
P.O. Box 105-231
Auckland Central
09-523-3462
e-mail: hkp@ihug.co.nz

CONTENTS

PREFACE

Social dancing can be a lifelong endeavor that offers many rewards and challenges. This book will help you get started with the basics. It is written for beginning social dancers who want to know how to do partner dances in recreational (rather than competitive) dance settings, and for those dancers who want the challenge of going beyond the traditional "packaged" dance steps. The basics presented in this book follow more closely the American styling at the bronze level (which is the first of three levels: bronze, silver, and gold). American styling is more popular on the social dance floor and will permit you to exchange with multiple partners wherever you might go to dance socially. It also offers more freedom in partner positions as both closed and open (or apart) partner positions may be used. In contrast, International styling permits only a closed dance position.

The purpose of this book is to simplify for beginning social dancers what is usually perceived to be a complex, difficult process. My experience with traditional methods of teaching social or ballroom dance, and my research on the process of acquiring sequential skills, motivated me to produce a course with a different approach. The uniqueness of this approach to learning social dance is its complete learning progression, which places skills and concepts along a continuum with uniquely designed practice drills for each learning step. Each learning step gradually builds in the necessary experiences you need to prepare you for the final outcome—to be able to dance with a partner to music on a crowded social dance floor.

In the second edition of *Social Dance: Steps to Success*, the sequence of learning steps has been (a) updated to reflect current terminology, (b) expanded to more clearly show the basic progression for learning a new dance, and (c) broadened to expand the number of dances covered. In particular, three popular Latin dances have been added. This second edition of *Social Dance: Steps to Success* provides clear guidelines on how to do eight different ballroom dances:

- Foxtrot
- Swing—including three different basics to fit three different tempos
- Waltz
- Polka
- Cha-cha
- Rumba
- Tango
- Salsa/mambo

The overall progression will help you understand how the basic step patterns are derived from everyday locomotor movements, how they are typically combined to create a repeatable rhythmic pattern, and how to fit the basic step pattern to the music. Once you know the basic step pattern(s) for a particular dance, you need to know the basic partner positions and how to transition efficiently from one partner position to another. The next challenge is learning variations of the basic step pattern(s) and identifying which variations combine together naturally. Once you have a repertoire of variations, the next challenge is to be able to spontaneously adjust your combinations according to the flow of traffic encountered on the dance floor. The final challenge is to create your own basic step patterns, combinations, sequences, and/or routines.

This second edition has expanded the number of sequential illustrations to show proper footwork, technique, and positioning with a partner. The Keys to Success for each basic step pattern detail those important footwork and timing cues that you may select from to help you both retain and recall relevant information. Each learning step includes drills that are ordered from easy to difficult, including options for increasing or decreasing the difficulty level of each drill—so that you can practice at your preferred learning pace.

A special feature of this second edition is the compact disc (CD) bound in the book. It offers not only practice music for all eight dances covered, but also training to help you hear and identify the beat, measure, phrase, tempo, and so forth. Very few classes have time to cover music structure and teach dance basics. Thus, this CD and its companion drills (see Step 2) will be invaluable, especially if you have not had much music experience such as playing an instrument or doing activities to music. If you have, you can move on to the next learning step; again, the goal is to self-pace your progress through the 16 learning steps in this book.

There are two ways that you might use this book. The ideal procedure is to read the introductory sections, then follow the learning steps (chapters) in the order presented. However, an alternative with the learning steps, especially if you have an interest in a particular dance, or dances, is to complete Steps 1-5, select specific dances from Steps 6-13, and finish with Steps 14-16 in order to be more comfortable on the social dance floor, to hone your technique, and to follow up with additional opportunities to get out social dancing! At the end of the book there is a glossary and a rating chart that you can use to assess your progress and target future goals. Whichever way you progress through this book, you'll soon find yourself pleasantly surrounded by others, enjoying their company, being challenged, and improving your fitness—all at the same time.

ACKNOWLEDGMENTS

I wish to acknowledge the contributions of my many hundreds of students, who taught me as much as I taught them. My constant goal is to create independent thinkers on the dance floor. It is rewarding to see students enjoying and expressing themselves on the floor. I am grateful for the opportunity to update my methods in this second edition. I want to thank Leigh LaHood, my developmental editor, for her insightful suggestions and constant guidance through the publishing process. I appreciate the time spent posing for the photographs used for the illustrations in this book by my models, Robert King, Jennie King, Valerie Hall, Brad Colson, Rosalva Torres, Tim Gallivan, Sam Wright, Leigh Gordon, and Mike Lockwood. I also thank Roger Francisco and Gordon Wilson for the original music used on the CD.

I especially want to thank my husband, Sam, for being my partner in life as well as on the dance floor—he is definitely my "Mr. Right." Lastly, I dedicate this book to my mother and late father, who have always supported me and encouraged me to be the best that I can be.

Key

CW = Clockwise

CCW = Counterclockwise

I = Instructor

LOD = Line of direction

L = Left

R = Right

O = Follower

O.F. = Original front

X = Leader

⟶ = Direction of movement

= Follower's footwork (right foot shaded)

= Leader's footwork (right foot shaded)

= Foot prepares to move

= Weight on ball of foot

= No weight on ball of foot

THE STEPS TO SUCCESS STAIRCASE

Get ready to climb a staircase—one that will lead you to become an accomplished social dancer. You cannot leap to the top; you need to get there by climbing one step at a time.

Each of the 16 steps you will take is an easy transition from the one before. The first few steps of the staircase provide a solid foundation of basic skills and concepts that are prerequisites to executing the basic steps. The concepts in Step 1 will help you understand how to move like a dancer, including the importance of posture, centering your body's weight over your base of support for balance, and positioning arms to create a frame. The concepts in Step 2 will help you to identify the more reliable (as well as the more unreliable) cues in the music and to understand how the music's structure can help you know what type of dance music is being played. The concepts in Step 3 will help you to connect your footwork to the tempo of the music, which sometimes is called a coincidence anticipation task (or being able to walk to an auditory cadence). The concepts in Step 4 introduce you to the general partner dynamics that occur in social dancing, both verbal and nonverbal, including general leading and following tips, basic partner positions, proper etiquette, and partner respect.

Step 5 prepares you for the progressions used within each specific dance style (shown in Steps 6-13). After a brief history, the basic step pattern is introduced, including rhythm, footwork cues, and timing cues (for both the leader and the follower). Easy-to-difficult drills provide practice experiences for understanding how to use transitions, add selected variations, combine variations, and review the options per dance in a summary chart in the last drill. Each dance included has a characteristic styling that needs to be added once the basic step pattern can be executed without much thought. After completing these learning steps, you will be more confident in your ability to execute eight different dances: foxtrot, swing, waltz, polka, cha-cha, rumba, tango, and salsa/mambo.

Step 14 will help you make the transition from practice to the social dance floor. It is helpful to be aware of the "rules of the road" that vary according to the dance style and music being played. Demonstrating good floor craft is part of the dance floor etiquette needed to avoid collisions with others. Thus, specifically designed drills will prepare you for the spontaneous decisions needed on the social dance floor.

As you near the top of the staircase, you can hone your turning technique with the concepts in Step 15. Then, Step 16 introduces you to some of the additional situations that you might encounter, which may require some modifications to your dancing. These include dancing to unfamiliar music, needing to adjust to different tempos, moving within restricted spaces, and creating or modifying basic step patterns, or variations, or combinations. The drills challenge you to do some problem solving as well as expand your opportunities to do more social dancing.

Familiarize yourself with this section as well as the "Why Social Dance?" section for an orientation and to understand how to set up your practice sessions around the learning steps.

Follow the same sequence of procedures for each learning step:

1. Read the explanations of what is covered, why it is important, and how to perform or apply the items focused on in the particular step, which may be a concept, a skill, a variation, a combination, or other options.

2. Follow the Keys to Success illustrations showing (like a demonstration) exactly how to position your body to execute successfully. Within Steps 6-13, there are two parts to the Keys to Success, including a variety of footwork cues and timing cues. You will need to select the cues that work the best for your learning style.

3. Where appropriate, become aware of the common errors that may occur and the recommendations for how to correct them.

4. Try the drills in order to help you improve your skills through repetition and purposeful practice. Use the Success Goal, the Success Checks, and suggestions (when appropriate) for either increasing or decreasing the difficulty level of the drill to self-pace your progress. Because the drills are ordered easy-to-difficult, you need to meet the Success Goal of each drill before moving on to the next drill. The drills are designed to give you successful experiences that prepare you for the next challenge.

5. After completing all of the drills in a learning step, you are ready to ask a trained observer, such as your teacher, coach, or trained partner, to evaluate not only your basic skill execution, but also your ability to demonstrate the appropriate styling.

6. Repeat these procedures with each of the 16 Steps to Success (learning steps) in this book. Then, rate yourself according to the directions in the "Rating Your Progress" section at the end of this book. Refer to the glossary, as necessary, at the end of this book as well.

Good luck on your step-by-step journey to developing your social dancing skills, building confidence, experiencing success, and having fun—see you on the dance floor!

WHY SOCIAL DANCE?

Looking for a way to meet new people and expand your social skills? Or perhaps you are looking for an alternative way to exercise and have fun at the same time. Try social dancing! Not only can you learn new skills, have an evening out, and share common interests, but you'll also receive both mental and physical benefits.

Social Needs

Throughout history, our social needs have been reflected in our dance forms. These social needs were first displayed in primitive courtship and tribal dances. Although primitive dances were often performed by members of the same sex with no bodily contact, social dance is essentially touch dancing and includes all forms of partner dancing done primarily for recreation or pleasure to a variety of musical styles.

The sometimes synonymously used term *ballroom dance* refers to partner dances done in a ballroom to traditional ballroom music. The earliest eighteenth- and nineteenth-century forms of ballroom dance were the minuet in France, the quadrille (a two-, four-, or more, couple dance) in France and England, the waltz in Austria, and the polka in France. It became fashionable during the Renaissance for ladies and gentlemen of the court to dress well and have polished manners. Soon, competition to outdo others led to elaborate balls and the hiring of dance masters to teach peasant dances to the aristocracy.

Additional partner dances done for pleasure and recreation were introduced early in the twentieth century, including the foxtrot, swing, tango, samba, rumba, and cha-cha. After World War II, traditional ballroom dancing and Big Band music went into a decline, but partner dancing continued in popularity throughout the rock-and-roll era and was perpetuated by the romantic disco era. Various movies featuring couples dancing reenergized interest in disco, country western, swing, Latin, club, and Big Band, or ballroom dancing. Although across time the categories of dancing may change, couples dancing continues to be popular—mainly due to the attractive benefits of social dancing.

Benefits of Social Dance

The foremost reason for participating in partner or touch dancing is the sheer joy of moving rhythmically in unison with a partner to music—regardless of your age. Being with a partner not only enhances the pleasure, but also highlights the social benefits, of meeting others (sometimes with romance in mind). Many married couples have first met on the dance floor—including my husband and me! Through dancing, partners can share common interests, learn to respect each other's rights, and show appreciation for each other's efforts.

An added benefit of ballroom dancing is being in pleasant, unstressful surroundings (large ballrooms) that emphasize proper etiquette and attire, which can be mentally refreshing. Listening to music is often very relaxing. Even if you are not dancing in a ballroom, you can be more in touch with your body and partner (be in the present) and, thus, less likely to worry about day-to-day events (either past or future).

A third major benefit of participating in partner dancing is the low-impact aerobic workout you receive by dancing continuously. Partner dancing is a great way to blend exercise and recreation because you can raise your heart rate up to 60 to 70 percent of its maximum, which boosts stamina safely. All you have to do to achieve aerobic benefit is gradually increase the amount of time you dance continuously. Start by dancing the length of one song, and gradually add more time until you are dancing 15 to 60 minutes nonstop, three times per week. Social dancing can add elegance to exercise! For many dancers, dancing is becoming the preferred way to be more active and improve fitness.

Lastly, you can experience great personal satisfaction from your accomplishments in dancing—including improved posture, coordination, balance, precision, timing, and concentration. Additional satisfaction comes from knowing how to ask a partner to dance (or how to accept a dance), how to lead (or follow), and how to adapt your variations to fit the traffic flow of other couples.

Social Dance Today

Numerous opportunities exist for recreational dancing. These include proms, cotillions, military balls, wedding receptions, and dances sponsored by schools, universities, colleges, parks, clubs, communities, and dance studios.

If you have the interest, you may also opt to dance on a competitive level. Competition may range from performing for yourself or others (the drills in Step 16 will help you explore some of these possibilities). Another performing option is to create a dance formation team—a group of two or more couples who constantly move from one formation to another (as does a marching band) as they dance.

Lastly, the United States Amateur Ballroom Dancers Association (USABDA)—a nonprofit organization—also promotes the physical, mental, and social benefits of ballroom dancing as a lifetime activity. USABDA supports both recreational ballroom dancing and DanceSport, the competitive form of ballroom dancing expected soon to become an Olympic event. Try to watch the annual ballroom championships aired on PBS. After you finish this book, you will certainly be more appreciative of these dancers' stamina and expertise. For information on USABDA membership and additional dance opportunities, go to **www.usabda.org** to locate a USABDA chapter in your area. Perhaps social dancing will bring excitement, challenge, romance, social interaction, and health benefits into your life, too!

STEP 1

POSTURE, CENTERING, AND FRAME:
MOVING LIKE A DANCER

When you watch couples on a crowded dance floor, which ones get your attention first? Most of us are drawn to those couples who move with confidence and have regal stature. Whether you're on or off the dance floor, your posture speaks volumes about you to others. Check yourself now. How are you sitting or standing? Are you slumped forward or leaning back? Are your feet flat on the floor? Is your lower back straight or excessively arched? Are you standing with your weight all on one leg? Are you looking at the floor? Are your arms hanging at your sides? In other words, are you demonstrating a balanced posture?

The purpose of Step 1 is to increase your awareness of correct body posture, which is called alignment when you are standing or carriage when you are moving. You'll also learn how to place your body's center of gravity over your base of support (understand the concept of centering) and where to place your arms (understand the concept of individual frame).

Why Are the Concepts of Posture, Centering, and Frame Important?

Your body is your instrument of expression. By dressing neatly and maintaining proper body alignment, you give the world the impression that you feel good about yourself. Proper body alignment allows you to use your muscles most efficiently, with the least amount of effort or extra muscular tension. Your standing posture is the standard to which you add the various dance stylings, or characteristics, that commonly describe particular dances. It is critical to

correct any deviations in standing posture, because they will be magnified tenfold when you move. Good dancers move with purpose and confidence, which is reflected in their posture.

The concept of centering helps you to be aware of where your center of gravity is located so that you can lift it (to capture the illusion of ease that is characteristic of good dancers) and to transfer your weight efficiently from one foot to the other. Centering is important in maintaining balance and being able to move smoothly and effortlessly as a dancer. Good dancers make it look easy.

Frame refers to the shape or positioning of your body, including your arms. You'll have better balance if your body's weight is above your base (in vertical alignment) and if you curve your arms in front of you with your elbows slightly away from the sides of your body. Positioning your arms is important whether you are dancing alone (for balance and appearance) or with a partner (for defining your half of the space between you and your partner).

Posture

Correct posture is usually thought to be somewhat like the weather: Everyone talks about it, but what can you do about it? You, too, may have fallen into the habit of taking posture for granted. However, now is the time to check your posture. Visualization techniques are particularly effective ways to learn how to align your body correctly. Try both of the following images. Which one helps you visualize proper vertical alignment? Perhaps other images come to mind.

First, stand with your hands at your sides, with your feet no more than shoulder-width apart and your knees slightly bent. As if you are balancing large blocks on top of one another, position your hips, shoulders, and head directly above your feet. Look forward with your head erect (it is helpful to look at an object that is at eye level). Think of both shoulders being pulled down and back, which brings your shoulder blades closer together. Contract your abdominals and lengthen (rather than arch) your lower back. You are now in proper standing alignment.

Another way to check your alignment is to imagine a plumb line (a string suspended from the ceiling with a weight on it) hanging at your side. Adjust your posture so that your ear, shoulder, hip, knee, and ankle align with the string. Again, check that your shoulders are back, your abdominals are firm, and your lower back is long (not curved sharply or hyperextended). Figure 1.1 shows the proper standing alignment with your hips level.

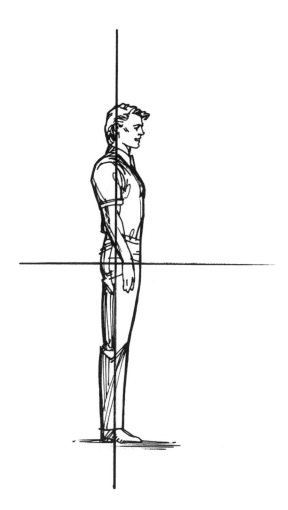

Figure 1.1 Proper vertical alignment when standing with hips and eyes level.

Centering

Once you can align your hips, shoulders, and head over your base of support (your feet), you need to become aware of where your center of gravity is located. It is a three-dimensional point near the center of your body where your body's weight is equally divided (i.e., half of your weight is above and half is below this point). Typically, the equal division of one's body mass is located a bit higher in males (i.e., at or slightly above the waist) than in females (i.e., at or slightly below the waist). However, in dance, a more universal term, *center point of balance*, or CPB, is often used to refer to a point just below your diaphragm. You can feel this point by making a fist and placing it at the base of your breastbone where your ribs start to separate. The advantage of the CPB is that it is slightly higher than your center of gravity. Take a deep breath from your diaphragm/abdomen and imagine your weight being lifted above your center of gravity. As your CPB is located in the center of your upper torso, you can easily move, or shift, your rib cage approximately five inches in any direction before losing your balance or having to take a step in the direction you shifted your weight. Dancers soon find that where their CPB goes, their feet will follow.

When you dance, your weight is rarely equally divided over both feet. It is more common to align or center your body's weight alternately over one foot, then the other. Stand with your feet a few inches apart. Shift your weight from both feet onto only one foot. Imagine that you are a puppet being suspended from a series of strings held high above your head. In particular, imagine an invisible vertical string lifting you from the inside of your ankle, the inside of your hip bone, the inside of your ear, and upward. From a front view, this line is just a few inches to either side of your body's vertical midline (see figure 1.2) and your CPB (which will shift toward the direction of your weight shift).

Frame

A typical question in dance is "Where do I put my arms?" The narrower your base of support, the more important it is to lift your arms and to look at a point in space that is at eye level—like a tightrope walker! However, it is not necessary to extend your arms out horizontally to mimic the tightrope walker. Rather,

your body. This position should be curved versus angular and is called your individual *frame* (see figure 1.3). Later, you will be connecting your frame with a partner's frame to dance in various partner positions.

Figure 1.2 Your image of vertical and center shifts slightly toward either side of your body when shifting weight from two feet to one foot.

Figure 1.3 Individual frame improves both balance and appearance.

you can improve both your balance and appearance if you curve your elbows, lift them slightly away from the sides of your body, and keep them in front of

POSTURE, CENTERING, AND FRAME SUCCESS STOPPERS

Start to become aware of your posture as you move throughout the day. Any alignment errors in standing posture are greatly magnified when you move, which will detract from your dance styling. These problems usually fade once you are able to align properly without conscious effort and have memorized

the basic step patterns. Making a postural change will require frequent and daily self-reminders for almost six months. Select only one error to correct at a time, and be persistent—you can succeed! Following are typical alignment, centering, and frame errors and corrections.

Error	Correction
Alignment	

1. Head is forward with eyes focused downward.

1. Even good dancers make mistakes. However, they do not telegraph their errors by looking at their feet. Try to focus on a point that is at your eye level, such that an imaginary line from your eyes to that point would be parallel to the floor (review figure 1.1). You can pick out a specific crack or line on the wall in front of you, or if necessary, place a piece of tape on the wall at your eye level. Notice that your spot corresponds to your height. Later, your spot will change depending on where you are on the dance floor and whether or not you are turning.

2. Lower back is curved too much, with hips and abdomen forward.

2. You need to increase your lower back flexibility as well as strengthen your abdominal muscles. Both problems can be corrected by doing exercises at home, lying on your back with your knees bent, feet flat on the floor, and arms at your sides. For flexibility, try a pelvic tilt. Concentrate on contracting your abdominal muscles, tilting your pelvis to gently press your lower back to the floor; hold the contraction for 10 to 30 seconds. For increasing your abdominal strength, try a curl-up. Fold your arms across your chest, inhale, tuck your chin, contract your abdominal muscles, and slowly curl forward to lift your shoulders off the floor. As you uncurl and lower your shoulders, gently press each vertebra down into the floor as you exhale. Repeat until you can do 8 to 25 repetitions.

3. Shoulders are rounded and forward of center.	3. Gently lift both shoulders up toward your ears, then circle them backward and downward. Repeat this a few times and become aware of bringing your shoulder blades closer together. You can also look in a mirror, using a side view, and check yourself to see whether your shoulders are rounded or back where they belong.
4. You are unable to balance on one foot.	4. Stand with your feet approximately shoulder-width apart and your weight on both feet. When you shift your weight onto any one foot (as when taking a step), be aware of a subtle shift of vertical from a midline position to the inside of your standing foot, approximately one to two inches in the direction that your weight shifts (review figure 1.2). Also notice where your arms are positioned and where your eyes are focused. Lifting your arms slightly and looking forward at a location at approximately eye level will also help improve your balance.

Error	Correction
Centering	
1. Body weight (CPB) is either back on heels or forward on toes. 	1. Move your torso (CPB) forward over the balls of your feet. This is similar to a ready position in sports. You'll need to move your CPB continuously over your base of support and onto the ball of each foot on each walking step.

Error	Correction
2. You have difficulty moving along diagonal directions.	2. Prior to taking a step in any diagonal direction, either start facing the diagonal (with either your front or back) or rotate your upper torso approximately 45 degrees to position your shoulders perpendicular to the intended diagonal direction (with either your front or back).

Error	Correction
Frame	
1. Arms hang or dangle at your sides.	1. Hold your arms in a curved position in front of your body to improve both your balance and your appearance (review figure 1.3). Avoid letting gravity take over.
2. You have limp or "spaghetti" arms when dancing with a partner.	2. Maintain a curved position with your elbows in front of your body. For example, when facing your partner in a two-hands-joined position, don't let your partner push your hands into your half of the space between you or let your elbows be pushed backward, beyond the sides of your body. If so, you've let your partner invade your half of the shared space.
3. Shoulders are raised along with arms.	3. Deliberately tense and raise your shoulders toward your ears, then circle your shoulders back and let them drop, or relax, with your scapulae wide and flat. Let only your arms lift for balance.

POSTURE, CENTERING, AND FRAME

DRILLS

1. Moving From Your Center

What part of your body moves first when you take a step forward? Some people might guess that it is their foot or their knee. This drill will help you discover the answer. Stand with your back to a wall and demonstrate good posture. Make sure that your heels, hips, shoulders, and the back of your head all touch the wall. Try to widen your shoulder blades so that they also touch the wall. Let your back curve naturally such that you could put your hand between the wall and the small of your back. Now try to take a step with either foot to move away from the wall. Notice what part of your body moves away from the wall first. Then continue walking at least four steps forward and notice what happens.

Success Goal = 10 repetitions of maintaining vertical alignment while taking a step forward (a) starting with your back to a wall and (b) on each walking step forward thereafter___

Success Check
- Imagine your body parts either as a series of blocks that align properly or as connected by a plumb line that passes through your ear, shoulder, hip, knee, and ankle___
- Keep your eyes focused on a point that is at eye level___
- Only your upper body (center, or CPB) moves at first when taking a step forward. Notice how your upper torso moves forward away from the wall as your body's weight shifts forward—all before you can even bend a knee or lift a foot___

2. Center Leads, Feet Follow

Review figure 1.1 to get a mental image of correct standing alignment. Start in a balanced stance, your feet approximately shoulder-width apart, and with good posture. Deliberately shift your CPB slightly beyond your base of support (your feet), and catch yourself before you actually fall (by stepping in the direction that you shifted your CPB). Experiment with shifting your CPB in eight different directions: forward, backward, right side, left side, diagonal left and right (forward and backward). In each case, notice how your torso (CPB) initiates the action in the intended direction. Each time, continue to walk at least four steps in the intended direction.

As a further challenge, what happens to your CPB when you need to reverse direction? For example, experiment with four walks forward, then four walks backward. Then combine any two opposite directions.

Success Goals = four walking steps in each of eight possible directions, then combine any two opposite directions using smooth transitions during the direction changes___

Success Check

- Notice that your CPB (torso) moves first regardless of which direction you move in___
- To reverse direction smoothly, slightly bend your knees prior to taking the last step in the intended direction, and don't continue to shift your CPB on that last step (that is, if walking forward, don't continue forward on the last step). Rather, keep your CPB between both feet, then reverse direction (i.e., to walk backward)___

3. Balance Test

Stand in proper alignment with your weight balanced over both feet. Review figure 1.1 (page 2), then position your arms for better balance. It may be helpful to stand next to a chair in case you need to support yourself. Shift your weight onto one foot (review figure 1.2). Keep your eyes focused on a spot at approximately eye level. Imagine a plumb line starting from the inside of your ankle and extending upward vertically. Notice that your CPB has shifted approximately one to two inches from center toward the leg you are standing on. Take a deep breath from your diaphragm and feel the air underneath your arms. Imagine the air enveloping your rib cage and gently supporting you (with CPB lifted). Gradually lift the heel of your standing foot off the floor. The higher you lift your heel, the more your CPB is shifted forward over the ball of your foot. Hold this position as long as you can. If you lift your heel too far off the floor, your CPB will go beyond your base of support and you will lose your balance. If so, just catch yourself by taking a step. Repeat this balance test with your opposite foot.

Success Goal = 5 to 30 seconds in balance while on one foot, then repeat on the other foot___

Success Check

- Improving your balance takes mental concentration and practice, as your CPB is a three-dimensional point___
- Follow the sequence described previously until all the components merge effortlessly___

4. Moving Within Your Frame

There are two fun ways to get the feel of how your arms can be a frame. Both require isolating either the upper or lower part of your body. These isolations will become useful when you start leading and following.

a. *Lower body isolation:* Stand in front of a wall. Position both hands in front of your shoulders, palms forward, then place them against the wall for support. Move closer to the wall until you can press your weight into your palms to keep your upper torso stationary. Stand with your feet together. With your CPB lifted, swivel, or twist, your lower body by lifting both heels off the floor, keeping your weight on the balls of both feet.

b. *Upper body isolation:* Move away from the wall. Stand with your feet approximately shoulder-width apart. Lift your arms in front of your chest and make a circle with your middle fingers touching. Lower your hands slightly so they are in front of your CPB. Imagine that there is a string connecting your CPB with your fingertips. Twist your upper torso from your waist such that the string remains taut as you rotate your entire upper body as far as you can to one side, then the other side.

Success Goal = 60 seconds of alternately twisting only the lower half of your body, then only the upper half of your body___

Success Check
• Twist, or rotate, from your waist___
• Let your frame move with your upper body twists, then keep it stationary during your lower body twists___

5. Movement Awareness

There is a reciprocal relationship between your mind and your body. Before you begin to dance, you need to get into the proper frame of mind and body. This means forgetting about those everyday tasks that need to be done and the problems that need to be solved. Think of temporarily shutting a door to the rest of your world, and enjoy the present. One way to do this is to become more aware of how you are moving.

In social dance, there are two contrasting movement qualities that can dramatically affect how you execute various dances: sustained and percussive. Sustained movements are continuous throughout, without any obvious starting or stopping points. In contrast, percussive movements both start and stop very sharply. Generally, these movement qualities are characteristic of the styling used with smooth dances versus Latin dances, respectively.

For practice, select a consistent pace and walk forward eight steps, then backward eight steps. How smoothly can you walk such that your movements have no obvious starting or stopping points? As you walk, pace each step evenly as you continue to bring your free leg alongside, then move it forward for the next step—without any obvious starting or stopping points. Sustained movements need control in order to be gradual throughout.

For contrast, repeat this walking combination, except quickly take a step and touch the inside edge of the ball of your free foot beside your standing foot. To do this, you'll need to change the styling to be more staccato, or do a step and hold or freeze. A karate kick is an example of a percussive movement. When walking, think of quickly taking a step, then quickly touching your free foot and freezing the position briefly before initiating another step. Percussive movements need control to initate and abruptly stop the movement flow.

Success Goal = 60 seconds of alternately contrasting sustained and percussive movement qualities___

Success Check

- Sustained movements have more continuous flow without obvious starting or stopping___
- Percussive movements both start and stop very sharply___
- As you walk along a straight line, place each foot either beside or no more than one or two inches to either side of the line___

POSTURE, CENTERING, AND FRAME SUCCESS SUMMARY

Proper body alignment and carriage create an impression—literally an image for others that can either enhance or detract from your performance. It is important to have your posture evaluated by your teacher or another trained observer, both when you are standing and when you are moving. Stand sideways in your best posture and ask your evaluator to place a check mark by each item from figure 1.1 that is observed. Walk eight steps forward, then eight steps backward, and ask your evaluator to evaluate your posture and how well you use your center point of balance and frame for effective balance during direction changes.

Do you have any postural deviations? If so, begin a daily self-check of your postural alignment—which may need to be repeated up to 30 times a day—until you have a strong mental image of vertical alignment. With practice, your posture, carriage, and individual frame will become more automatic.

STEP 2

MUSIC STRUCTURE: HEARING RELIABLE CUES IN THE MUSIC

A frequently asked question is "How do I know when to start moving with the music?" To those with a musical background, or who have played an instrument or participated in other rhythmical activities, the answer to this question seems obvious, yet it is a critical and difficult question to answer if you have not had any rhythmical experiences. When you listen to music, any of several different aspects could grab your attention. For example, you could focus your attention on the melody, particular instruments, the tempo, various accents in the music, and so on. The more aspects you can recognize, the more difficult it is to know where to focus your attention. Because it is possible to attend to any one of these aspects in the music, the question becomes "What should you focus your attention on?"

From a dancer's viewpoint, the underlying beat is the most reliable cue because it has a high probability of recurring in a predictable manner. Thus, your first challenge is to separate the rhythm in the music (often called the melody) from the beat (often called the underlying beat). Once you've identified the beat, you'll know the tempo, or how much time elapses between the beats. With very few exceptions, once a tempo is established, it will repeat at that same speed throughout a particular musical selection. Sometimes musicians may slow down the tempo near the end of a song; however, any easy-to-dance-to song will maintain a consistent tempo throughout. Additional cues that have a high probability of consistent recurrence include the number of beats per measure, the duration of each beat (the time signature), the downbeat, the upbeat, and how songs are put together (i.e., measures are grouped into phrases).

You may remember a game show that asked contestants to estimate how many notes they would need to hear of a song before coming up with the song's title: "I can name that tune in six notes (or eight notes, etc.)." Dancers are challenged like this every time a musical selection is played. If you can identify what type of music is being played, for example, a waltz, a foxtrot, or a swing, then you'll know which basic step pattern (described in Steps 6-13) to use to fit the music being played. Once you develop your auditory perception of the underlying beat and the type of music being played, you'll be ready to learn the basic footwork. For your convenience, special practice drills at the end of this step will help you enhance your auditory discrimination skills (in conjunction with the accompanying auditory selections on the enclosed CD).

Why Is It Important to Understand Music Structure?

Social dance music has a hierarchical arrangement of beats, measures, and phrases that can not only help you quickly identify the tempo, but can also provide cues as to which dance music is being played. It is advantageous to know that for all practical purposes, social dance music can be categorized into two basic time signatures: 3/4 and 4/4. This means either three or four beats are combined to form a measure, with each beat getting a quarter note, or one count. If three beats are grouped, waltz music is being played. If four beats are grouped, the music being played could be one of a variety of other dance music (e.g., foxtrot, swing, cha-cha, or rumba). One exception is polka music, but even though musicians will play a polka in 2/4 time, it is often easier for social dancers to count it in four counts.

Reason, Not Rhyme

If you are mathematically inclined, you will appreciate the hierarchical relationships among musical notes. But even if you are not mathematically inclined, music has an order and consistency—it is not random. You need only be able to recognize and identify which cues in the music provide order and consistency and thus provide dancers with the most reliable information. The most reliable cue in the music is the underlying beat. Once you can distinguish the underlying beat, you'll be able to notice that the beats are clustered into groups of either three or four. Once identified, the measures may be clustered into phrases. The following sections describe five cues that illustrate the order and consistency that can be identified after listening to any one song.

Cue 1: Underlying Beats Provide a Consistent Tempo

How can you locate the underlying beat? One way is to listen for the heavier sounds in the music, such as the bass player's or the drummer's sounds, rather than the lighter sounds. Typically, the lighter sounds reflect the melody within a song. The melody is superimposed over the underlying beats and is variable; that is, it changes the duration, or extends the time, of certain notes. The melody is typically played by the wind instruments. As the duration of the notes within the melody may vary, the melody becomes an unreliable cue for dancers. Typically, it is the bass drum that keeps all the musicians together at a certain consistent tempo, which is called the underlying beat. You may have heard band leaders say "and-a-1, 2, 3, 4" to give the tempo of the underlying beat. Likewise, dancers and dance teachers often say "5, 6, 7, 8" after mentally counting 1, 2, 3, 4, to establish the tempo of the underlying beat.

Cue 2: Beats Are Clustered Into Measures

Why are beats grouped into measures? A good analogy is that of listening to a metronome clicking at a constant tempo (see figure 2.1). In this example, you

— — — — — — — — — — — — — — —

Figure 2.1 Continuous beats without measures.

can start and stop counting the beats (metronome clicks) whenever you want. You can also group these isolated metronome clicks into multiples of either three or four beats (see drill 1 on page 17). Social dance music clusters these isolated beats into measures. Within a particular song, the measures will be clusters of either three or four beats. The measures provide definite starting and stopping points that are regular within a particular song.

So, how do you know how many beats to group together? If you look at sheet music, vertical bars separate the beats into measures. Also, the time signature is often shown at the left of the first measure. The time signature is advantageous for dancers to know because it indicates not only how many beats are in a measure, but also how much time duration to give each beat.

Common time signatures in social dance music include the fractional signs 2/4, 3/4, and 4/4. The numerator indicates the number of beats per measure, whereas the denominator indicates the duration of a particular beat. For example, the numerator values in figure 2.2 signify that there are, respectively, two, three, and four beats per measure. The denominator value, 4, signifies that each quarter note in each example gets one count (i.e., one beat gets one count). In social dance music, it is safe to assume that the denominator will be 4, which means that each beat (each quarter note) always gets one count. You might hear dancers using a shorthand version by saying "4/4 time music" versus "music with a 4/4 time signature."

Cue 3: Time Signatures Are Consistent Within a Song

Typically, dancers do not have access to sheet music to help them identify the time signature. Thus, you'll need to be able to identify the time signature after hearing a portion of the music. Start by focusing your attention on the underlying beat, then identify the number of beats per measure.

The easiest way to identify the number of beats per measure is to count in multiples of either three or four (the most common numerators). First, try counting with the music in sets of four (1-2-3-4, 1-2-3-4, etc.). If counting in sets of four does not match the beats of the music, then switch to counting in sets of three. One of these methods will work better than the other. You may need to close your eyes to

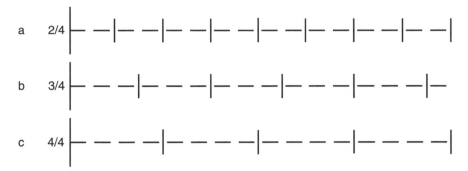

Figure 2.2   Underlying beats per measure for *(a)* 2/4 time, *(b)* 3/4 time, and *(c)* 4/4 time signatures.

reduce outside distractions and focus all your attention on the music.

One exception is polka music. From a musician's viewpoint, polka music has a 2/4 time signature; that is, two beats per measure with each beat getting one count. Yet from a dancer's viewpoint, due to the speed of polka music and the difficulty of repeatedly saying "1, 2, 1, 2, 1, 2, etc.," it is often easier to count in sets of four counts, which groups two traditional measures of polka music. You may memorize the fact that music with a 2/4 time signature indicates polka music. It is your option whether to count it in sets of two or in sets of four.

Cue 4: Measures Are Clustered Into Phrases

The measures within a particular social dance song are organized in an exponential fashion that applies to both 4/4 time and 3/4 time music. As an example, in 4/4 time music, one measure equals four counts. These four counts may be grouped into multiple measures as follows:

- 2 measures, or 8 counts (i.e., 2 measures times 4 counts equals 8 counts),
- 4 measures, or 16 counts (i.e., 4 measures times 4 counts equals 16 counts),
- 8 measures, or 32 counts (i.e., 8 measures times 4 counts equals 32 counts), or
- 16 measures, or 64 counts (i.e., 16 measures times 4 counts equals 64 counts), and so forth.

Within 3/4 time music, each measure is equal to three counts. Thus, waltz measures may be grouped into multiple measures as follows:

- 2 measures, or 6 counts (i.e., 2 measures times 3 counts equals 6 counts),
- 4 measures, or 12 counts (i.e., 4 measures times 3 counts equals 12 counts),
- 8 measures, or 24 counts (i.e., 8 measures times 3 counts equals 24 counts), or
- 16 measures, or 48 counts (i.e., 16 measures times 3 counts equals 48 counts), and so forth.

When the measures are grouped this way, they are called phrases. There are many ways of defining a phrase. Some might call the examples given a mini-, a minor, and a major phrase for the 2-, 4-, and 8-measure groupings, respectively. A 16-measure grouping typically, but not always, reflects a chorus or verse within a song.

Dancers and/or teachers tend (a) to use mini- and minor phrases more often and (b) to use one of the following two methods of counting the phrases: grouping either one measure or two measures. It is a matter of preference. As an example, one way of phrasing 4/4 time music is to mentally count in eight sets of 4 counts (i.e., for a total of 32 counts) as follows:

1,2,3,4
2,2,3,4
3,2,3,4
4,2,3,4
5,2,3,4
6,2,3,4
7,2,3,4
8,2,3,4

Another way of phrasing 4/4 time music is to mentally count in four sets of eight counts as follows:

1,2,3,4,5,6,7,8
2,2,3,4,5,6,7,8
3,2,3,4,5,6,7,8
4,2,3,4,5,6,7,8

These two methods of counting, or phrasing, may also be used with 3/4 time music. Thus, one example for phrasing waltz music is to group eight measures as follows:

1,2,3
2,2,3
3,2,3
4,2,3
5,2,3
6,2,3,
7,2,3
8,2,3

Another way to phrase waltz music is to group four sets of six counts (i.e., two measures) as follows:

1,2,3,4,5,6
2,2,3,4,5,6
3,2,3,4,5,6
4,2,3,4,5,6

The previous examples show how social dance music has structure. Dancers have less to remember when they phrase counts versus isolating counts. It is easier to remember sets of four or eight measures versus individual counts of 32 or 24.

The arrows in figures 2.3 and 2.4 indicate the first count (or downbeat) within each phrase grouping, for both 4/4 and 3/4 time signatures. In 4/4 time music, it may be more difficult to hear the downbeat because the even counts represent upbeats; that is, counts 1 and 3 are downbeats while counts 2 and 4 are upbeats. It is not as hard to find the first beat

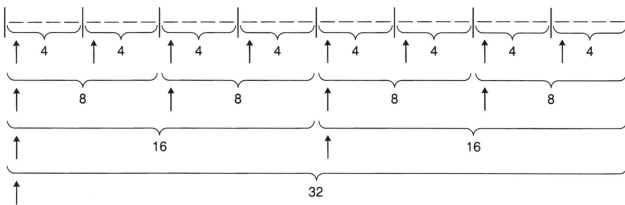

Figure 2.3 Phrase hierarchy for 4/4 time music, with the first beat within the selected phrases marked by arrows.

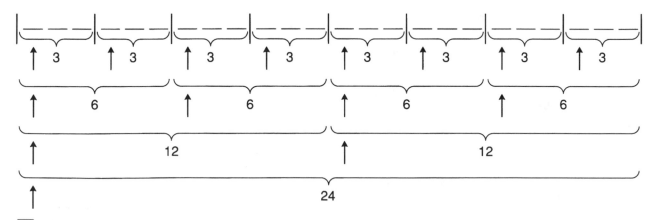

Figure 2.4 Phrase hierarchy for 3/4 time music, with the first beat within the selected phrases marked by arrows.

(downbeat) with 3/4 time music because the first count typically has a stronger emphasis (heavier sound versus lighter sounds on counts 2, 3). If you can also identify the beginning or end of a phrase grouping, you'll get an additional cue as to when the next measure will occur.

Cue 5: Tempo Remains Consistent Within a Song

How fast should you move? As discussed earlier, because each beat gets one count in social dance music, you only need to know how much time occurs between the underlying beats. Basically, three different speeds or tempos are used in social dance music: slow, moderate, and fast. Tempo may vary between songs, but it is likely to be constant within a particular song. Thus, once you have identified the tempo, you need only repeat that particular speed, or tempo, for the length of that song. Exceptions may occur at the end of a song when the tempo may slow down or fade out.

Also, the tempo may be expressed as *beats per minute*, or bpm—literally, the number of beats are counted for one minute. Or a shorthand method may be used. As an example, count the number of beats for six seconds and multiply by 10 to get the number of beats per minute. If the number is 12, then multiply by 10 to get 120 bpm. Table 2.1 shows typical song tempos for different types of social dance music. You can get an idea of the type of music being played from the tempo.

Table 2.1	Average Song Tempos for Selected Social Dances
Social dance	**Tempo (bpm)**
Foxtrot	120
Waltz	90 to 105
Swing	120 to 170
Polka	96 to 130
Cha-cha	120
Rumba	120
Tango	130
Salsa/mambo	150

Determining When to Begin Moving With the Music

A logical place to start moving is right after the introduction. There is a high probability that the introduction consists of either four or eight measures; however, you may find exceptions in both the number of measures and in the tempo. Thus, you may want to wait until after the song's introduction and you've identified the underlying beat and tempo.

Once the song is in progress, you may begin on the first beat of any measure or any phrase, or you might use some combination of the first beat within the measure and the phrasing. Most dancers use a combination of methods. Except for the polka, all of the basic step patterns covered in this book begin on the first beat within a measure. However, in the early stages of learning, it is helpful to also start the polka on the first beat of the measure by eliminating the hop prior to the first step. Then, once you are in motion, it is easier to add the hop prior to the next measure of music (the basic footwork/step pattern will be covered in detail in Step 9).

More experienced dancers often start after hearing two measures of music, especially with waltz and polka music. Grouping two measures together corresponds to the time it takes to complete the basic step pattern on both sides of the body, which is a way to match movements with the phrasing of the music. The basic step patterns for both the waltz and the polka are executed on one side of the body (for one measure), then repeated on the other side of the body (for the second measure). Thus, it takes two measures before your starting foot is free to start again. This point will become clearer after you learn the basic step patterns for the waltz and the polka (in Steps 8 and 9). Notice that two measures equals a miniphrase of either eight counts (4/4 time music) or six counts (3/4 time music).

If the first downbeat of a measure is too difficult to locate, or if the tempo seems too fast, you might think about slowing down the time between each underlying beat. Typically, more experienced dancers separate the underlying beats within each measure into either duple or triple divisions. Musicians may subdivide the beat even more, but social dancers do not find further subdivisions of the beat very useful. With duple division of the beat, any one beat may be split into two halves, with each getting one-half count. For example, using duple division, one measure of 4/4 time music may be counted as follows:

1 &, 2 &, 3 &, 4 &

Or, using duple division, one measure of 3/4 time music may be counted as follows:

1 &, 2 &, 3 &

With triple division of the beat, any one beat may be split into three parts, with each getting one-third of a count. For example, using triple division, one measure of 4/4 time music may be counted as follows:

1 & a, 2 & a, 3 & a, 4 & a

Or, using triple division, one measure of 3/4 time music may be counted as follows:

1 & a, 2 & a, 3 & a

Beginning dancers find it helpful to know that they can use either duple or triple division of the last beat of the measure as a ready signal to improve their reaction time. Even in a race, the runners are given warning signals, such as "On your mark," "Get set," and "Go," to alert them when to move. In social dancing, the goal is to take a step on the first downbeat (count 1). Thus, you might interpret the "&" to be a trigger to start moving. Initiating movement prior to count 1 will help you coincide your step (weight change) on count 1.

Likewise, a triple division of the beat may be used as a ready signal to locate the first downbeat within a measure. In this case, on the last beat within a measure, you might mentally think of replacing the "& a" with "Ready, move." More experienced dancers find it challenging and exciting to use triple division of the beat as a place to add syncopation steps (i.e., either extra or fewer steps) or flair moves. Either method of dividing the beat provides a consistent structure that dancers can use to account for the time between the underlying beats.

Identifying the Type of Music

Because the denominator stays the same in social dance music (giving each beat one count), all you need to recognize is how many beats are grouped together. For example, if three beats are grouped, the music is structured in 3/4 time, which is waltz music. If two beats may be grouped together, the music is structured in 2/4 time, which is used in polka music. If four beats may be grouped together, the music is structured in 4/4 time, which is used for the majority of social dance songs, including swing, foxtrot, cha-cha, rumba, tango, and salsa/mambo.

In addition, certain accents are used within a measure that can alert you to what type of dance music is being played. If, for example, count 1 is stronger than counts 2 and 3, then a 3/4 time signature is being used, which is waltz music. On the other hand, if both counts 2 and 4 are stronger (or accented), then a 4/4 time signature is being used, which is most likely to be either foxtrot or swing music. Other accents are subjective and may be altered by different musicians' interpretations of a particular song.

A less reliable cue is the melody. The melody, as reflected in the lyrics of a song, provides an overlying rhythmic pattern superimposed on the underlying beats. The melody does not provide reliable rhythm cues because it does not have to correspond exactly to the number of beats per measure, nor does it have to exactly fit one measure. However, particular styling cues that are characteristic of certain music are introduced through the melody or overlying rhythmic patterns. For example, a Latin flavor may be added with certain instruments and multiple accents that are more characteristic of cha-cha, rumba, samba, and the like.

DRILLS

Locate the CD bound in this book, gently remove it from the sleeve, and use it to answer the practice drills. Feel free to listen as many times as necessary to answer the following questions. You may refer to the correct answers that are located at the end of this learning step, as needed. Once you get the main idea, listen to a variety of other music sources as a self-test to find out if you can transfer your auditory perceptual skills to different musical selections.

1. Count the Underlying Beat

Listen to the metronome clicks on track 1. Mentally count in multiples of either two (2, 4, 6, 8, etc.) or three (3, 6, 12, etc.) counts. Which counting method works best for you?

Success Goal = Count using any multiple of two, then any multiple of three___

Success Check

- Maintain a recurring unit of musical time, or count per click of the metronome___
- Surprise! Any counting method works because there are no definite starting or stopping points___

To Increase Difficulty

- Listen to track 2 and repeat this drill, or ask a partner to provide a recurring clap or tap. Do you notice a difference in tempo? Is any one tempo easier for you to maintain?
- Try counting by using different multiples of two and three. Are any combinations easier for you? It is often easier to group at least 4 or 8 counts (with 4/4 time music) and to group at least 6 or 12 counts (with 3/4 time music).

To Decrease Difficulty

- Either close your eyes or narrow your focus to one spot in the room as you listen to the metronome clicks.
- Listen to the counting examples on track 3, then repeat this drill and verbally count the clicks.

2. Identify the Number of Beats per Measure

Listen to the counting examples identifying the beats per measure for the selected song segments on tracks 4 and 5. Each song has its own recurring structure, starting with an introduction, followed by either the chorus or verses of the song. The vocal cue "& a" will help you know when the introduction is over on track 4, while the vocal cue "&" occurs at the end of the introduction on track 5.

Now it's your turn. Listen to the song segments on tracks 6 and 7. Use the following procedures each time: (a) listen for the pause (almost like taking a breath at the end of a sentence) at the end of the introduction, then (b) experiment with counting in either threes or fours.

Once you know the number of beats per measure, you'll also know the time signature. The number of beats per measure represents the numerator in the time signature. The denominator is a 4 because, in social dance music, a quarter note typically gets one beat. Then, calculate the beats per minute (bpm) and the type of music being played for tracks 4 through 7.

Success Goal = Correctly identify the number of beats per measure, then list the time signature, tempo, and type of music for the song segments on tracks 4 through 7___

Success Check
- Measures provide starting and ending points for identifying the tempo___
- Typically, the tempo is consistent within a particular song___
- Introductions have measures that are often, but not necessarily, in multiples of two___
- Once the introduction is over, the number of measures and the tempo will be more predictable___

To Increase Difficulty
- Listen to songs on the radio or at home and repeat this drill. Notice how the tempo changes between songs yet remains constant within any one song. Notice that most popular songs on the radio use one of these time signatures. Which one?
- Count the number of measures within the introductions for the song segments on tracks 4 though 7.

Track number	Number of beats per measure	Time signature	Tempo (bpm)	Type of music
4				
5				
6				
7				

3. Locate the Accents

Listen to the song segments on tracks 6, 7, and 8. After the downbeat, identify any beats that are either stronger or heavier (accented). There is subjectivity involved in identifying accents. When in doubt, be sure that you can hear the downbeat (count 1) in each measure.

Success Goal = Correctly identify the count(s) accented on tracks 6 through 8___

Track number	Count(s) accented
6	
7	
8	

✔**Success Check**

- Accented beats (or counts) are either stronger or heavier to make them different from the other beats within a measure___
- Downbeats are the odd-numbered beats within any measure. They may or may not be accented___
- Upbeats are the even-numbered beats within any measure. They may or may not be accented___
- Multiple accents are characteristic in Latin music___

To Increase Difficulty

- Identify the time signature used for track 8.
- Identify the type of music played for tracks 6, 7, and 8.

4. Name That Dance Tune

As you listen to various dance songs, you'll soon find that there are three different tempos: slow, moderate, and fast (compare tracks 9, 10, and 11). The distinctions between these three different tempos are very subjective, however. What may be slow to one person may be considered fast to another. Thus, some decision making is needed on your part to identify the tempo, what type of dance music is being played, and eventually, which dance steps to execute to that music. For example, on the social dance floor, both foxtrot and swing music are somewhat overlapping. It is common to see some couples doing foxtrot steps traveling around the outside of the floor while other couples are doing swing steps in the center of the floor—all to the same music—depending on the tempo (compare tracks 9 through 12). As another example, some couples may choose different swing basic step patterns, depending on the tempo of the music. Ultimately, the choice will be yours—you'll only need to avoid bumping into anyone else.

Each dance has its unique characteristics that are reflected both in the music and in the way the basic step patterns are to be presented. At this point, another important aspect to become aware of is the different stylings possible in the music for the same dance (compare tracks 15 and 16). One example is a Polish polka, characterized by a light quality in the music. It is typically danced with the body weight lifted and the landing precisely controlled (lifted) so that very little sound is made when contacting the floor. Another example is a German polka, characterized by a heavy quality in the music. It is typically danced with stomps, using a flat-footed landing to increase the sound when contacting the floor. Listen to each of the selected songs on tracks 9 through 19 to identify the type of dance music being played as well as its tempo, count(s) accented, and time signature.

Success Goal = Correctly identify the type of dance music, tempo, count(s) accented, and time signature for each of the tracks listed___

Success Check

- Foxtrot music is smoother when compared to swing music, which is more energetic, jazzy, and syncopated___
- Waltz music is in 3/4 time and accents the downbeat of each measure___
- Cha-cha music has a Latin flavor to it___
- Polka music is lively and accents the downbeat of each measure. German polka styling is heavy (base instruments) compared to Polish polka styling, which is light and airy (wind instruments)___
- Rumba music is romantic and sultry___
- Tango music intermixes soft, flowing crescendos with sharp staccato notes___
- Salsa/mambo music is faster than cha-cha music; both have multiple accents and a variety of Latin instruments___
- Which type of dance music is most difficult for you to recognize___
- Which type of dance music is the easiest for you to recognize___

 To Increase Difficulty

- At random, identify the appropriate dance music being played.
- Listen to a variety of popular songs to identify the downbeat, tempo, accent(s), and time signature.

To Decrease Difficulty

- Ask a partner to call out the appropriate dance style prior to playing any music.

Track number	Type of music	Tempo	Count(s) accented	Time signature
9				
10				
11				
12				
13				
14				
15				
16				
17				
18				
19				

MUSIC STRUCTURE SUCCESS SUMMARY

Two important auditory skills for dancers are (a) to recognize the hierarchical structure of music and (b) to identify the most reliable cues in the music. By knowing which aspects of the music have a higher probability of recurrence, you'll have a perceptual edge over those who do not know what to listen for, where to focus attention, or how to predict the tempo and type of music being played.

The most reliable cue is the underlying beat. The underlying beats are grouped into measures and then phrases. After you've identified the tempo, you'll also be able to predict with high probability the speed for the remainder of that song and the type of social dance music being played. You'll need to apply these auditory skills automatically whenever you dance.

Social dance music is generally categorized as having either a 4/4 or a 3/4 time signature. In either case, the denominator of 4 tells you that each quarter note, or beat, gets one count. The numerator (i.e., either 3 or 4) tells you how many beats there are in each measure.

Thus, for the duration of any particular song, the following aspects have a high probability of being constant: the number of beats per measure and the value of each underlying beat being one count. Both aspects tell dancers the tempo to maintain throughout that particular song.

DRILL ANSWERS

Drill 1

Any counting method works with the metronome clicks (tracks 1, 2, and 3) because there are no definite starting or stopping points. Track 2 uses a faster tempo than track 1.

Drill 2

Track 4—three beats per measure; 3/4 time signature; 90 bpm; waltz music

Track 5—four beats per measure; 4/4 time signature; 140 bpm; swing music

Track 6—four beats per measure; 4/4 time signature; 120 bpm; foxtrot music

Track 7—three beats per measure; 3/4 time signature; 105 bpm; waltz music

To Increase Difficulty—4/4 time signatures are typically used with popular songs

Track 4—four-measure introduction

Track 5—eight-measure introduction

Track 6—four-measure introduction

Track 7—four-measure introduction

Drill 3

Track 6—counts 2 and 4; foxtrot music

Track 7—count 1; waltz music

Track 8—multiple accents; cha-cha music

To Increase Difficulty—track 8 uses a 4/4 time signature

Drill 4

Track 9—swing; moderate tempo (150 bpm); counts 2 and 4; 4/4 time signature

Track 10—swing; slow tempo (120 bpm); counts 2 and 4; 4/4 time signature

Track 11—swing; fast tempo (170 bpm); counts 2 and 4; 4/4 time signature

Track 12—foxtrot; slow to moderate tempo (118 bpm); counts 2 and 4; 4/4 time signature

Track 13—waltz; slow to moderate tempo (105 bpm); count 1; 3/4 time signature

Track 14—cha-cha; slow to moderate tempo (120 bpm); multiple accents; 4/4 time signature

Track 15—polka; slow to moderate tempo (100 bpm); count 1; 2/4 or 4/4 time signature; German styling

Track 16—polka; moderate to fast tempo (120 bpm); count 1; 2/4 or 4/4 time signature; Polish styling

Track 17—rumba; slow to moderate tempo (120 bpm); multiple accents; 4/4 time signature

Track 18—tango; slow to moderate tempo (130 bpm); multiple accents; 4/4 time signature

Track 19—salsa/mambo; slow to moderate tempo (150 bpm); multiple accents; 4/4 time signature

STEP 3

EAR-FOOT COORDINATION: CONNECTING WITH THE MUSIC

Have you ever been part of a marching band, or in the military? If so, you know the importance of recognizing an external cadence and marching to it. These same skills are essential in social dance. The music gives us the cadence, or tempo, via the underlying beats. Once a tempo has been established, it tends to remain the same throughout a particular song. Thus, your first task is to recognize the tempo of the music being played. Your second task is to walk and become aware of transferring your center of gravity, or torso, over the ball of your foot on each step.

Next, have you ever thought about what part of your foot should hit the floor when you step to the music? This sounds easy, yet it is more difficult than you might think. Your third task is to not only take a walking step (making a weight change), but also to time your center of gravity's shift onto the ball of your foot to coincide precisely with a specific beat or count. In motor learning terminology, these three tasks combined are called a *coincidence anticipation task*. In other words, you'll need to spontaneously time your walking steps to coincide with an external tempo, which requires ear-foot coordination. It takes concentration to be able to walk according to the tempo of the music—versus at your own pace!

Why Is Ear-Foot Coordination Important?

You're probably most familiar with eye-hand coordination tasks such as seeing, tracking, and catching or batting a ball. Dancing requires you to make a similar type of perceptual-motor match—with ear-foot coordination tasks. First, you need to be able to hear and recognize the underlying beats in the music. Second, you need to be able to walk efficiently with proper body mechanics and alignment. Third, you need to be able to put these two prerequisites together. A perceptual-motor match is achieved when you can precisely coincide your walking steps with an external pace provided by the music. Achieving this perceptual-motor match also will facilitate your execution of the basic foot patterns for various dance styles because you will be more aware of how the footwork needs to connect with the music's underlying beats.

Your dancing is greatly enhanced when it is connected with the music versus being "off beat" with the music. Good dancers make it look easy. One secret for looking good on the dance floor—whether dancing alone or with a partner—is to connect your movements with the music. When you can connect with the music, it becomes both intrinsically satisfying and pleasing for others to watch. Don't ignore the music—let it help you.

Two Basic Rhythm Types

Two basic types of rhythm, even and uneven, describe the number of weight changes in relationship to an underlying beat. These rhythms can be observed in the eight basic locomotor movements that take us from one place to another, as follows: walk, run, jump, leap, hop, skip, slide, and gallop. The first five locomotor movements use an even rhythm, whereas the latter three locomotor movements use an uneven rhythm. Each rhythm type will be described in the next two sections using the most common locomotor movements for social dance.

Walking in an Even Rhythm

An even rhythm reflects a repetitive action that has a steady, soothing quality to it. The best example of an even rhythm is walking at a constant tempo. Each whole count of the music corresponds to one foot action; that is, one weight change. The rhythmic repetition of even-rhythm locomotor movements is part of the appeal and satisfaction for those who enjoy weight-bearing aerobic activities such as walking, running, or social dance.

When you walk in an even rhythm, notice that, alternately, one foot (i.e., your trailing foot) pushes off the floor to provide momentum for your other foot (i.e., your leading foot) to contact the floor in a heel-to-toe manner. To connect with the music, coincide your walking steps to transfer your body's center of gravity over the ball of your foot on each whole count of the music. This is not as easy as it sounds because you incorporate at least seven different actions in each walking step: a shift of your center of gravity forward toward the direction you want to walk, a push-off with your trailing foot, an initial knee bend, an extension of your leg forward from the hip, a heel contact on the floor with your leading foot, a weight shift forward onto the ball of your leading foot, and a rolling forward to push off again—all done to an external tempo. In fact, if you watched a film of yourself walking, you would be able to break down these actions into even more subparts! See figure 3.1 for the Keys to Success for walking forward in an even rhythm. When you walk backward, the weight shifts backward, rolling from the toe to the ball of the leading foot (without a heel strike).

FIGURE 3.1 KEYS TO SUCCESS: WALKING IN AN EVEN RHYTHM

Count "&"

1. Push off with trailing foot

Count "a"

2. Shift weight forward
3. Heel strike with leading foot

Count 1

4. Continue shift forward onto ball of leading foot
5. Leading foot becomes trailing foot as movement repeats on other side

Tempo Modifications. Be aware that the tempo will dictate how many actions are possible to execute. For example, when you speed up the tempo, at some point a walk becomes a run. A faster tempo doesn't permit enough time for your heel to contact the floor; rather, your weight shifts from the ball of your trailing foot directly onto the ball of your leading foot. In addition, the length of each step is shortened when the tempo is increased. However, both the walk and the run are still examples of an even rhythm. With the run, the tempo is faster, yet the amount of time per weight change from one foot to the other remains constant, with an equal time duration for each foot during the established tempo or pace.

Execution of a Hop. A hop is defined as a push-off from one foot and a landing on the same foot. A true hop is executed in an even rhythm. However, a walking step and a hop may be combined, which creates a skip that is more commonly used in the polka basic step. The timing of a skip is faster and is more difficult because of the number of movements that need to be done in a very short time frame. The skip will be described further with the other uneven-rhythm locomotor movements (see next section). Obviously, to execute the skip, you'll need to know how to execute both a walking step (review figure 3.1) and a hop. The hop entails a few critical execution points.

To perform a hop in an even rhythm, stand on one leg and think of Newton's law of action and reaction: For every action there must be an equal and opposite reaction. Thus, bend your standing knee, push off from the ground, rise into the air, and then bend that same knee to absorb the force as you land. All actions (including the bend, push, rise, and land) must be consecutively repeated so that the timing of the *landing* coincides with each whole count. With repeated hops, the landing actually becomes the preparation for the next push-off (see figure 3.2). Make sure that your hopping foot begins and lands in the same location—with only upward (i.e., vertical and not forward or horizontal) motion. When you practice consecutive hopping, be sure to alternate feet after a while to avoid overworking one leg.

FIGURE 3.2 **KEYS TO SUCCESS: HOPPING IN AN EVEN RHYTHM**

Count "&"

1. Weight on one foot
2. Bend weight-bearing knee
3. Push off

Count "a"

4. Rise slightly off ground

Count 1

5. Land on ball of same foot
6. Bend knee to absorb force

Walking in an Uneven Rhythm

Combining three walks together creates a triple step. A triple step will be used in the waltz basic step, and it will have an even rhythm (i.e., each weight change gets the same duration). On the other hand, a triple step will be used in a variety of other social dances, such as the cha-cha, polka, and swing, where it will have an uneven rhythm. When using an uneven rhythm, the timing needs to be altered such that three weight changes are made within two beats of music. Typically, it is cued as "quick, quick, slow" to indicate that the first two weight changes are faster (quicker) than the third (which is slower relative to the quicks). Uneven rhythms reflect the unexpected, which adds variety and interest to dance step combinations. In social dance, examples of uneven-rhythm locomotor movements include both the triple step (which is an execution and styling variation of the gallop) and the skip (which is a combination of a walk and a hop). Additional uneven-rhythm alternatives occur when only one weight change is made within any two beats of music (which requires a hold or a pause).

Execution of a Triple Step.   The three footwork actions for executing a triple step may be cued in sev-eral ways, such as "step, push, step," "step, ball, step," or "step, close, step." These three weight changes occur within two beats of music, which means that some of the weight changes will need to be executed faster or more quickly. The timing for the triple step's three weight changes is "1-&, 2," or QQS. Take a walking step on the first count, a half step on the "&" count, and a walking step on count 2 (the second beat in 4/4 time signatures).

Notice that you are splitting the first count into two halves, giving each weight change a half beat or count. Take a small walking step on the "1" cue and use a pushing action with the ball of your trailing foot on the "&" cue. During the "&" or the "push" action, place the ball of your trailing foot either just beside or slightly behind the heel of your leading foot—there is not enough time to put your whole foot down. Whether you travel forward or backward, it helps to keep one foot in the lead on each whole count; for example, "left, push, left" then "right, push, right." Keep your knees slightly bent during the push with the ball of your trailing foot (on the "&"). This will ensure that your head and shoulders remain level (and you travel forward versus rising in the air). See figure 3.3 for the triple step Keys to Success.

FIGURE 3.3 KEYS TO SUCCESS: TRIPLE STEP IN AN UNEVEN RHYTHM

Count 1

1. Step forward onto ball of leading foot

Count "&"

2. Place ball of trailing foot beside heel of leading foot
3. Push off with ball of trailing foot
4. Start to take next step with leading foot

Count 2

5. Shift weight forward onto ball of leading foot

Execution of a Skip. Unlike the hop, a skip alternately switches from one foot to the other. The combining of a walk and a hop is not difficult; however, it is the timing of these actions that makes a skip more difficult. The walk portion coincides with each whole count or underlying beat. The hop portion takes place between each whole count; that is, during the "&-a" counts. Thus, on the first whole count, take a walking step and also bend that knee (in preparation for the push-off). Do both a push-off and rise in the air on the "&" count, then land on that same foot on the "a" count. It helps to practice at a slow tempo until these actions merge smoothly and can be more automatic. Make sure that you coincide your walking step with a whole count (or underlying beat of the music). Figure 3.4 shows the Keys to Success for executing the skip starting with your right foot. Repeat with your left foot to alternate the skip on both sides of your body

| FIGURE 3.4 | KEYS TO SUCCESS: SKIP IN AN UNEVEN RHYTHM |

Count 1

1. Step forward onto ball of leading foot
2. Bend and push off the floor

Count "&"

3. Rise in the air

Count "a"

4. Land on that foot

Timing Options. One timing option is to make fewer weight changes than beats per measure. This typically combines a weight change with a non-weight change within any two beats of music and may occur in almost every dance. For example, you might take a walking step on the first whole count and hold (or freeze) on the second whole count (to make it different or dramatic). Instead of a hold, you might consider substituting a non-weight action during the hold. A variety of non-weight actions are possible (e.g., a touch, tap, point, kick, heel, scuff, brush, scoot, hitch, or clap). Non-weight actions are useful with slow-tempo music because they give you something to do during the extra count versus holding it. These non-weight actions can be used to personalize your dancing or to alter the timing to make it easier (and more compatible with even rhythms, as you can do something on each underlying beat).

Another timing option is to take a longer stride on the first whole count and not actually change your weight, or step, until the second whole count. This option is useful when the goal is to travel or when the tempo is very fast. It gives you more time to execute your walking step to coincide with each second count (when grouping two beats of the music).

EAR-FOOT COORDINATION

DRILLS

1. Establish a Personal Pace

In a large open space, without music, begin walking forward in a counterclockwise (CCW) direction. Use regular walking steps. Establish a comfortable pace that you can easily repeat. What part of your foot hits the floor first? If you are using a typical heel-ball-toe walking motion, your heel will hit the floor first. However, some may notice other parts of the foot hitting the floor first, perhaps more of a flat or whole-foot motion, which is also possible.

Next, try walking backward. Be sure to look over one shoulder to see where you are going. Notice that the motion now reverses such that your toe touches first with each backward step in a toe-ball-heel motion. Remember to keep your weight centered over the ball of your foot on each step. This means that your heel may touch the floor when walking backward, but don't shift your weight backward onto or above your heels. It is important to keep your weight centered over the ball of your foot, which will also help you change direction very quickly.

Success Goal = Two minutes of walking using an even rhythm (a) forward, then (b) backward___

Success Check
- Push off with the ball of your trailing foot against the floor for momentum into the next step___
- Make sure your weight moves over the ball of your foot with each whole number___
- Walk in an even rhythm with each weight change getting one count___

To Increase Difficulty
- Modify your personal pace to match a partner's pace.
- Repeat this drill using a different tempo each time.

To Decrease Difficulty
- Walk with the purpose of moving at a constant speed and in a recurring rhythm (e.g., as if in a walking race or a marching band).
- Ask an observer to count out loud each time that you shift your weight onto the ball of your leading foot. Are you moving at a consistent pace or speed?

2. Using an Even Rhythm

The purpose of this drill is to connect your walking steps not only with the underlying beats, but also with the measures in music. Whenever you take a step onto the ball of your foot to coincide with each beat of the music, you are walking using an even rhythm. Start this drill by asking a partner to give you either four preparatory claps or four verbal counts that will provide you with an underlying beat at a moderate tempo. Your partner should then clap or count out loud continuously in sets of four beats (which is reflective of music with a 4/4 time signature) and maintain the established tempo. The first count should be louder so that you can identify the beginning, or downbeat, of the measure. Mentally count with your partner's claps (or counts) to identify the tempo, then take one walking step per clap (or count). As you discovered in the previous drill, it will be a challenge to execute a weight shift forward, a heel strike, and a transfer of your body weight forward onto the ball of each foot with each clap (or count) that you hear.

Next, ask your partner to clap (or count) in sets of three counts (which is used in music with a 3/4 time signature) and to accent or make the first beat/count of each measure louder and stronger. Match your walking pace to coincide with your partner's claps (or counts). With each three-beat measure, notice that you'll be grouping your steps as follows: either left, right, left or right, left, right, depending on which side of the body you started with.

Success Goal = Two minutes of walking while using an even rhythm (a) to match four beats to a measure and (b) to match three beats to a measure___

✔ Success Check

- Adjust your pace to match your partner's established auditory tempo___
- Regardless of which time signature is used, your weight should still shift onto the ball of each foot with each clap (or beat/count) when using an even rhythm___
- The tempo (walking pace) should remain constant for the length of each trial or song___

To Increase Difficulty

- Repeat the drill using a different tempo.
- Repeat the drill, except walk backward to a partner's claps (or counts). Remember that your weight should not shift onto the heel with each backward step; rather, it should remain over the ball of each foot.

To Decrease Difficulty

- Close your eyes to block out all distractions and focus on the auditory cues, identify the tempo, then repeat this tempo by mentally counting it in measures. Once you have the tempo, walk to it (making sure that no obstacles are in your path).
- Compare the difference between placing your weight over the ball of your foot on a backward step versus shifting your weight onto the heel of your foot. The latter will stop your momentum, causing you to be late or off beat with the verbal counts.

3. Using an Uneven Rhythm

Ask a partner to either clap in sets of four beats or to verbally count out loud using four-beat measures. After listening to at least one measure (to identify the established tempo), experiment with walking at this tempo until you can solve each of the following uneven-rhythm movement challenges:

a. Step on only the odd-numbered claps (or counts 1 and 3).
b. Step on only the even-numbered claps (or counts 2 and 4).

Both ways of coordinating your steps to an external pace using 4/4 time may occur in social dance. Which way is easier for you?

Success Goal = Two minutes of walking using two different uneven rhythms: (a) single step on odd-numbered counts or beats and (b) single step on even-numbered counts or beats___

Success Check
• Time your weight changes to occur only on the odd-numbered claps or counts___
• Time your weight changes to occur only on the even-numbered claps or counts___
• Both ways use a walking pace that reflects an uneven rhythm___

To Increase Difficulty
• Try this drill while walking backward and looking over one shoulder to see where you are going.
• Repeat this drill using a different tempo.

To Decrease Difficulty
• Accent the count (or beat) either mentally or verbally to reinforce when to make a weight change (for example, either "1, **2**, 3, **4**," or "**1**,2,**3**,4").

4. Rhythm Affects Stride Length

The purpose of this drill is to combine both even and uneven rhythms and to notice how your stride length is affected by each. Ask a partner to clap in four-beat measures to establish a tempo. Take one walking step with each clap for two measures (i.e., eight walks with one weight change per count), then take one walking step on only the even-numbered claps (i.e., four walks only on claps/counts 2 and 4) for the next two measures (eight counts). Thus, the actual number of weight changes is 12 (i.e., alternating eight walks, then four walks) within four measures of claps (or 16 counts).

Consecutively repeat this two-part rhythmic combination (which becomes a rhythmic pattern) for the length of one song (in 4/4 time). In which part do you have the shorter strides?

Reverse roles with your partner, and give each other feedback on the actual lengths of your walking steps. Which walking pace gives you more time to take a longer stride?

Success Goal = Noticing the stride length differences when stepping (a) on each count, then (b) only on even-numbered counts___

Success Check
• A faster pace prompts a shorter stride___
• A slower pace prompts a longer stride___
• A very fast pace shortens the time for each weight change such that weight transfers from the ball of one foot directly onto the ball of the other foot, as in running___
• A very slow pace allows more time for a heel-to-ball weight change for each foot, as in walking___

To Increase Difficulty

- Repeat this drill while stepping only on the odd-numbered counts (i.e., counts 1 and 3) during the second part of this rhythmic pattern.
- Repeat this drill while walking backward in a CCW direction around the room.

To Decrease Difficulty

- Practice each part separately.
- Substitute a non-weight action for the hold (during the uneven rhythm portion), such as closing your feet briefly and adding a tap or a touch, on those counts without a weight change. Notice that this works better when stepping (making a weight change) on counts 1 and 3 because it gives you something to do during counts 2 and 4. In contrast, it is easier to extend and reach out (i.e., push off with the trailing foot in order to take a longer stride) on counts 1 and 3 prior to actually stepping on counts 2 and 4.

5. Changing Directions Efficiently

The purpose of this drill is to practice how to change directions quickly and smoothly and still match your footwork to an external tempo. Face one wall to establish a "front." Using your right foot to start, take four walking steps forward, then four walking steps backward. Try this pattern without any cues. Then ask a partner to count in four-beat measures to give you a tempo. Try the pattern again. Can you keep up with the established tempo? The ability to change directions quickly is called *agility*. This drill and dancing in general can improve your agility!

There are a few secrets to making efficient changes of direction—in this case, from forward to backward and from backward to forward. First, lower your center of gravity by bending your knees. Second, keep your weight over the balls of your feet. To make the transition smooth, you need to anticipate the upcoming direction change by slowing down at the end of the third step, whether it is forward or backward. Keep your feet in a forward-backward stride position with your weight centered between them. When you walk to a tempo, these transitions become a rocking motion (either forward-backward or backward-forward) in that your weight is centered and you can slightly lift one foot and then the other off the floor without losing your balance.

Because dancing often requires you to be ambidextrous, repeat this walking sequence starting with your left foot. Again, make the transitions between the direction changes as smooth as possible and correctly time them with the music. These "secrets" apply regardless of which direction or which foot you start with. Sometimes a change of direction may be called a check stop.

Success Goal = Two minutes of alternating four walks forward with four walks backward to 4/4 time music, starting with (a) the right foot, then (b) the left foot___

To Increase Difficulty

- Repeat the drill using a different tempo.
- Systematically vary the number of repetitions of walking steps taken in each direction. Experiment with a decelerated rhythm pattern such that you walk as follows: 16 steps forward and 16 steps backward; 8 steps forward and 8 steps backward; 4 steps forward and 4 steps backward; and finally, 2 steps forward and 2 steps backward.
- Experiment with an accelerated rhythm pattern such that you walk as follows: 2 walks forward and 2 walks backward; 4 walks forward and 4 walks backward; 8 walks forward and 8 walks backward; and finally, 16 walks forward and 16 walks backward.
- Experiment with putting both rhythm patterns together using the following number of repetitions: 16 forward, 16 backward, 8, 8, 4, 4, 2, 2, 1, 1, 1, 1, 2, 2, 4, 4, 8, 8, 16, 16. Quick direction changes test your balance and control!

To Decrease Difficulty

- Stand in a forward-backward stride position with your weight centered between your feet and alternately rock your weight from one foot to the other (to any four-beat measure tempo) without permitting your upper body (center of gravity) to shift either forward or backward.

6. Triple Step Challenge

How might you take six steps within four counts (or one measure of 4/4 time music)? Some of your steps will need to be executed more quickly than the rest. To solve this challenge, you'll need to subdivide the beats into half counts and group three steps together. Take two steps to one count by cueing it "1-&"; take your third step on the second count. Repeat this uneven-rhythm pattern (or triple step) starting with the other foot. Notice that the phrase "tri-ple step" can be broken into three syllables, which is an easy way to remember the number of weight changes in a triple step—three. Due to the quickness of the first two steps, the triple step may also be cued as "quick, quick, slow." The footwork cues for the triple step are "step, ball, step," with the middle half count getting half a foot and the two steps staying in the lead on one side of the body; that is, step on right foot, push (with left), step on right foot; or step on left, push (with right), left.

Success Goal = 16 consecutive triple steps (a) with counts, then (b) with music___

Success Check
- The six-count cues become "1-&-2, 3-&-4"___
- Make one weight change on each cue___
- Group three steps starting with one foot, then group three steps starting with the other foot___

To Increase Difficulty

- Increase the tempo.
- Repeat triple steps while moving backward.
- Alternate directions; for example, repeat four triple steps forward, then four triple steps backward.
- Experiment with decelerated and accelerated rhythm patterns to repeat the triple step in both directions as follows: 8 forward, 8 backward, 4, 4, 2, 2, 1, 1, 2, 2, 4, 4, 8, 8.
- Create a rhythmic pattern that combines both even and uneven rhythms, such as walking steps and triple steps; for example, two triple steps and two walking steps, two walking steps and one triple step, a hop and a triple step, and so on. Some of these patterns will become familiar (as universal basic step patterns) as you progress in this book!

To Decrease Difficulty

- Use slow counts and slow music.
- More measures or repetitions in any one direction allow more time for the direction change (giving you more time to prepare and to react).

7. Double-Circle Walking Mixer

If you have a group, a mixer can add fun to your practices. A mixer calls for switching partners at some point, usually within an easy-to-follow sequence, although it does not require any leading, as both partners do the same set routine. It is a great culminating activity or a unique way to review steps. It can be more social if you introduce yourself to each new partner, or just a fun, rhythmic experience shared with others.

Pair up with a partner (side by side with your left shoulders toward center) to form a large double circle facing counterclockwise (see figure 3.5). Walk through each part of the following sequence, gradually adding another part, until the entire sequence can be done to counts, then to slow 4/4 time music.

This mixer includes four direction changes: forward, backward, left diagonal, and a clockwise (CW) rotation. The challenge is that two direction changes are used within each measure. The secret is to group three walking steps together in any one direction, then make the second direction change on the fourth count of each measure. In total, this mixer uses four measures, or 16 counts. You may start with either foot; just maintain the tempo with each weight change. Verbal cues for the direction changes follow:

a. *Forward and face:* Walk forward three steps, face your partner (inside circle makes a quarter turn clockwise and outside circle makes a quarter turn counterclockwise).

b. *Backward and diagonal:* Walk backward three steps and face your left-front diagonal. You will be facing a new partner.

c. *Forward and hook:* Walk forward three steps in your left-front diagonal direction and hook elbows with a new partner.

d. *Rotate and release:* Walk clockwise with this new partner for three steps, then release elbows and face the CCW direction to start over again (the partner in the outside circle has the greater distance to turn to be in position to start the sequence again). Figure 3.5 is a diagram of the double-circle formation.

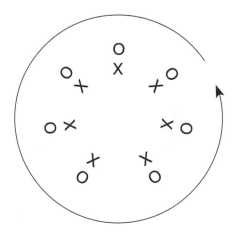

■ Figure 3.5 Diagram of double circle.

Success Goal = Two minutes of continuous repetition of the double-circle walking mixer to slow 4/4 time music___

✔ Success Check
• Change to a new direction on count 4 of each measure___
• Take small backward steps to avoid bumping into others (if on the inside of the circle) or getting too far apart (if on the outside)___
• Step on each beat using an even rhythm___

To Increase Difficulty
• Increase the tempo.
• Repeat this mixer with the inner circle starting with the left foot and the outer circle starting with the right foot.
• Repeat this mixer substituting an uneven locomotor step for the walks; for example, try skips or triples.
• Repeat this mixer intermixing both even and uneven rhythms in a novel way.

To Decrease Difficulty
• Without a partner, assume you are on the outside (or the inside) of the double circle and repeat the mixer. If you keep the pace going, this becomes a great aerobics routine!

EAR-FOOT COORDINATION SUCCESS SUMMARY

There are two prerequisites to dancing. First, you need to know how to execute the basic locomotor movements—if you can walk, then you can dance! Second, you need to recognize (or perceive) the tempo. These skills were covered in the two previous learning steps. This learning step focuses on how to make a perceptual-motor match, which occurs in dancing when you can coordinate your walking steps to an external tempo. This sounds easy, yet it requires you to know exactly what part of your foot should hit the floor to match your footwork exactly with the beats of the music—think of it as an ear-foot coordination task. Typically, the external pace may be provided by either a partner counting out loud or by the underlying beats of the music. In either case, you'll be moving to an external tempo or pace rather than your own pace. In addition, you must coincide your weight shift onto the ball of your foot with the appropriate underlying beat of the music (review figure 3.1).

Social dancing uses two types of rhythm, even and uneven, that describe the number of weight changes in relationship to an underlying beat. If the weight changes each get one beat, then it is an even rhythm. If the weight changes get either less or more time than any one beat, it is an uneven rhythm. Three walking steps may be used as an example. If three walking steps are executed with an even rhythm, then each beat gets one count, or one weight change occurs on each beat (which will be used later in the waltz basic step pattern). If three walking steps are executed with an uneven rhythm, then each weight change does not correspond to each beat in a one-to-one manner; rather, one of the steps occurs between the whole counts, which is called a triple step (and later will be used within the swing, polka, and cha-cha basic step patterns). It is critical that you be able to match your footwork with the intended beat and to be in tempo with the music. Ask a trained partner or your teacher to use the checklists in figures 3.1 through 3.4 to evaluate your ability to execute both even- and uneven-rhythm locomotor movements properly without getting off beat with the music.

STEP
4

PARTNER DYNAMICS AND ETIQUETTE:
COMMUNICATING EFFECTIVELY

Before dancing with a partner, it is natural to have some uncertainties, such as: How should you ask a partner to dance? Who asks whom to dance? What do you do if a partner does not want to dance? Will your partner know how to give the proper leads? What do you do when your partner doesn't follow? Why does the man always get to be the leader and the woman have to follow? What do you do if your partner doesn't know the basic step? What do you do if your partner criticizes you? You can be more in control of these uncertainties if you know your responsibilities and how to communicate effectively in a social dance setting.

Basically, there are two ways of communicating with your partner: verbally and nonverbally. Both ways contribute to making the "social" in social dancing a more pleasant experience. Verbal communication includes knowing and practicing proper social dance etiquette, as well as promoting and practicing a respectful attitude toward your partner and others. Nonverbal communication includes knowing and practicing how to connect with a partner, how to lead, how to follow, and how to create a three-way partnership—involving you, your partner, and the music.

Why Are Partner Dynamics and Etiquette Important?

Social dancing involves very traditional roles for leaders and followers, as well as proper etiquette. Just as when driving a car, there can be only one driver. In social dance, the leader's primary role is to "drive the car"; that is, to plan and signal direction changes

to a partner and to initiate choreography (put moves together) without bumping into other couples. However, neither partner is literally a car, so this analogy must be modified a bit. Thus, the interpretation of leading has evolved from thinking of it as a dictatorship situation to viewing it as a partnership. A successful partnership combines an awareness of moving not only yourself, but of moving both yourself and your partner in unison to the tempo of the music. Blending these three elements together is intrinsically satisfying.

Good communication is said to be made up of the following components:

- 7 percent words
- 38 percent voice quality
- 55 percent body language

On the dance floor, your actions literally speak louder than your words! When you say something to a partner, how you say it is as important as what you say. We all like to receive positive strokes. If you are polite and respectful of both your partner's and others' space, they will be more likely to treat you in the same manner. A social setting presents numerous opportunities to practice social etiquette, such as introducing yourself to others, politely asking a partner to dance, graciously accepting a dance invitation, thanking your partner for the dance, and generally working with a partner. The main advantage of demonstrating these social graces is that they encourage positive interactions and continual interchanges. A sponsored evening of social dancing is similar to a group date because the group members constantly interrelate with each other, fulfilling the role of a good host or hostess.

General Partner Etiquette

In a social setting, it is considered good etiquette to introduce yourself to someone new. Likewise, whenever you meet a new partner, make it a point to introduce yourself. At least three potential situations exist where you may demonstrate social dance etiquette: prior to dancing with a partner, while dancing with a partner, and after sharing a dance with a partner.

Before Dancing With a Partner

The traditional expectation in social settings is that the male take the initiative. However, the most important thing is that both partners are polite to each other. Thus, either partner may ask the other to dance. Following are some examples of how to politely ask a partner to dance:

- "May I have this dance?"
- "Would you like to dance?"

Here are some examples of how to accept an invitation graciously:

- "Certainly."
- "Yes, you may."
- "Yes, I would like to."
- "I would love to."

The following rules provide some examples of etiquette practices typically found in sponsored, nondate events:

- It is more polite to ask a partner to dance than to stand on the sidelines watching.
- Politely ask a partner to dance.
- The follower graciously accepts. (If the follower truly does not want to dance, she can say so, but she should not dance with another partner until that particular dance is over.)
- There is a "no monopolizing" rule, meaning that the follower may excuse herself after two successive dances to provide the leader with an opportunity to ask another partner. (This rule encourages mixing and more opportunities for all to dance.)
- A leader should not cut in on a dancing couple without first asking any follower who is not dancing whether she would like to dance.
- Followers should not huddle in groups, which

makes it harder for the leaders to ask them to dance.
- Introduce yourself, as well as other people who do not know each other.

When Dancing With a Partner

Once on the dance floor, one partner needs to lead and the other needs to follow. Traditionally, the male takes the initiative to lead and invites the female to follow. In this case, tradition is practical in that one person, the leader, becomes the designated driver. Following are selected social etiquette tips to use when dancing with a partner:

- Be considerate of your partner. Avoid giving helpful hints, or criticizing, or dancing for the benefit of onlookers—showing off at the expense of your partner.
- Move in unison with your partner. Avoid leading your partner like an object—versus a person.
- The leader is the one responsible for choreography on the dance floor. Avoid elaborate and complex combinations with a new partner. Focus on the basic step to the music, then gradually add variations.
- Be considerate of other couples. Avoid executing long routines and horizontal arm extensions, especially when the floor is crowded.
- The follower should let the leader lead (i.e., have patience that the leader is doing his best).
- Do *not* offer advice on the dance floor unless you are specifically asked for your opinion.
- The follower's arms should not rest heavily on the leader's arm and hand.
- The leader's right hand should not slip down below the follower's left shoulder blade.
- Avoid singing, counting out loud, or chewing gum to the music as you dance.
- Offer an apology if you accidentally bump someone.
- Inconspicuously and gently lead a partner through an unknown step, or move to the side to avoid blocking traffic.

After Dancing With a Partner

Etiquette doesn't stop when the dance is over. Following are some examples of how to treat a partner after sharing a dance:

- The leaders escort their partners back to where they asked them to dance.
- Both partners thank each other for the dance.
- During an evening of dance, share the fun by dancing with many different partners.
- At the end of the evening, thank the official host or hostess.

Connecting With a Partner

When you dance with a partner, you are sharing space that includes both of you. The basic partner posi-

tions used in this book are commonly used in social dancing (see figure 4.1, a-g). Each partner position described in the following paragraphs requires you to connect with a partner in a slightly different manner.

Shine Position

The shine position is used whenever you are facing a partner but not touching hands. It is called "shine" because each partner has more freedom to express him- or herself when apart and not touching. Another interpretation of the shine position is that a

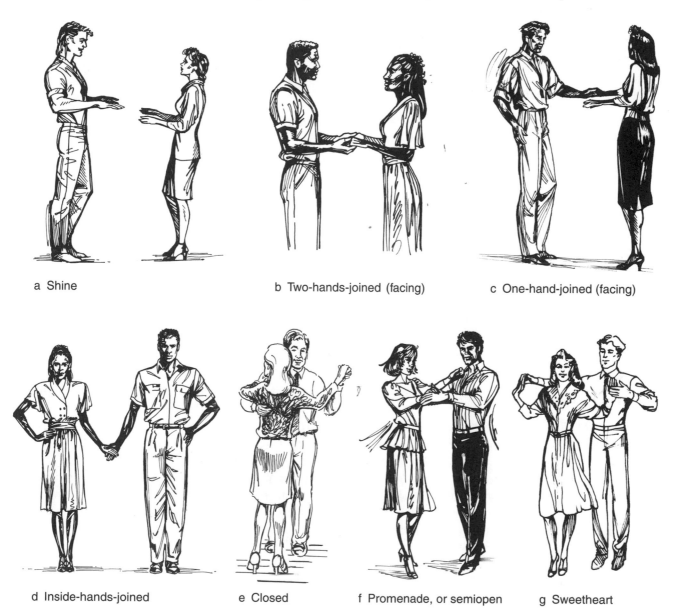

a Shine

b Two-hands-joined (facing)

c One-hand-joined (facing)

d Inside-hands-joined

e Closed

f Promenade, or semiopen

g Sweetheart

Figure 4.1 Basic partner positions.

spotlight is shining on your chest and you are "in the spotlight" to present your moves with flair. The shine position is typically used in the cha-cha and the salsa/mambo.

Two-Hands-Joined Position

The partners face each other a comfortable distance apart. The leader opens his palms for the follower to put her hands (palm down) into them. The leader then gently grasps the follower's hands. Avoid gripping too tightly. A modification of this two-hands-joined position is used in the cha-cha. Specifically, the leader separates his thumb from his fingers and lets the follower curl her fingers around his thumbs—much like a bird on a perch. The leader then gently rests his fingers on top of the follower's fingers.

One-Hand-Joined Position

Start with a two-hands-joined position, then release one hand. Typically, a one-hand-joined position is used for leading either sideways or rotational moves. For example, the leader's left hand may be brought across his midline toward his right side, or conversely, the leader's right hand may be brought across his midline toward his left side.

Inside-Hands-Joined Position

The inside-hands-joined position is most often used in the polka. The leader extends his right hand, palm up, toward his partner. The follower places her left hand, palm down, in his hand. Another characteristic of the polka is for each partner to place the outside hands on the hips.

Closed Position

The closed position is a very regal position reflecting the origin of ballroom dancing in the royal courts of Europe when soldiers wore swords on their left hip. Thus, the follower is positioned more on the leader's right side so as to keep the sword out of the way. An offset position also keeps the leader from stepping on the follower's toes and from stepping around the follower with his feet too widely spaced. In social dancing and within the American styling, the closed position, or "closed hold," consists of at least four points of contact between partners: The leader's right hand is placed on the follower's left shoulder blade; the follower's left arm is gently placed on top of the leader's right arm; the follower's left elbow is resting on, or slightly touching, the leader's right elbow; the leader's left hand is extended with palm up for the follower to place her right hand with palm down. In International style, an additional contact point is required; that is, the right side of each partner's diaphragm must be touching. Because the International styling requires closer contact, it is not commonly used on the social dance floor, especially when dancing with a variety of partners.

Promenade, or Semiopen, Position

The promenade, or semiopen, position is a modified closed position with outside shoulders angled toward the joined hands. In the swing, the hand grasp changes slightly such that the hands are lower and the leader rotates his left-hand fingers clockwise approximately 90 degrees before grasping his partner's fingers.

Sweetheart Position

The sweetheart position is used in the polka and the cha-cha. It starts with a right-to-right hand grasp. The leader then brings his right hand to his right side to guide the follower in front and to his right side. Her palms are facing out and placed at approximately shoulder height. The leader's fingers gently connect with the follower's fingers. The follower stands approximately a half step in front of the leader.

Within each partner position, notice that there is a center point between the partners. If either partner gets too far away from or too close to the other, it is more difficult to lead and follow. You can use your arm positions to give your partner a reference base for where you are. If you permit your arms to hang freely at your sides whenever you are in an open or apart position, it will be difficult to find your partner's hand(s) whenever a hand grasp is needed. On the other hand, if you bend your elbows and keep your forearms more parallel to the floor, you are splitting the distance between you and your partner such that your hands can meet in the middle (for example, in a two-hands-joined position). Thus, your arm placements, or positions in space, provide a frame that defines your personal space. Following are three example situations where one's frame affects how partners connect with each other.

Example 1: In a closed dance position, if the leader signals a forward direction move, the lead will not be effective if the follower lets her arms collapse, which permits the leader to move into her space (see figure 4.2a). Conversely, if the leader moves in a backward direction and lets his elbows collapse, the follower moves into his space (see figure 4.2b). Basically, each partner is responsible for maintaining his or her half of any partner dance position. The amount of pressure or tension to maintain is often a matter of trial and error. It is not necessary to tense your arms all the time. Rather, it is a matter of not letting your partner move into your space, and vice versa. In the example of a forward direction lead, once the leader moves forward, the follower can feel the movement initiation and can move backward with arms defining her space. She only needs to hold her arms up against the pull of gravity and avoid letting her elbow extend back behind her body. The follower needs to avoid resting the weight of her arms on her partner, and the leader needs to avoid letting his elbows droop toward his sides. For both partners, holding the arms up and not dangling them becomes an isometric exercise that will strengthen the triceps muscles (posterior upper arms). Note that these same points apply to the sweetheart position, too.

Example 2: From a two-hands-joined position, avoid straightening your elbows, which increases the distance or space between partners. Figure 4.3 shows the results of this common error. Notice that straightening your elbows permits your head and upper torso to lean backward, throwing you off balance and slowing down your timing with the music. Correct this potential error by using your elbows like shock absorbers; that is, keep your elbows slightly bent with enough tension or resistance to keep them in front of your body. Be aware that this error may also occur when using a one-hand-joined position.

Example 3: On rotational moves, the distance between partners should also be split. As an example, stand beside a partner and find the center point between your feet. Imagine stretching a string from this center point and drawing a small circle on the floor connecting both partners' feet to outline both an inner and an outer circle. Now both partners may take walking steps either clockwise or counterclockwise within this small circular floor path (see figure 4.4). By splitting the distance that either partner has to travel, you are connecting with your partner to make the entire rotational move look effortless. On the other hand, if one partner acts like a post, the other partner must walk around this post, which is more awkward. By splitting the distance that each partner has to move, you are working together, which is an important part of social dancing.

a   b

■ **Figure 4.2** Without individual frame, each partner's half of the shared space may be invaded when the leader wants to travel *(a)* forward or *(b)* backward.

■ **Figure 4.3** Avoid straightening your elbows when using a two-hands-joined position.

Figure 4.4 On rotational moves, imagine a small circular area that connects both partners' feet.

General Tips for Leading a Partner

To be a good leader, you first need to be able to repeat your basic steps until you can do them almost without thinking. Note that the learning progressions from basic steps to combinations will be explained in Step 5, then applied to each dance in Steps 6 through 13. Once you can repeat the basic step(s) to the music without looking at your feet, you are ready to think about other aspects of dancing with a partner (for example, how much force to use on leads, when to signal a lead, how to smoothly connect any two or more partner positions, and how to combine steps into short, sequential combinations). As the leader has a lot to think about, it helps to focus on only one aspect at a time and to gradually add another aspect as you execute the appropriate basic steps.

How much force should you use to lead? In general, "leads" involve gentle pressure to indicate a direction change. They are subtle, nonverbal indicators of where you intend to move next. Typically, a lead comprises a combination of actions. For example,

from a closed partner position, the leader may initiate a couple's turn by facing, or rotating, his chest (upper torso, including arms) in the intended direction, either clockwise or counterclockwise. This example lead involves upper body isolation to twist the upper body in the direction of the desired turn. The leader should keep his arms curved and move his entire frame (i.e., shoulders, arms, and torso move as one unit) until his chest is facing the intended direction. It is important to maintain a solid frame, which means that the lead is less effective if either partner lets only his or her arms move.

When does the leader give the lead? All leads must be given immediately prior to the intended move, so that your partner has enough time to respond. If you intend to stay in the direction indicated, then it is not necessary to give a new lead until you want to move in another direction. Thus, the leader is always thinking ahead to what direction to move in and signaling the lead early enough that the follower can recognize and respond to it. In general, leads occur at the end of a basic step. If the basic step is very short, such as in the waltz, where the basic step gets only three beats of music, then it is helpful for the leader to repeat the basic step at least twice. The advantages of this strategy are that the leader has time to think about the next move and the follower has time to react to the lead—before another lead is given. Use this strategy as long as you find it helpful; for example, when dancing with a new partner for the first time.

In general, as the leader, you are responsible for doing the following:

- Executing the basic in tempo with the music
- Adjusting the length and width of your steps to your match partner's (i.e., you may need to use smaller steps)
- Keeping your elbows positioned against gravity (slightly bent, away from the sides, and in front of your body to establish a frame)
- Signaling the lead prior to the next basic step (i.e., indicating the direction)
- Signaling a turn by lifting your hand above your partner's head
- Ending a turn by lowering your hand below your partner's head
- Keeping your weight centered over the balls of your feet (in a ready position)

General Tips for Following a Partner

To be a good follower, you also need to be able to repeat the basic steps without much thinking. In addition, the follower must be ready to respond to various nonverbal signals. This means that the follower must be versatile in order to reverse directions and sides of the body (from that used by the leader). The follower potentially may move in the same eight directions that the leader may move in. However, whenever the follower is facing a partner, the follower's directions are the mirror opposite. For example, the follower travels backward in response to the leader's signal to move forward, or the follower moves to her right side in response to the leader's signal to move to his left side. Or, from a closed dance position, the leader moves forward with his left foot while the follower moves backward with her right foot.

At first, followers can be confused because instructors typically call out cues for the leaders to know when to give the lead. The order of sequence should be hearing the instructor's cue, giving the lead, then following, which means that you can expect a subtle delay after the instructor's cue and the actual lead before the follower needs to respond. Otherwise, a common error for followers is to anticipate the lead (as given by the instructor's verbal cues to the leader) and move to the vocal cues. Neither anticipating the leads nor responding early will help the leader understand how to lead a particular move when the instructor's verbal cues are not given.

How can followers pick up the leads for direction changes? One tip is to use your peripheral vision to focus on your partner's shoulders, because they indicate direction changes, especially rotations. Avoid the habit of watching your own feet, which indicates that you need more practice without a partner to ingrain the basic steps. If the leader is moving forward, backward, or sideways, his shoulders will be perpendicular to the line of dance (LOD). On couple's turns, the leader's shoulders typically angle approximately 45 degrees either clockwise (to face diagonal toward the wall) or counterclockwise (to face diagonal toward the center) from the LOD (see figure 4.5).

In general, as the follower, you are responsible for the following:

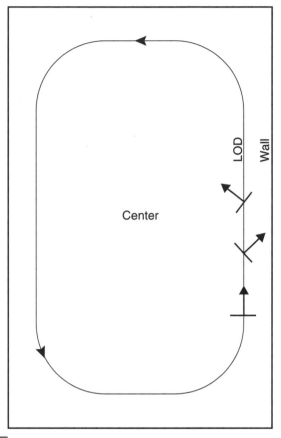

Figure 4.5 Diagonal paths possible along the LOD.

- Executing the basic step at a consistent tempo (set by the leader)
- Waiting for the lead (versus anticipating or "helping" the leader)
- Repeating the basic step until given a new lead
- Holding your own frame (arm positions) against gravity (versus resting weight on your partner's arms)
- Maintaining your frame so as to provide gentle feedback to define your space (avoid either very rigid or very limp arms, sometimes called "spaghetti" arms)
- Keeping your weight over the balls of your feet (in a ready position)
- Executing the turn (after the leader signals when to start; the leader then stops the turn)
- When traveling in the LOD, reaching backward from the hip (versus bending your knees)

Handling Criticism

Unfortunately, some of the following comments may be heard on the dance floor:

> "You're hard to lead."
> "Dancing with you is like moving a tank around the floor."
> "When are you going to add a turn?"
> "You didn't do that right—you need to lift your arm like this."
> "You're pushing too hard."
> "You can't lead."
> "You can't follow."

Perhaps the worst scenario on the dance floor is to be criticized by a partner, even if it is well intended. You've probably either heard others disagree or been involved in disagreements about the "correct" order, timing, way to move, and so forth. It is not a pleasant experience. The best way to handle criticism is to make it a practice to notice what your partner is doing right and compliment him or her on it. Have patience that your partner is doing the best he or she can at any point in time. Have confidence and trust that your partner will get there eventually and at his or her own rate. It is not helpful to provide verbal reminders to your partner as to what to do or how to do it. Your role is to cooperate with your partner. You can only be responsible for your own actions. The only time advice is welcome on the floor is when a partner specifically asks for it. Otherwise, social dancing should be for meeting others, improving/practicing your own skills, accepting differences, and sharing the experience of dancing with a partner. It is a great way to have fun and get some exercise too.

With experience, you'll soon find that there is an evolution of "blame" in couples dancing starting from directly criticizing your partner to taking responsibility for your own actions to finally acknowledging that something didn't work out as planned and laughing about it or just trying it again, as follows:

> "You did that wrong."
> "I did that wrong."
> "We did that wrong."
> "Let's try that again."

Or

> "You made a mistake."
> "I made a mistake."
> "We made a mistake."
> "That didn't work."

Or

> "You're off."
> "I'm off."
> "We're off."
> "That's one way."

At both the third and fourth levels of blame, it is shared, so there are often a few laughs at the same time the couple acknowledges that things didn't go right and decides to "try it again." No one person is to blame; rather, it is a consequence of a particular trial. We all learn by trial and error. Give yourself some leeway to make mistakes on the dance floor—this is how we learn and have some fun along the way.

In summary, some suggestions for handling criticism follow:

- Compliment your partner on something he or she did correctly ("I liked the way that you timed the lead for my turn. I knew just which way to turn.") or mention something about the experience that you enjoyed ("That was fun," or "I really like this song," or "Thanks so much for the dance.").
- Use a cooperative approach (e.g., "Would you try it again?" or "Let's do that again.").
- Ask an unbiased observer, ideally an instructor, to watch and provide constructive criticism (e.g., "When should I give the lead?" or "Where should I be standing in relationship to my partner?" or "What should my footwork be ?").
- Take a time-out if at an impasse (e.g., "Time for a break. Let's try it again later.").
- Take responsibility for your own contribution to the partnership (e.g., "I missed that lead. Would you please try it again?" or "I was trying to lead a turn. Let me do it again.").
- State your position, then use "would" versus "could" in your comments (e.g., "I'm a beginning dancer. Would you please go easy?" or "I don't like to go that fast. Would you please slow it down?" or "I want to make sure that I understand my part. Would you please walk through that again?").

Notice that the previous suggestions assume that it is *not* acceptable to offer advice or criticism on the social dance floor. It is more important to appreciate different role responsibilities and to cooperate with your partner. It will not matter in five years whether one person or the other was "right." On the other hand, it could matter greatly if you're establishing a new friendship or meeting a potential life partner.

Creating a Three-Way Partnership

The ultimate goal on the social dance floor is to dance with your partner in time to the music. This shared experience provides intrinsic rewards. Once you go to a dance, you may become aware of spectators watching you dance. However, you need to shift your focus away from any observers and instead focus first on the music for the tempo, then on moving with your partner to that tempo. The ideal three-way partnership consists of you, your partner, and the music. If only one or two elements come together, then you'll experience a feeling of being at odds with either your partner or the music. If all three elements mesh together, then dancing becomes a pleasure to do as well as enjoyable to watch.

PARTNER DYNAMICS AND ETIQUETTE

DRILLS

1. Whole-Body Leads

Face a partner and match both your facing palms such that your fingers are pointing toward the ceiling, like a stop sign. Adjust your facing palms so that only your fingertips are touching. The best leads are those that are subtle. One partner can be designated as the leader, who starts this drill by shifting his weight forward to signal the forward direction. For example, once the leader has shifted his weight forward over the balls of his feet, the follower can detect this subtle shift forward—even before the leader can take a step. Walk at least four to eight steps in the leader's forward direction (which is backward for the follower).

After a few trials, alternate roles such that the follower initiates the direction forward by shifting her weight forward over the balls of her feet. The leader should be able to detect this subtle shift forward (which is backward for the leader). Walk in the direction indicated. Notice that this drill will not work if either partner lets the elbows or arms move in isolation from the rest of the body. Frame refers to the entire hand, arm, and shoulder relationship—with elbows positioned in front of the body, and hands in the middle to define each half of the shared space.

Next, the leader can practice subtle whole-body leads to indicate travel to either side. Remember that the center point of balance should shift in the direction of travel. The follower should be able to pick up the leader's weight shift from both feet to one foot prior to actually taking a step to that side—all without any verbal cues from the leader. Walk to the side indicated by the leader. After a few trials, reverse roles and let the follower initiate the side direction (either right or left) prior to both partners stepping to that side so that the leader may feel the lead. Again, this will not work if either of you isolates and only moves your arms (versus your entire body, i.e., from your center).

Success Goal = 10 repetitions of shifting weight to indicate direction, (a) either forward or backward, then (b) either left side or right___

Success Check
- Shift your weight (CPB) in the intended direction prior to actually taking a step in that direction___
- When facing a partner, shift your weight forward to indicate the follower should move backward___
- When facing a partner, shift your weight to the left side to indicate the follower should move to the right side, and vice versa___
- Maintain your half of the shared space between you and your partner (versus letting only your arms move)___

To Increase Difficulty

- Start on the outside of the room with a partner such that the leader can travel forward in a CCW direction around the perimeter of the room (which is the line of dance, or LOD). Practice walking to any 4/4 time music or at a set pace with a partner, and notice how you need to incrementally angle your center (much like turning the wheel of a car) on the curves. This challenge is much like playing "bumper cars" when there are multiple couples on the floor. The leader must be aware of other couples and safely maneuver the follower in the LOD.
- Repeat this drill from a closed dance position.
- Repeat this drill from a shine position. (Tip: Watch the leader's upper torso to detect the direction being led.) Be aware of maintaining the distance between yourself and your partner.

To Decrease Difficulty

- Start the drill with the leader standing with his back to a wall, then repeat the drill.

2. Frame and Rotational Leads

Whether you are dancing in a shine (apart position) or with a partner, it is important to establish and maintain your frame. Stand without a partner. Notice where you have positioned your arms. If they are dangling by your sides, then you do not have frame. Make a conscious effort to bend your elbows and lift your forearms until they are parallel with the floor, with your palms facing downward. This is the arm position used in the two-hands-joined position. What is different is that you need to maintain this position even when you turn or rotate to either side. For example, rotate your upper torso 45 degrees both left and right. Notice that your entire upper torso rotates from your spine or midline. As your sternum faces either side, your arms move as well. It is not a matter of reaching your arms across your body.

Another critical position for frame is in the closed dance position. Stand in the closed position with a partner. Now take at least two steps backward and away from your partner. You may lower your arms slightly to make the position more comfortable, but keep the same semicurved shape from your fingertips through your arms and shoulders. Imagine that you are holding a large beach ball, so that you become aware of the space inside the semicircle. Maintain this shape as you rotate your upper torso 45 degrees both to the left and to the right. Think of turning your chest or sternum in the direction of the turn, and your arms will follow if you keep them moving as one unit.

Success Goal = 10 repetitions of demonstrating frame while rotating your upper torso to one side, then to the other side___

Success Check
- Maintain an arm position whether dancing alone or with a partner___
- Keep forearms parallel to the floor when in a two-hands-joined position___
- Create a semicurved shape that slopes in a descending manner from shoulders to elbows to hands___
- Initiate a turn by rotating your upper torso and arms in the direction of the turn___

To Increase Difficulty

- Alternately, from a two-hands-joined position, practice rotating your upper torso and arms to one side (e.g., to leader's left side) and release one hand (e.g., leader's left hand) to make the transition to a one-hand-joined position (leader's right hand holding follower's left hand). Face your partner to resume a two-hands-joined position, then continue rotating to face the opposite side and release one hand to make the transition to a one-hand-joined position (leader's left hand holding follower's right hand).

To Decrease Difficulty

- Check yourself in a mirror to see whether you have positioned your arms correctly.
- Start in a closed position with a partner and rotate your upper torso 45 degrees to either side while keeping a circular shape with your partner—that is, each partner's arms create a semicircle that together with the partner's makes a full circle.

3. Getting Started With a Partner

Imagine that you are at a social dance with the goal of dancing with a variety of partners. If you are the leader, practice how you might ask a partner for a dance. If you are the follower, practice how you might accept a dance with a partner. How would you introduce yourself before the dance? What would you say if you wanted to compliment your partner, as appropriate (and avoid any criticism)? If you are the leader, practice how you would escort the follower back to the location where you asked her to dance.

Success Goal = Appropriate dialogue for dancing with at least five different partners___

Success Check

- Politely ask a partner to dance___
- Graciously accept a partner's invitation to dance___
- Correctly name and demonstrate with a partner each of the seven basic partner positions shown in figure 4.1___
- Thank your partner after the dance___

To Increase Difficulty

- Dance with a variety of partners.
- Indicate a forward direction lead in the LOD.

To Decrease Difficulty

- Challenge yourself to dance with at least one or two new partners each time you go social dancing.

PARTNER DYNAMICS AND ETIQUETTE SUCCESS SUMMARY

Social dancing may be both exciting and a bit unnerving if you've never done it before. You can be more in control of the uncertainties if you know your responsibilities on the dance floor and know how to communicate effectively with your partner. Verbal communication is important when asking for or accepting a dance and generally making the time shared on the dance floor enjoyable for both partners. Nonverbal communication is important for indicating direction of travel, connecting with a partner, and moving in unison with the music. What you say and how you move with a partner can show either respect or disrespect. Obviously, the goal is to work together to make dancing a more pleasant experience for everyone.

STEP
5

BASIC STEPS, TRANSITIONS, AND VARIATIONS:
PREPARING TO DANCE

During an evening of ballroom dance, an orchestra will typically play a majority of foxtrot and swing songs, a few waltz songs, and one or two songs each for rumba, cha-cha, polka, tango, and mambo or salsa. These dances reflect the most popular ballroom dances and are specifically covered in this book in Steps 6 through 13. Once you learn the basic step patterns, transitions, variations, and how to create combinations, you'll be able to go out dancing too!

The purpose of this learning step is to prepare you for the progression used with each dance style covered in this book (i.e., in Steps 6 through 13). For each dance style presented, the following elements will be featured:

- A brief history
- A basic step pattern description, including rhythm, footwork cues, and timing cues (for both the leader and the follower)
- Easy-to-difficult practice drills for executing the basic step patterns, for adding appropriate transitions, and for expanding your repertoire of moves (called variations)
- Sample combinations (linking any three or more variations)
- A summary chart listing the variations and transitions covered for each dance style and categorized either by the type of rhythmic pattern or by the partner position from which the variation is executed

Why Are Basic Steps, Transitions, and Variations Important?

Even though you may be "dancing" by repeating a rhythmic pattern, your rhythmic pattern may be different than someone else's rhythmic pattern, which makes it difficult to dance with a variety of partners. The basic step patterns represent a "packaged" version that is both traditionally and universally associated with a specific type of dance.

Transitions function as bridges to connect any two partner positions. How you get from any one partner position to the next makes a big difference in your presentation of any particular dance style. Many dancers either ignore or forget about transitions in their rush to learn as many "cool" moves or variations as they can. It is important to take time to understand how transitions can make your dancing look more polished and flowing. Smooth transitions will also make it easier for leaders to lead and for followers to follow.

Some dances have more than one transition option either into or out of specific partner positions. Once you know which transition options exist for particular dances, you can select the one you prefer to use at any one time. Because there are a finite number of possible transitions, you may select your favorite ones to create a flowing sequence of moves that connect any two or more partner positions. With practice, your transitions soon become automatic, which makes it easier for the leader to focus on other things.

Once you can move smoothly from one partner position to another, you can add variations of the basic step that are appropriate for any particular partner dance position. For example, an underarm turn is a popular variation. Typically, an underarm turn may be executed from a closed position, a two-hands-joined position, or a one-hand-joined position. The actual timing of the leads to indicate an underarm turn varies with the basic step selected and the tempo of the music.

Variations provide fun challenges because you may repeat the basic step pattern yet modify the interaction with your partner. For example, some modifications for either or both partners might include the following: a turn or spin, a change in direction, a subtle timing change, use of multiple turns, linking variations together, and so forth. The fewer basic step patterns executed between these modifications or variations, the more challenging they become. As you practice, you'll soon find that some variations are more appealing to you and link together more naturally than others.

The more variations you know how to execute, the more difficult it becomes to remember both how and when to do them on the dance floor. One way to trigger your memory of the possible variations is to associate them with the various dance partner positions from which they are executed. Another way to remember them is to group any three or more moves together into a cluster of moves to create a combination. Thus, once you start any particular cluster or combination, the next two or more moves are naturally linked without the need to think about them

purposefully. The moves emerge without much thought, much like a chain reaction.

Common Footwork Positions

There are five common foot positions that can enhance your balance and execution of the basic step patterns. You'll be using one of these foot positions on every step (weight change) that you take. A chart of selected examples of when you might use these different foot positions is at the bottom of this page.

Once you can recognize these foot positions, you can use them as visual references for better understanding where to position your feet. Figure 5.1 shows the five footwork positions commonly used in social dancing.

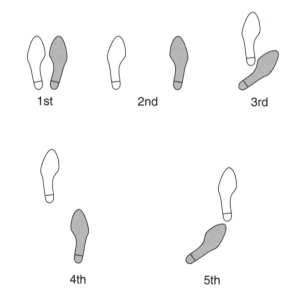

Figure 5.1 Five footwork positions commonly used in social dancing.

Foot position	Movement purpose
First position (feet parallel and side by side)	Closing feet or spinning
Second position (feet parallel and shoulder-width apart)	Stepping left or right
Third position (feet perpendicular, heel to instep)	Balance and turning
Fourth position (feet parallel, forward-backward stride)	Stepping forward or backward
Fifth position (feet perpendicular, heel to toe)	Balance and turning

New Skill Expectations

Sometimes it can be frustrating to learn new skills. Even if you are highly skilled at one dance, when you learn a new dance, a new variation, or a new combination, you are starting the learning process over again. With any new skill, your first goal is to get an idea of what to do, including exactly where to position your feet, your body, your hands, how fast or slowly to move, and so forth. At this point, it is necessary for you to think more cognitively about what to do and to get an image of the desired skill. With practice, you'll soon be able to repeat the basic step patterns without much thought. With more practice, you'll soon want more variety and will be ready for the challenge of learning different variations (i.e., off the basic step pattern and in different partner positions). Once you know how to execute many different variations, the challenge is how to remember them all! You'll need to choose a strategy not only to help you combine the variations in a meaningful way, but also to recall them on the dance floor when under pressure. Everyone goes through this general learning process when learning something new. Don't expect to do things perfectly the first time you are introduced to a new skill. It takes a lot of practice to make your dancing look easy, which is the ultimate goal. Again, the order of presentation of the dances in Steps 6 through 13 is specifically designed to take you through the learning process in a fun and engaging manner.

How do you approach learning a new skill? When someone demonstrates a new skill, do you prefer to focus on one thing at a time, add on the next part, and so forth, until the entire skill is learned? Or do you prefer to see what the entire skill involves, including the timing, rhythm, and how to relate with your partner? If you prefer to focus on each part, then, for example, your attention would be only on what your feet do, then only on what your body does, then only on what your arms do, and so forth, until the entire skill is learned. This is a part-to-whole method of approaching new skills. If you prefer to focus on the entire skill first, then you would not be concerned with specific parts, but more with how the parts merge to create a flow of energy, including timing, rhythm, coordination with your partner, and the like. This is a whole-to-part method of approaching new skills. Both methods work equally well. Neither method is better than the other. It is a matter of what you prefer and what helps facilitate your learning. Once you know your preferred method of approaching new skills, you can be more tolerant of others who may use a different method. Again, remember that each method gets you to the same end—it's simply a matter of using different ways of getting there.

PREPARING TO DANCE

DRILLS

1. Recognizing Foot Positions

Review the five foot positions shown in figure 5.1, then practice positioning your feet in each of them. After you are comfortable defining these foot positions, ask a partner to help you test your application of them. Take turns with your partner such that one person demonstrates a particular foot position, then the other states the name of that foot position.

Success Goal = Correctly name and demonstrate each of the five foot positions___

Success Check
• Compare your answers with the illustrations shown in figure 5.1___

To Increase Difficulty
• Use a random order.

To Decrease Difficulty
• Use a sequential, numerical order.

2. Presentation Preferences

When someone demonstrates a new skill to you, what do you focus on? For example, how would you best learn to execute the following sequence: walk two steps forward, do one triple step, then repeat these actions starting with your other foot?

Can you take each separate part and gradually add them together until the entire sequence is completed? Was there enough information for you to understand how to execute this sequence? Or do you need to see someone demonstrating this sequence for you to identify the timing, rhythm, direction, and total flow of the sequence?

Success Goal = Decipher the sequence and demonstrate it for a partner. Ask your partner what he or she focused on. How do your approaches compare___

Success Check
- Both methods of focus (either part-whole or whole-part) are equally effective___
- Become aware of both your (and your partner's) preferred method of approaching new skills___

To Increase Difficulty
- Vary some aspect of the sequence, such as the direction or the number of repetitions of each part. How does your partner notice the difference between the original sequence and your modified sequence?

To Decrease Difficulty
- Use a combination strategy to focus on the whole sequence, then on selected parts of the sequence, or vice versa.

BASIC STEPS, TRANSITIONS, AND VARIATIONS SUCCESS SUMMARY

For each dance style presented in this book, a specially designed progression is used to introduce you to the basic step pattern(s), appropriate transitions and variations, and strategies for creating combinations. This progression reflects the typical learning process that everyone goes through when learning new skills. A summary chart within the last drill for each of these dance styles (Steps 6 through 13) provides a handy reference for helping you remember and recall which basic step pattern(s), transitions, and variations are associated with each dance style.

Before going to the specific dance styles, it is helpful to know that common foot positions are used each time you take a step (i.e., make a weight change from one foot to the other). You can enhance your balance and execution by being aware of these different foot positions, which are shown in figure 5.1 and will be specifically identified as appropriate to each dance style covered in this book.

In addition, it is helpful to recognize that there are different methods and approaches to learning. Once you can identify both your own and your partner's learning preferences, you can be more tolerant of the process, especially if your partner's rate of progress is different from yours. It is unrealistic to expect everyone else to learn in the same way that you do.

Now you are ready to go directly to any one or all of the eight dances presented in this book: foxtrot (Step 6), swing (Step 7), waltz (Step 8), polka (Step 9), cha-cha (Step 10), rumba (Step 11), tango (Step 12), or salsa/mambo (Step 13). Enjoy the process!

STEP 6

FOXTROT: DANCING REGALLY

There are many variations to the foxtrot, an American dance first introduced in 1913 or 1914. The foxtrot got its name from Mr. Harry Fox, a musical comedy star who performed a fast, trotting step to ragtime music in a Ziegfeld musical. As the result of a publicity stunt, Mr. Oscar Duryea, who was a star nightclub performer, was hired to teach this step to the public. However, the original version was too exhausting, so it was modified to alternate four walking steps with eight quick running steps.

Later, Vernon and Irene Castle and other professional dancers helped shape the foxtrot into a smooth, graceful dance. An erect posture and stationary torso and arm movements lend elegance as the partners move around the floor counterclockwise.

An alternative variation, the magic step, was created by the famous dance instructor Arthur Murray. He and his wife Katherine used a six-count combination of slow and quick beats (the magic step) in several "surprising" ways. The magic step is one of two popular basic steps in foxtrot today. It uses a slow, slow, quick, quick (SSQQ, or six-count) rhythmic pattern.

The other popular basic step in foxtrot uses a slow, quick, quick (SQQ, or four-count) rhythmic pattern, which is typically used in a box step. Foxtrot music is the most frequent type of music played during an evening of ballroom social dancing. The basic foxtrot uses a closed dance position. Both basic step options will be addressed.

Slow, Quick, Quick (Four-Count) Rhythm

The SQQ rhythmic pattern may be executed forward, backward, sideways, or turning, making it a versatile step. Initially, it is helpful to use only forward and backward directions, such as combining two

basics, or two measures of music, to create a box step. Imagine a box shape on the floor, and then divide it in half along the diagonal. It takes two repetitions of this SQQ rhythmic pattern, or two half-box basics, to complete a full box step.

Although the term "box step" implies a square, its shape actually becomes more rectangular. The sides of the box should extend approximately 18 inches (or longer than your side step), and the side steps should be no wider than your shoulders. The leader starts with the left foot to execute the forward half of the box while the follower starts with the right foot to execute the back half of the box. The follower both mirrors and reverses the leader's part. When the leader moves forward, the follower moves backward, and vice versa.

Throughout the following descriptions, two terms often get confused. Note that "together" means bringing the feet together with a weight change, whereas "close" means bringing the feet together with no weight change.

For the leader: To execute the forward half-box basic, bend your standing knee (i.e., your right knee), push off to extend your left leg forward, and step onto your left foot (and shift your weight) on count 1. For styling on count 2, you may bring the ball of your right foot beside the ball of your left foot to close your feet briefly, but do not shift your weight. Then continue moving your right foot directly sideways (notice that your right foot traces a 90-degree angle along the floor). On count 3, step to your right side onto your right foot (your side step should be no wider than the width of your shoulders). On count 4, bring your left foot beside your right to bring your feet together and transfer your weight onto your left foot. Then reverse these actions to execute the backward half-box basic (see follower's footwork, which starts with the backward half-box basic).

Notice that the leader uses the following foot positions: starts in parallel first position, steps forward (or backward) into parallel fourth position, steps sideways into second position, then brings the feet together to return to parallel first position.

An alternative is to continue to travel forward on the second half-box basic. You'll then be executing half-box progressions forward.

For the follower: To execute the backward half-box basic, start with your right foot. For momentum, bend the knee of your standing leg (i.e., your left leg), push off to extend your right leg backward, and step onto the ball of your right foot on count 1. For styling on count 2, you may bring the ball of your left foot beside the ball of your right foot to close your feet briefly, but do not shift your weight. Then continue moving your left leg directly sideways to step (on count 3) onto your left foot (both feet should be no more than shoulder-width apart). On count 4,

bring your right foot beside your left to bring your feet together (and transfer your weight onto your right foot). Then execute the forward half-box basic (see leader's footwork, which starts with the forward half-box basic step).

Notice that the follower uses the following foot positions: starts in parallel first position, steps backward (or forward) into parallel fourth position, steps sideways into second position, then brings the feet together to return to parallel first position.

An alternative is to continue to travel backward on the second half-box basic. This alternative starts the half-box progressions backward for the follower.

Figure 6.1 shows the various ways you might organize the counts and footwork for the foxtrot basic four-count rhythm. Some cues will be more helpful to you than others. Select those cues that most help you retain how to execute both the foxtrot box step and the half-box progression step.

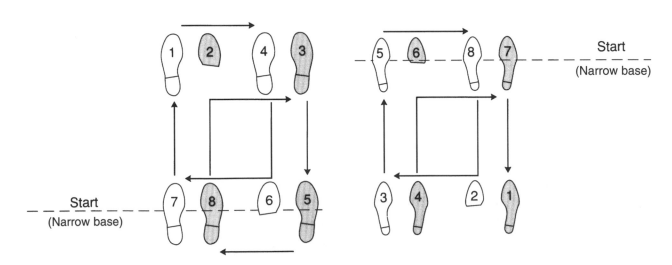

FIGURE 6.1 **KEYS TO SUCCESS: FOXTROT BASIC FOUR-COUNT RHYTHM (SQQ)**

Footwork Cues

a Leader's box step

b Follower's box step

Box Step

a. Leader: Forward, close, side, together;
   backward, close, side, together
b. Follower: Backward, close, side, together;
   forward, close, side, together

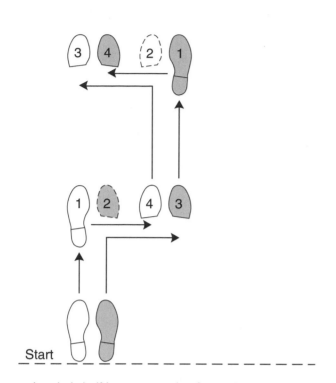

c Leader's half-box progression forward

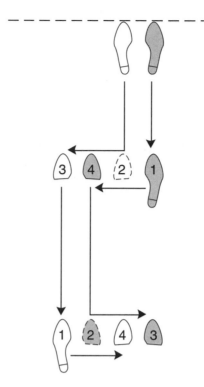

d Follower's half-box progression forward

Half-Box Progression

a. Leader: Forward, close, side, together;
   forward, close, side, together
b. Follower: Backward, close, side, together;
   backward, close, side, together

Timing Cues

4/4 time signature:	Four beats to a measure, each beat gets one count
Total counts:	Eight (accents on even counts)
Rhythmic counts:	1-2, 3, 4; 2-2, 3, 4 or 1-2, 3, 4; 5-6, 7, 8
Weight changes:	Six (in two measures; on counts 1, 3, 4 and 5, 7, 8)
Duration of steps:	Slow, quick, quick (repeat twice); 2:1 ratio of counts to beats
Direction of steps:	a. Box step: Forward half box, then backward half box (leader); backward half box, then forward half box (follower)
	b. Half-box progression: Forward half box, forward half box (leader); backward half box, backward half box (follower)

Slow, Slow, Quick, Quick (Six-Count) Rhythm

The six-count rhythm in foxtrot gives you a lot of traveling options and is used in the magic step. The leader starts with the left foot while the follower starts with the right foot. After one repetition of the basic step, each partner's original starting foot is free again.

For the leader: Stand in correct body alignment with your feet in a narrow base (feet parallel in first position and no more than two to three inches apart). To extend your reach to approximately 18 to 24 inches, bend your standing knee (i.e., right knee), push off, and step forward (and transfer your weight onto your left foot) on count 2. Repeat on the opposite side to step forward (and transfer your weight onto your right foot) on count 4. For styling at the end of count 4, you may briefly bring your left foot up beside your right foot (close) without shifting your weight. Then take a shoulder-width side step onto your left foot on count 5. Bring your feet together (and transfer your weight onto your right foot) on count 6.

For the follower: Stand in correct body alignment with your feet in a narrow base (feet parallel in first position and no more than two to three inches apart). To match the extension of your partner's reach, bend your left knee, push off, extend your right leg backward, and step onto the ball of your right foot (and transfer your weight) on count 2. Repeat on the opposite side to step backward (and transfer your weight) onto the ball of your left foot on count 4. For styling at the end of count 4, you may briefly bring your right foot beside your left foot (close) without shifting your weight. Then continue to take a shoulder-width side step onto your right foot on count 5. Bring your feet together (and transfer your weight onto your left foot) on count 6.

Notice that the foot positions for the basic six-count rhythm are to start in parallel first foot position, move to fourth position with feet parallel (whether traveling forward or backward), then take a side step in second foot position, and bring the feet together to return to first position with feet parallel.

Figure 6.2 shows the various ways you might organize the counts and footwork for the foxtrot basic six-count rhythm. Some cues will be more helpful to you than others. Select those cues that most help you retain how to execute the foxtrot basic six-count rhythm.

FIGURE 6.2	KEYS TO SUCCESS: FOXTROT BASIC SIX-COUNT RHYTHM (SSQQ)

Footwork Cues

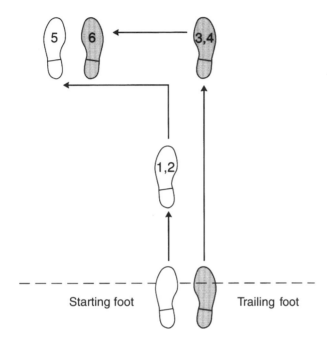

a Leader

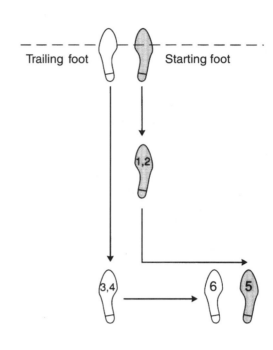

b Follower

a. Leader: Forward reach, forward reach, side, together
b. Follower: Backward reach, backward reach, side, together

Timing Cues

4/4 time signature:	Four beats to a measure, each beat gets one count
Total counts:	Six (accents on even counts)
Rhythmic counts:	1-2, 3-4, 5, 6
Weight changes:	Four (in 1 1/2 measures, or on counts 2, 4, 5, 6)
Duration of steps:	Slow, slow, quick, quick
Length of steps:	Long, long, short, together
Direction of steps:	a. Leader: Forward, forward, left side
	b. Follower: Backward, backward, right side

FOXTROT BASIC STEP PATTERN

DRILLS

1. SQQ Execution Challenges

You have two step options with the basic four-count rhythm: a box step or a half-box progression. The first option is a good choice when space is tight, whereas the second option is a good choice when there is room to travel.

a. *Box step:* Imagine the outline of a rectangular-shaped box drawn on the floor. Without music or a partner, step in each corner of this rectangular-shaped box. Notice that you will need to step with one foot either forward or backward (along the length of the rectangle), then make two weight changes (along the width of the rectangle). Review figure 6.1, as necessary, for the specific footwork and timing cues. Practice starting with either the forward or the backward half box. Notice that a different foot starts each half box. Try this with a partner in closed dance position.

b. *Half-box progression:* Repeat the first half box forward as you did with the box step. However, if no other couples are immediately in front of you and your partner, then the leader may choose to continue forward on the second half box. Try this with a partner in closed dance position.

Success Goal = Two consecutive minutes of the SQQ rhythm, first executing (a) a box step, then (b) half-box progressions___

Success Check
- Width of the rectangle should be no wider than your shoulders___
- Length of the rectangle should be longer than the sides___
- Take two counts for the "slow" (along the length of the rectangle)___
- Take one count for each "quick" (along the width of the rectangle)___

To Increase Difficulty
- Execute each of the basic box step options to slow foxtrot music (use track 12).
- Alternate the basic box step options.

To Decrease Difficulty
- Place tape or string (or cut out and place footprints) on the floor to outline a rectangular-shaped box, then follow this floor shape as you execute the box step.
- Match an action with each underlying beat such that you do a "forward, close, side, together" or a "backward, close, side, together" pattern, matching an action with each beat within a measure. This alternative gives you a head start on styling your free foot (i.e., to move through your base of support).

2. SSQQ Execution Challenge

The timing in the basic six-count rhythm alternates two "slows" and two "quicks" within six total beats of music. This basic step combines two reaching steps with a small side step and together (review figure 6.2). You give each reaching step two counts by extending your leg prior to making a weight change (stepping on alternate feet on counts 2 and 4). Then take a shoulder-width side step and bring your feet together. Give each "quick, quick" one count (changing weight on both counts 5 and 6). Try the basic six-count rhythm with a partner in a closed dance position.

Success Goal = Two consecutive minutes of executing the SSQQ rhythm___

✔**Success Check**
• Keep a narrow base on forward or backward steps (feet two to three inches apart)___
• Notice that the basic six-count rhythm not only travels forward, but also moves you closer to the center of the room___

To Increase Difficulty
• Use a variety of slow foxtrot music.
• Combine two basics forward, then do two basics backward—for practice only—as this would be difficult to do on a crowded dance floor.

To Decrease Difficulty
• Place tape or string (or cut out and place footprints) on the floor as a guide for both the direction and length of steps to be taken.
• Gradually increase the tempo of the counts until you are up to the tempo of the slow music selected.

3. Lengthening Your Stride
Because the smoothness of the foxtrot depends so much on the long, reaching step with each "slow," it helps to practice how to modify your regular walking step to achieve the proper length. The actual reaching length varies, depending on your height and your leg length, but it should be longer than your regular walking stride. The purpose of this drill is to identify your walking versus reaching stride.

To start this drill, place your heels on a line and stand with your feet two to three inches apart. Ask a partner to put one end of a yardstick beside you and perpendicular to the line your heels are touching. Take one regular walking step forward, transfer your weight forward onto the ball of your foot, and freeze your position. Use the yardstick to measure the distance from your starting heel position to the tip of the toe of your front foot. Record this measurement.

Now place your heels back on the starting line and modify your previous actions by bending your trailing knee and pushing off against the floor with the ball of your trailing foot as you take one step forward. Again, transfer your weight onto the ball of your foot and freeze your position. Use the yardstick to measure where the tip of the toe of your front foot ends. Record this measurement. Compare the two measurements just taken. Which is longer?

Success Goal = Awareness of the lengthening effect that a knee bend and a push-off add to your reach on each "slow"___

✔**Success Check**
• Keep your center over the foot and leg that bear your weight___
• Bend one leg to lower your center of gravity___
• Connect with the floor by pushing down and in the direction opposite to your intended direction (e.g., push down and back with one foot to move the other foot forward). This provides more momentum to go in the desired direction (Newton's law of action and reaction)___

To Increase Difficulty
• Extend your reach twice within your basic six-count rhythm execution to maintain the flow (momentum) on both of your "slow" timing cues. Watch for any tendency to reach on only the first "slow" step.
• Gradually increase the tempo of your selected foxtrot music.
• Alternate SQQ and SSQQ rhythms.

To Decrease Difficulty
• Face a partner and match facing palms. Experiment with taking a step, first without and then with a knee bend, prior to your "slow" step. A knee bend should give you more connection with your partner (lowering your center), making it easier to start in unison.

4. Using the Rule of Two Repetitions

When you are first learning a new step, it is helpful to do a minimum of two repetitions of any basic step before switching to something new. The purpose behind this rule is to make a combination that is both easy to remember (if you are the leader) and easy to recognize (if you are the follower). For example, without a partner, do two box steps, then two basic six-count rhythm steps. Continue to alternate these two basic steps. After you can do this combination without music, try it to slow foxtrot music.

Success Goal = Two consecutive minutes of alternately executing two box steps and two basic six-count rhythm steps___

Success Check

• Avoid watching either your own or someone else's feet___
• Keep your eyes level and stand tall___
• Use any cues that will help you mentally visualize the steps prior to executing them___

To Increase Difficulty

• Vary both the order and the number of repetitions (i.e., 2, 4, 6, 8, and so on) of any of the three basic step patterns learned so far. For example, combine two basic six-count rhythm steps and four half-box progression steps, or four box steps and six basic six-count rhythm steps, or two box steps and eight half-box progressions. Which combinations are most natural for you?

To Decrease Difficulty

• Use at least four repetitions of any one basic. For example, combine four box steps and four basic six-count rhythm steps, or four half-box progressions and four box steps. Notice that more repetitions allow more time to think about what to do next. Which order is most natural for you?

FOXTROT TRANSITION

DRILL

1. Leads From a Closed Position to a Promenade Position and Back to Closed

Using box rhythm, the cross step may be executed in either the foxtrot or the waltz. It uses two half-box basics (two measures of music) and includes a transition between a closed partner position and a promenade position. What makes this transition more challenging is that it requires isolation such that your hands and arms remain stationary while your torso and lower body angle 45 degrees. To get an idea, stand facing a wall without a partner. Place your hands against the wall at about shoulder height. Position your weight over the balls of your feet and twist your feet such that your toes alternately face either your right hand (for followers) or your left hand (for leaders).

You don't need to be extremely flexible, as you'll only need to rotate from your hips 45 degrees to either side, or 90 degrees total. The most common error is to move your arms. The second most common error is to rotate or twist too far to the side (beyond 45 degrees). Practice this subtle lower body rotation alone, then with a partner.

For both the foxtrot and the waltz, the box rhythm uses three weight changes. However, the counts are different due to the different time signatures (four beats to a measure in the foxtrot

Foxtrot: Dancing Regally • 61

versus three beats to a measure in the waltz). Thus, in the foxtrot, the lead to angle 45 degrees occurs at the end of count 3 and prior to count 4. The cross step includes one half-box basic to move into a promenade position, then another half-box basic to move back to a closed position (see figure 6.3).

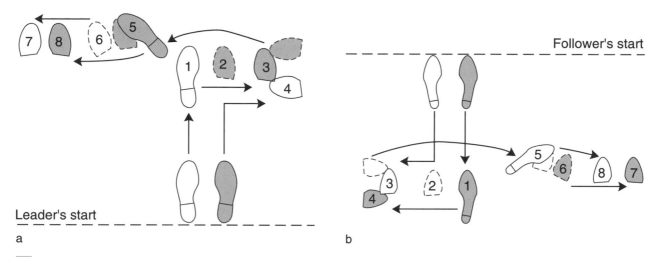

Figure 6.3 Cross step footwork and counts.

a. *Transition to promenade:* From a closed partner position, start to execute a half-box basic. Both partners take a normal step on the first "slow." Take your regular side step. At the end of the side step, the leader needs to twist or rotate his hips, legs, and feet counterclockwise approximately 45 degrees and to gently press with the heel of his right hand on the follower's left shoulder blade. Both partners swivel to face their extended hands, bringing their feet together on the third weight change to be in a promenade position.

b. *Transition to closed:* In the promenade position, both partners' inside feet should be free (his right foot and her left foot) to start the second half-box basic step. On the first weight change, the leader crosses his right foot over his left foot while the follower crosses her left foot over her right foot. At the end of this step, both partners swivel on the ball of their weighted foot in order to face each other in closed position again. Then both partners execute their "side, close" steps (i.e., their second and third weight changes) in the closed dance position.

Success Goal = 10 correct hip rotation leads of the cross step from a closed partner position to a promenade position, then back to a closed position___

Success Check

a. *First half-box basic*
- Leader: Forward (left foot), side (right foot and swivel counterclockwise), together (left foot)___
- Follower: Backward (right foot), side (left foot and swivel clockwise), together (right foot)___
- Angle lower body 45 degrees from partner when in the promenade position___

b. *Second half-box basic*
- Inside feet cross on first weight change, then swivel___
- Square up shoulders (to be parallel) with partner when in the closed dance position___

To Increase Difficulty

- Repeat this transition only once, then alternate it with either the basic four-count rhythm or the basic six-count rhythm.
- Practice to a variety of tempos.

To Decrease Difficulty

- Place your hands on a wall at approximately shoulder height. Keep your weight on the balls of your feet as you practice the entire cross step in place without a partner.
- Repeat at least twice before changing to something different.

FOXTROT VARIATIONS AND COMBINATIONS

DRILLS

1. Left Box Turn

A left box turn rotates counterclockwise and is a variation of the box step. For each half-box basic step taken, a degree of upper body rotation is initiated prior to the "slow" step, then the "side, together" steps are executed. This process of rotating slightly with each foxtrot half-box step gradually achieves a left box turn. How much rotation is done with any half-box step is optional. Figure 6.4, a and b, shows one example in which the leader may execute a left box turn with four half-box steps (and making a quarter turn to face a new wall on each half-box step, for a total of 16 counts).

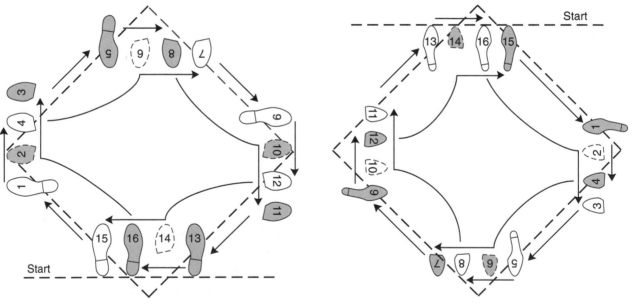

a Leader's left box turn

b Follower's left box turn

Figure 6.4 Left box turn footwork for the foxtrot (16 total counts).

a. *For the leader:* The lead occurs just prior to the downbeat of a measure and prior to executing a forward half-box basic. The lead consists of a slight CCW rotation of the upper torso while keeping the chest and shoulders firmly connected with the arms (maintaining a frame). This upper torso rotation facilitates an outward-angled left foot position on each forward half-box basic and an inward-angled right foot position on each backward half-box basic. When a quarter-turn rotation is desired with each half-box basic, then the foot placements occur along a 45-degree angle (i.e., either the left-front diagonal or the right-back diagonal). Continue the CCW momentum while executing the backward half-box basic. Alternately repeat the forward and backward half-box basics. To signal that the turn is over, the leader must firmly keep his upper torso in a closed dance position and avoid any momentum tendencies to continue the CCW rotation.

b. *For the follower:* Starting with a backward half-box basic, the follower should be aware of the upper torso rotation lead just prior to taking her first step. This signals the follower to angle the toes of her right foot slightly inward rather than stepping straight backward. Then the "side, together" steps are finished as usual. As the CCW momentum continues, the follower should be aware of the natural toes-out position, or angle of her left foot, just prior to executing a forward half-box basic. Continue rotating counterclockwise as you alternately repeat backward and forward half-box basics.

Success Goal = Two left box turns, rotating to complete a 360-degree turn on each turn___

Success Check

• Rotate a quarter turn with each half-box basic, using a total of four quarter turns for each full turn___
• Maintain a closed dance position___

To Increase Difficulty

• Experiment with a CW box turn by taking a half-box progression forward, four CW quarter turns, then a half-box progression forward (for a total of six half-box basics).
• Combine two CCW quarter turns, then two CW quarter turns (the leader needs to step diagonally backward with his left foot on the CW quarter-turn rotation, then step diagonally forward with his right foot to continue with the second CW quarter-turn rotation).

To Decrease Difficulty

• Reduce the amount of rotation on each half-box basic so that you gradually turn counterclockwise—that is, slowly rotating a few degrees prior to each half-box basic.
• Practice without a partner to a slow tempo.

2. Combine Two Variations

As soon as you know at least two variations, you are ready to connect them into a practice combination. Some variations will flow together better than others. Try each of the following combination suggestions and identify which ones feel best to you:

• Two box steps and a left box turn
• Two box steps and four half-box progressions forward
• Four half-box progressions forward and a left box turn
• Two box steps and two basic forward steps (six-count rhythm)
• Four half-box progressions forward and four basic forward steps (six-count rhythm)
• One box step and a cross step

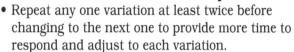**Success Goal =** Eight consecutive repetitions of each of the listed foxtrot combinations, in correct position and with proper leads, to slow foxtrot music___

✔**Success Check**
• Maintain a closed dance position___
• Maintain the tempo established___
• Make smooth transitions between variations___

To Increase Difficulty
• Execute the suggested combinations in reverse order.
• Use a faster tempo.
• Vary the number of repetitions for each variation selected.

To Decrease Difficulty
• Repeat any one variation at least twice before changing to the next one to provide more time to respond and adjust to each variation.
• Use a slow tempo.

3. Basic Rock Step

The basic rock step is an agility variation of the basic six-count rhythm in foxtrot. It requires a shift of weight in two directions: forward and backward. Each weight shift gets two counts, then the "side, together" steps each get two more counts (see figure 6.5, a-d). Remain in a closed dance position for this variation. After a few trials, notice that multiple repetitions of the basic rock step move both you and your partner toward the leader's left side.

a. *For the leader:* Step forward with your left foot on count 1. Either keep your feet in a parallel fourth position or draw up your right foot by sliding it just above the floor and placing the ball of your right foot on the floor to touch or tap it on count 2. Repeat in the opposite direction, stepping backward onto your right foot and either keeping your

a Leader rocks forward on counts 1, 2

b Leader rocks backward on counts 3, 4

c Side step on count 5

d Close feet on count 6

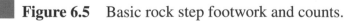**Figure 6.5**   Basic rock step footwork and counts.

feet in a parallel fourth position or drawing your left foot beside your right foot to touch the floor. Finish by stepping sideways onto your left foot and bringing your right foot beside your left foot, shifting your weight onto your right foot.

The leads for the basic rock step require a firm right hand position to stop the forward momentum on count 2. The leader then pulls gently toward his own midline to shift, or rock, both partners' weight in the opposite direction. Keep the upper torso and arms firm as you gently press with the heel of your right palm toward your left side to signal the "side, together" steps.

b. *For the follower:* Start with a backward step onto your right foot on count 1. Become aware that the leader is limiting further backward motion so that you may either keep your feet in a parallel fourth position or have time to touch your left foot beside your right foot during count 2. The leader will then shift directions to pull you slightly toward him. Reverse your actions to step forward onto your left foot and either keep your feet in a parallel fourth position or touch with your right foot. The last two counts occur as you step sideways with your right foot, then bring your feet together and shift your weight onto your left foot.

Success Goal = Four correct repetitions of the basic rock step to slow music___

Success Check
- Keep side steps no wider than the width of your own shoulders___
- Maintain frame throughout___

To Increase Difficulty
- When executing more than approximately four repetitions of this variation—or when you run out of space to move sideways—start to gradually rotate counterclockwise (see the next drill, which expands on this strategy).
- Vary the tempo.
- Combine this variation with any other variation that you know so far.

To Decrease Difficulty
- Practice without a partner.
- Keep your feet in a forward-backward placement (fourth foot position) and shift, or rock, your weight from one foot to the other on each "slow."

4. Left Rock Turn

Once you are comfortable with the basic rock step, then adding CCW rotation is a popular variation. As with any turn, the amount of rotation may vary from a gradual rotation to a quarter-turn rotation with each basic (or more, once you get really good at it). If you decide to make quarter turns, you can use the walls of the room as location references (see figure 6.6, a and b). With each quarter turn, face a new wall; four walls equals a full turn.

a. *For the leader:* During your second "slow," keep the weight on the ball of your right foot. Swivel or rotate your foot approximately 90 degrees. You can check yourself by observing where your toes point when you start compared to after your swivel. The timing of the lead needs to take advantage of the momentum as you shift back on count 3 and rotate your upper torso counterclockwise on count 4 as you swivel on the ball of your right foot. Finish with your normal "side, together" steps. Repeat this six-count basic four times to complete a full turn.

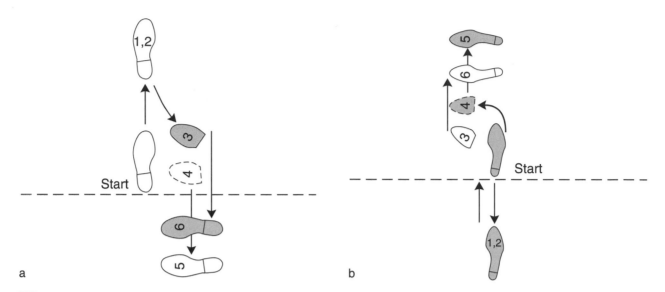

a   b

Figure 6.6   Left rock turn footwork and counts *(a)* for the leader and *(b)* for the follower.

b. *For the follower:* During your second "slow," keep the weight on the ball of your left foot. Swivel or rotate your foot approximately 90 degrees. Observe where the toes of your right foot point prior to, then after, the swivel. Continue with your normal "side, together" steps. Repeat this six-count basic four times to complete a full turn.

Success Goal = Four correctly executed left rock turns___

Success Check

- Make sure that your closed dance position includes your feet being offset from your partner's versus standing toe-to-toe with your partner___
- Maintain a firm frame throughout___
- Use the momentum of changing directions to facilitate the CCW rotation___

To Increase Difficulty

- Vary the degree of rotation with each basic.
- Combine this variation with any other variation that you know so far (e.g., alternately execute the six-count basic forward step for the length of the room, then do a quarter-turn rotation with a basic rock step to "square the corner" when you get to each corner of the room). You can also substitute half-box progressions for the basic forward steps. Which is easier for you? The first combination uses all six-count basic steps, whereas the latter combination option intermixes a four-count basic rhythm with a six-count basic rhythm, which is more difficult.

To Decrease Difficulty

- Isolate the foot position to be used with a partner during the rotation. The leader's right foot is back while the follower's left foot is forward—and to the inside of the leader's right foot (between his feet).
- Without a partner, use your own momentum to rotate counterclockwise approximately 90 degrees on each six-count basic (until you've executed four quarter turns).

5. Side Rock Step

Another variation of the rock step is to transfer your weight from side to side. Sometimes this is called a side sway. This variation is also executed from a closed dance position.

a. *For the leader:* Step to your left side with your left foot on the first "slow" and touch your right foot beside your left (without changing weight). Repeat to the opposite side by stepping to your right with your right foot on the second "slow" and touching your left foot beside your right (without changing weight). If the leader keeps his frame firm and moves his entire body to the side, it will be easy for the follower to recognize the lead. In addition, the leader may gently press with the heel of his right hand prior to moving to his left side, then gently pull with the fingers of his right hand prior to moving to his right side. Finish the "quick, quick" steps with the normal "side, together" steps (changing weight on both counts 5 and 6, respectively). Notice that this variation takes you to your left side. Thus, after so many repetitions, you may not have room to continue to your left. You can then alternate this variation with other variations that you know.

b. *For the follower:* Step to your right side with your right foot on the first "slow" and touch your left foot beside your right foot (without changing weight). Repeat to the opposite side by stepping to your left with your left foot on the second "slow" and touching your right foot beside your left foot (without changing weight). Take your regular "side, together" steps to finish this six-count variation. Notice that this variation takes you to your right side.

Success Goal = Eight correctly executed side rock steps___

Success Check
- Keep your side steps approximately the width of your own shoulders___
- Tap or touch your foot by placing the ball of your free foot beside the instep of your weighted foot___

To Increase Difficulty
- Experiment with gradually rotating counterclockwise by turning prior to taking your second "slow" step.
- Experiment with gradually rotating clockwise by turning prior to taking your second "slow" step.
- Let your upper torso sway (or lean slightly) to each side on the "slow" cues.

To Decrease Difficulty
- Stand with your feet approximately shoulder-width apart and shift from one foot to the other to get the rhythm—two counts or beats per side or per weight change.
- Either verbally or mentally use the cues "side, touch; side, touch; side, together" as you execute this six-count variation.

6. Conversation Step

The conversation step is a popular six-count basic variation that alternately uses a closed dance position and a promenade position. It is called the conversation step because the promenade position permits a conversation to occur between partners. This variation has sometimes been called the promenade step (due to the use of the promenade position). The promenade position may be led in two different directions—either toward the center (described below), or toward the LOD (see "To Increase Difficulty" option).

a. *For the leader:* From a closed dance position, the leader rotates his torso and lower body toward his left hand to signal a transition into the promenade position. Facing his left side, the leader can now take two walks in this turned-out, or promenade, position. Return to closed position to face your partner on the "side, together" steps.

b. *For the follower:* Respond to the leader's signals by rotating your torso and lower body to face your right hand. Take two walking steps to your right while in promenade position. Return to face your partner again in closed position during the "side, together" steps.

 **Success Goal** = Eight correctly executed conversation steps___

 Success Check
• Cross your inside foot on the second "slow" as you walk sideways in promenade position___
• Turn back to your partner for the "quick, quick" steps in closed position___

To Increase Difficulty
• Combine this variation with any other variation that you know so far.
• Add an underarm turn for the follower between the two "slow" rhythms.
• Execute three left rock quarter turns to face the outside wall. Do at least two conversation steps in the LOD. End with a left rock quarter turn.

To Decrease Difficulty
• Take small steps.
• Use a slow tempo.

7. Combine Three Variations

Experiment with connecting three variations to create a practice combination. Do any number of repetitions of each variation selected. Remember that the directions are from the leader's point of view. Start by executing each of the following three variations to identify the combinations you like best:

• Box step, basic forward step and a left rock turn
• Side rock step, cross step, and a left box turn
• Side rock step, half-box progressions forward, and a left rock turn
• Basic forward step, basic rock step, and a box step
• Two CCW half-box quarter turns, four (or two) half-box progressions backward, and two CW half-box quarter turns

Success Goal = Eight consecutive repetitions of each of the listed foxtrot combinations, in correct position and with proper leads, to slow foxtrot music___

Success Check
• Make smooth transitions between variations to create a flowing sequence___
• Maintain a constant tempo___

To Increase Difficulty
• Vary the order of the variations presented (e.g., do them in reverse order). Which orders are more natural combinations?
• Create your own three-variation combinations by using any foxtrot variation that you know so far.

To Decrease Difficulty
• Practice combining two variations, then add the third variation in the suggested combination.
• Practice only the first three combinations suggested in drill 7.
• Do at least two repetitions of each variation.

8. Weave Step

The weave step is a variation of the cross step that you used as a transition between a closed dance position and a promenade position earlier in Step 6. In this modification, three cross steps are taken with the outside arms opening to each side for a total of four half-box basics (see figure 6.7, a-d).

a Half-box basic to promenade position

b Cross inside feet, and open arms on second half of box

c Cross inside feet, and open arms on third half of box

d Cross inside feet, and regrasp hands on fourth half of box

 **Figure 6.7** Weave step.

a. *For the leader:* The weave step starts the same as a cross step with a half-box basic to promenade, except the leader releases his left hand as both hands open to the side (i.e., extending his left and her right hand). A cross step is taken during the next half-box basic but is modified such that more rotation is taken in order to face the opposite side with outside hands open (i.e., extending his right hand and her left) to that side (his right side and her left). Repeat for two more cross steps and move back to a closed dance position on the fourth half-box basic.

b. *For the follower:* During the three cross steps, if the follower holds her frame without dropping her elbows, then the leader may reach under either her right or left arm to place one hand on that shoulder blade, which signals the follower to open to the opposite side.

Success Goal = Four consecutive repetitions of the weave step___

Success Check
- Keep your weight over the balls of your feet in order to swivel prior to the cross steps to each side___
- Keep your outside (free) arm gently curved and symmetrical with your partner's arm position. Avoid opening your arms behind your own shoulders___

To Increase Difficulty
- Alternately combine the weave step with any other variation that you know so far, such as a box step, then a weave step, or a left box turn into a weave step.
- Experiment with creating combinations of any three variations that include the weave step.

To Decrease Difficulty
- Without a partner, stand facing a wall with your hands placed at shoulder height. Press into the wall with your hands to keep your upper torso stationary. Stand with your feet together and center your weight over the balls of your feet. Swivel on the balls of your feet to isolate your lower body. Then do consecutive cross steps to get an idea of the importance of the swivel in executing the weave step easily.

9. Rollovers

Rollovers are a fun way to progress in the LOD. In this variation of the half-box progression, the leader brings the follower to his right side and releases his left hand so both open up facing the LOD. The person on the left side then moves across in front of the person on the right (by rolling over to the opposite side) while the person on the right does a basic half-box progression almost in place. In this manner, places are alternately switched.

a. *For the leader:* Start in a closed dance position. During the first four-count basic step, three things occur. During the slow, quick, quick rhythm, companion cues are "forward, side, and open." Thus, on the first "slow," step forward. Prior to your side step on the first "quick," rotate your right shoulder back, or clockwise, and gently press with the heel of your right hand. These leads facilitate the follower to execute a half turn and end up on the leader's right side. On the second "quick," release your left hand as you both face the LOD standing side by side.

The leader's right foot is now free to do the next four-count basic step along his right-front diagonal, facing his partner and ending up on the right-hand side. As you roll over, you need to release your right hand and place your left hand on the follower's right shoulder blade, just as you did in the weave step. Then it is the follower's turn to roll over when her right foot is free. Continue to exchange sides. When you want to end the rollovers, just bring the follower into a closed position when facing you (instead of letting her continue to roll over to your right side). Finish with a half-box progression forward.

b. *For the follower:* At the end of the first "quick," the follower needs to swivel 180 degrees clockwise on the ball of her left foot to face the LOD. On the second "quick," extend your right hand and arm, keeping it curved and symmetrical to your partner's left hand. Do a basic in place as the leader moves from your left to your right side. Then, on the next basic, travel along the right-front diagonal as you roll over from the leader's left to his right side. Continue until the leader brings you back to a closed position. Finish with a half-box progression forward.

(((Success Goal = Eight repetitions of the rollovers___

✔ Success Check
• Travel along a diagonal when switching places___
• Open up toward the LOD during the rollovers___

■ To Increase Difficulty
• Do any even number of repetitions of the four-count basic step.
• Combine this variation with any other variation that you know so far.

To Decrease Difficulty ■
• Use a total of only four basic steps: (1) to get the follower to the right-hand side, (2) for the leader to roll over, (3) for the follower to move in front and back into a closed position, and (4) to do a half-box progression forward.

10. Basic Forward and Backward Combination Using Parallel Positions

This variation travels in the LOD and requires both the leader and the follower to pivot 180 degrees on the "quick, quick" steps. It also uses a modification of the closed position to include both right and left parallel partner positions.

a. *For the leader:* Start in a closed position. As you take two walks forward, step slightly along your diagonal left front in order to move up beside your partner so that she is on your right side (and your right shoulders are almost touching in a right parallel position). Between the "quick, quick" steps, lead the CW pivot by pulling the heel of your right hand toward your midline and gently pressing your left hand clockwise. You'll end up facing the reverse line of dance (RLOD) with the follower on your left side, which is a left parallel position. Take two walking steps backward, then reverse directions with your leads to pivot counterclockwise back to face the LOD again at the end of the "quick, quick" steps. Continue alternating the basic forward step and the basic backward step. When you want to end this combination, square up your shoulders to resume a closed position at the end of any second repetition of the basic step.

b. *For the follower:* Your movements are the reverse. Take two walking steps backward. Notice that the leader has moved beside you on your right-hand side. In place, pivot clockwise to face the LOD and execute the two "quick" steps. The leader will now be on your left-hand side. Execute two walks forward, then pivot counterclockwise to face the RLOD, and take two "quick" steps while in a right parallel position with your partner. To end this combination, the leader will remain facing you to resume a closed position.

Success Goal = Eight consecutive repetitions of the basic forward and backward combinations using right and left parallel positions___

Success Check
- Alternately keep your right and left shoulders parallel to your partner's shoulders___
- Use small steps on the pivots to step more "in place, together," with the pivot executed between these two weight changes___
- Keep your weight on the balls of your feet during the pivots___

To Increase Difficulty
- Vary the tempo and the number of repetitions.
- Alternate this variation with any other variation that you know so far.

To Decrease Difficulty
- Without any footwork, practice just the arm switch needed to rotate or pivot clockwise, then counterclockwise.
- From a closed position, the leader needs to take longer strides and the follower needs to take shorter strides in order to move to a right parallel position by the end of the second walk.

11. Combine Four or More Variations

Once you are comfortable with the individual variations, experiment with combining them so that you don't have to think about what you want to do next. Rather, the combination should flow naturally. Now that you've tried linking any two or three variations, it's time to lengthen your combinations to link any four or more variations. The following chart lists the variations covered in this book, indexing them according to the rhythm, whether a four-count or a six-count basic step. The leader has the option of doing either rhythm separately or intermixing these rhythms. Have fun identifying your favorite combinations.

Foxtrot Variation Summary

A. Basic Four-Count Rhythm Variations
1. Box step
2. Half-box progression (forward and backward)
3. Box turn (left and right)
4. Cross step
5. Weave step
6. Rollovers

B. Basic Six-Count Rhythm Variations
1. Basic step (forward and backward)
2. Basic rock step
3. Rock turn (left and right)
4. Side rock step
5. Conversation step
6. Basic forward and backward combination (using right and left parallel positions)

Success Goal = Eight different combinations that link any four or more variations together___

Success Check
- Make smooth transitions from one partner position to the next, as appropriate for your selected combination___
- Maintain the tempo and flow throughout___
- Make a list of your favorite eight combinations for future reference___

To Increase Difficulty
- Create longer combinations that intermix variations from either of the two basic foxtrot rhythms.
- Use a variety of tempos.
- Switch partners frequently.

To Decrease Difficulty
- Create shorter combinations that link variations from only one of the two basic foxtrot rhythms.
- Use a slow tempo.

FOXTROT SUCCESS SUMMARY

The foxtrot is one of the most popular dances on the social dance floor. It has two basic rhythmic patterns: a four-count basic and a six-count basic. Both basic step patterns may be executed during a dance. In the foxtrot, the closed dance position is used the majority of the time; however, it is helpful to know how to make the transition to the promenade, or semiopen, position and back to closed position again. The variations for the foxtrot are categorized according to their rhythmic pattern to help you remember which variations use which pattern.

Optional: If you ever have the opportunity, join in a mixer that focuses on changing partners in a random way. For example, the popular waterfall mixer (see figure 6.8) starts with the danc-

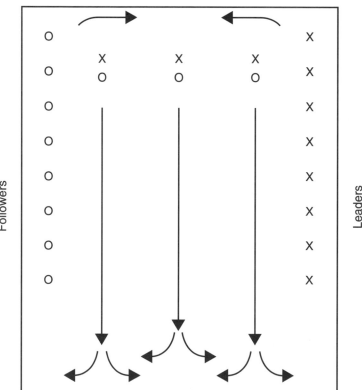

Figure 6.8 Waterfall mixer.

ers forming two lines on each side of the room (leaders on one side, followers on the other), then coming toward each other at the top of the room, which is usually on the end where the music is located. The first person in each line walks to meet the other in the center. They introduce themselves, then dance down the middle of the floor (foxtrot music is usually played). At the other end of the room, they thank each other and walk back to start over again with a new partner. When the first row gets a third of the way down the middle of the floor (approximately two basics), the next row should be ready to start, and so on. More than one couple may dance down the middle at a time, depending on the space available.

STEP

7 SWING: LOOKING JAZZY

The swing is fun to do because of its styling freedom (erect posture is not as important in the swing). It is characterized by torso leans and a jazzy, syncopated style. The swing is a spot dance—each couple stakes out a small circle, or spot, on the dance floor. The many variations within the swing allow partners to rotate around each other within a circle approximately 10 feet in diameter.

The swing, which evolved from the jazz era of the 1920s, was first known as the jitterbug. The first jitterbug step, the shag, was inspired by the boogie-woogie. The shag had a slow, slow, quick, quick rhythm that is still used today. Later, an American dance evolved that was called the "lindy hop" in honor of Charles Lindbergh, who flew solo across the Atlantic in 1927. In time, the lindy hop became known simply as the lindy. Typically, lindy steps involve eight-count patterns executed in a circular spot on the floor. However, sometimes these terms were interchanged with the earlier shag step—according to the tempo of the music—with a single, double, or triple basic step within any two beats of music. Because of the popularity of swing bands during the 1930s and 1940s, the lindy became known simply as the swing. Swing was popular throughout the rock-and-roll era (the 1950s and 1960s).

Two additional forms of swing emerged, East Coast Swing and West Coast Swing, which are very popular today. The East Coast Swing is a circular dance also known as the Triple Swing, due to its use of a triple step that is very effective with slow swing music (earlier known as the triple lindy). The West Coast Swing is a slot dance that uses both six- and eight-count patterns done to either medium or slow tempos. A European version of the East Coast Swing is called the Jive. Characterized by sharp kicks and flicks, the Jive is typically used in competitions and is done to a fast tempo. Neither of these latter dances will be covered directly in this book. As you gain more experience and confidence, you may want to try the East Coast Swing's triple steps to a very fast tempo—but remember that it is easier to practice with slow tempos first.

The East Coast Swing remains the foundation for the other swing dances. It is easily adaptable to three different tempos: fast, moderate, and slow. For each tempo, the basic is modified to include three steps (triple step), two steps (double step), or one step (single step) within two beats of music. The basic footwork for each of these modifications takes a total of six counts, or 1 1/2 measures of 4/4 time swing music. You may choose to execute any of these three modifications—even if your partner chooses a different one. Initially, it is easier to start with the same tempo and basic step modification.

Notice that throughout the following descriptions, the term "ball-change" is purposefully substituted for the often-used term "rock step." In particular, "ball-change" presents a better image for shifting your weight onto the ball of your foot (versus onto the entire foot) and for keeping your upper torso above the center of gravity and the feet (versus letting your upper torso lean backward beyond a vertical alignment). Either literally rocking your weight too far back or stepping back onto a flat foot on the rock step are typical errors that greatly affect your balance and timing with the music—causing you to be late or behind the tempo. Be aware that in some geographic locations, it is preferred to start with the ball-change portion. On the social dance floor, either way is acceptable.

You may find that you have certain tempo preferences, which is fine too. Feel free to start with the tempo you prefer. Once you know all three swing basic step patterns, you may select the one that best fits the tempo of the swing music being played. Think of it as three ways to have more fun on the dance floor. Typically, the three swing basics are initiated either from a two-hands-joined position or in a semiopen position with a partner. Figure 7.1 shows the triangular partner orientation when in a semiopen position. The leader is on the left side, the follower on the right side, and the hands are placed in the middle toward the top of the triangle. Notice that the hand position is a bit different in the swing in that the hands are grasped at approximately waist height with the leader's thumb on top (pointing toward his midline).

Outside foot

Inside foot

Outside foot

■ **Figure 7.1** Suggested hand grasp in the semiopen starting position for the swing.

Single-Time Swing Basic Step Pattern (Fast Tempo)

Listen for the tempo (it should be fast). Mentally count in sets of four counts to identify the tempo, and prepare to step on any first count with your starting foot (i.e., left foot for the leader, right foot for the follower).

For the leader: In a two-hands-joined position, stand with your feet together and shift your weight onto your right foot (versus being centered over both feet) in order to free your left foot. Take a small side step onto your left foot, then a small side step onto your right foot. Keep your steps no wider than the width of your shoulders. Both of these weight changes take two counts during each of the "slow" timing cues. Two more weight changes follow for a ball-change. On the "ball" step, place the ball of your left foot approximately two to three inches from your right heel and change your weight. On the "change" step, shift your weight back onto your right foot, which remains in place (that is, in the same place as it started). Thus, the ball-change steps are similar to in-place "left, right" marching steps. The ball-change steps move you away from and then toward your partner like stretching a rubber band.

When in a two-hands-joined position, start with your feet side by side or in a parallel first foot position. Notice that your two side steps are taken in a parallel second foot position, then the ball-change steps are taken in either a third or a fifth foot position.

For the follower: In a two-hands-joined position, stand with your feet together and shift your weight onto your left foot (versus having it centered over both feet) in order to free your right foot. Take a small side step onto your right foot, then a small side step onto your left foot. Keep your steps no wider than the width of your shoulders. Both of these weight changes take two counts during the "slow" timing cues. Two more weight changes follow for a ball-change. On the "ball" step, place the ball of your right foot approximately two to three inches from your left heel and change weight. On the "change" step, shift your weight back onto your left foot, which remains in place. These actions are similar to a mirror reverse except during the ball-change steps, when both partners move away from and then toward each other.

When in a two-hands-joined position, start with your feet side by side or in parallel first foot position. Notice that your two side steps are taken in a parallel second foot position, then the ball-change steps are taken in either a third or a fifth foot position.

For styling and to maintain the tempo, you may add a slight knee bend on counts 2 and 4, instead of pausing or holding these counts. Figure 7.2 shows the two-hands-joined position footwork and timing cues for the single-time swing basic step pattern.

FIGURE 7.2 KEYS TO SUCCESS: SINGLE-TIME SWING BASIC (FAST TEMPO)

Footwork Cues

Leader

Left, right, ball-change

Follower

Right, left, ball-change

Timing Cues

4/4 time signature:	Four beats to a measure, each beat gets one count
Total counts:	Six (accents on even counts; weight changes on counts 1, 3, 5, 6)
Rhythmic counts:	1-2, 3-4, 5, 6
Weight changes:	Four
Duration of steps:	Slow, slow, quick, quick
Length of steps:	Short or in place (under center of gravity)
Direction of steps:	a. Two-hands-joined position: Side, side, backward, replace
	b. Semiopen position: Forward, backward, backward, replace

In the semiopen position (see figure 7.3), when both partners angle 45 degrees toward the middle, the same timing is used, but the direction changes. Now both partners take a small step forward, then shift their weight backward and do a ball-change (step backward, then replace your weight in the same position). You may start either with your feet together (in parallel first foot position) or with one foot slightly ahead of the other (in third foot position) for better balance. The ball-change steps should be in either third or fifth foot position.

The characteristic upper torso leans used in the swing (for all three basic step pattern modifications) follow.

On the "slow" (counts 1-2), let one shoulder dip slightly in the same direction as your weight change (see figure 7.4a), letting your knee bend as you step

to absorb the weight change. This additional action helps you time your footwork to fit two counts of the music, so that you step on count 1 and bend your knee on count 2.

On the next "slow" (counts 3-4), reverse your footwork and styling actions; that is, lower your other shoulder slightly in the direction of your second step (see figure 7.4b). After you step onto the other foot, slightly bend that knee, which again gives you two actions to fit two counts of the music.

On the "quick, quick" (counts 5, 6), keep your torso more upright so that you can execute your ball-change steps under your center of gravity (see figure 7.4c). You might think of marching in place when making these two weight changes versus actually rocking your weight.

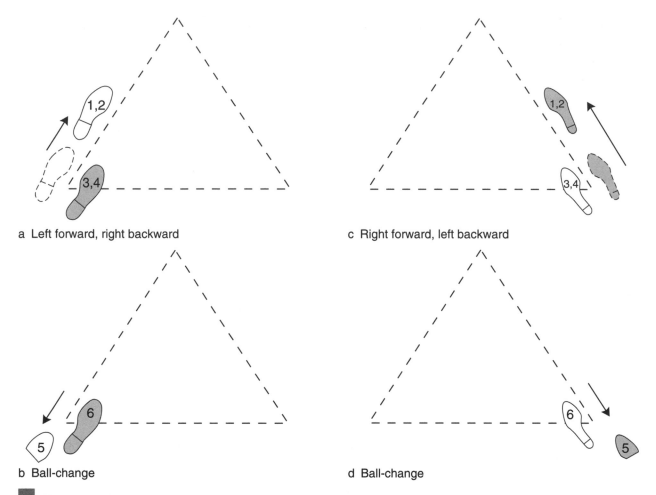

a Left forward, right backward

c Right forward, left backward

b Ball-change

d Ball-change

Figure 7.3   Basic single-lindy swing footwork from a semiopen position for *(a* and *b)* the leader and *(c* and *d)* the follower.

a

b

c

Figure 7.4   Swing torso leans demonstrated from a semiopen position.

Double-Time Swing Basic Step Pattern (Moderate Tempo)

An alternative to the single-time swing is the double-time swing basic pattern. It is used with moderate-to fast-tempo music. This swing basic step pattern allows you to select any of a variety of non-weight moves followed by a weight change within two beats of music, which delays your weight change. Examples of non-weight moves are a toe touch, a tap, or a small kick. These non-weight moves are executed prior to making a weight change, or step, on the second beat of any two beats of music. It is easy to keep the tempo, as an action occurs on each underlying beat of the music. Thus, each action, "touch, step," gets one count or beat. On a crowded dance floor, substituting a toe-heel drop is a useful variation because it takes less space (i.e., tap your toe on the first count, then drop the heel of that same foot without moving the ball of your foot on the second count).

For the leader: From a semiopen position, stand with your feet together and shift your weight onto your right foot (versus having it centered over both feet). Moving your left foot slightly forward, dig the ball of your left foot into the floor on count 1 and drop your left heel on count 2. Repeat on the other side to dig the ball of your right foot, then drop onto your right heel. The ball-change is the same as described earlier for the single-time swing.

When in a semiopen position, both partners start in parallel first foot position. The toe-heel actions use a parallel first foot position. The ball-change uses either a third or fifth foot position. When in a two-hands-joined position, both partners start in parallel first foot position. Both of the side steps use a parallel second foot position, then the ball-change uses either a third or a fifth foot position.

For the follower: From a semiopen position, stand with your feet together and shift your weight onto your left foot. Moving your right foot slightly forward, dig the ball of your right foot on count 1 and drop your right heel on count 2. Repeat on the other side to dig the ball of your left foot, then drop onto your left heel. The ball-change is the same as described earlier for the single-time swing.

Figure 7.5 shows the semiopen position footwork and timing cues for the double-time swing basic step pattern.

FIGURE 7.5 | **KEYS TO SUCCESS: DOUBLE-TIME SWING BASIC (MODERATE TEMPO)**

Footwork Cues

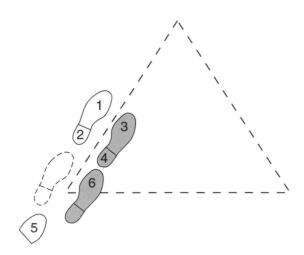

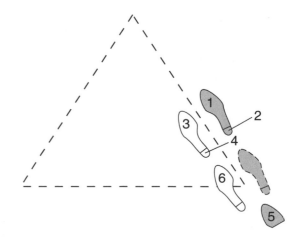

Leader

Toe dig, heel drop; toe dig, heel drop; ball-change

Follower

Toe dig, heel drop; toe dig, heel drop; ball-change

Timing Cues

4/4 time signature:	Four beats to a measure, each beat gets one count
Total counts:	Six (accents on even counts)
Rhythmic counts:	1, 2, 3, 4, 5, 6
Weight changes:	Four (on counts 2, 4, 5, 6)
Duration of steps:	Quick, quick, quick, quick, quick, quick
Direction of steps:	a. Two-hands-joined position: Side; side; backward, forward (to replace)
	b. Semiopen position: Forward; backward; backward, forward (to replace)

Triple-Time (or Triple-Step) Swing Basic Step Pattern (Slow Tempo)

As mentioned earlier, the third swing basic step pattern variation, the triple-time swing, is synonymous with the triple-step swing, the triple swing, and the East Coast Swing. It is typically used with slow swing music. What makes the triple-step swing basic pattern a bit more difficult is that you need to execute three weight changes (or three steps) within two beats of music—twice. Thus, a slow tempo gives you more time to execute these extra steps to each side.

For the leader: From a two-hands-joined position, stand with your feet together and shift your weight onto your right foot. This frees your left foot to move quickly. To execute three steps (a triple step) within two beats of music, use the cues "step, ball, step." When you execute a triple step on each side of your body, the cues become "left, push, left," and "right, push, right." This means that you take a step onto your left foot, put your weight only on the ball of your right foot as if you are pushing downward and backward on the floor, then step onto your left foot again. These three weight changes require you to do the first two weight changes more quickly, using a quick, quick, slow rhythm. Now repeat a triple step on your right side, then add the ball-change steps (as previously described for the single-time swing).

When in a two-hands-joined position, start in parallel first foot position. Each of the triple steps to the sides uses a parallel first (or small second), third, second foot position. The ball-change uses either a third or a fifth foot position.

For the follower: From a two-hands-joined position, stand with your feet together and shift your weight onto your left foot. This frees your right foot to move quickly. To execute three steps (a triple step) within two beats of music, use the cues "step, ball, step." When you execute a triple step on each side of your body, the cues become "right, push, right" and "left, push, left." Thus, step onto your right foot, push downward and backward against the floor with the ball of your left foot, then step again onto your right foot. Repeat a triple step to the opposite side such that you step left, push with your right foot, and step onto your left foot again. Then add a ball-change as you did with the other swing basic step patterns.

When in a two-hands-joined position, start in parallel first foot position. Each of the triple steps to the sides uses a parallel first (or small second), third, second foot position. The ball-change uses either a third or a fifth foot position.

If you choose to start from a semiopen position, it is the same as described for the single-time swing. Again, the direction of the basic step pattern changes. Figure 7.6 shows the semiopen position footwork and timing cues for the triple-step swing basic pattern.

FIGURE 7.6 KEYS TO SUCCESS: TRIPLE-TIME (OR TRIPLE-STEP) SWING BASIC (SLOW TEMPO)

Footwork

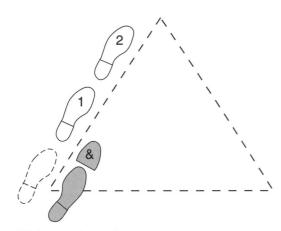

a Triple step forward

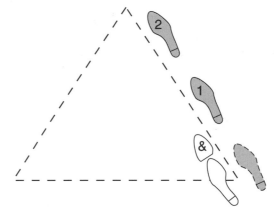

d Triple step forward

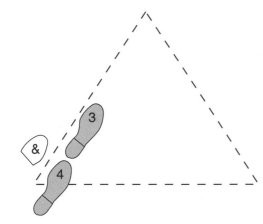

b Triple step backward

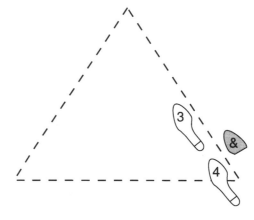

e Triple step backward

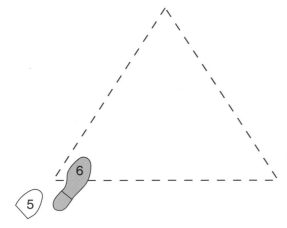

c Ball-change

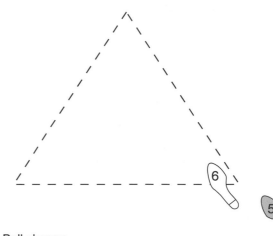

f Ball-change

Leader

Triple step (or left, push, left), triple step (or right, push, right), ball-change

Follower

Triple step (or right, push, right), triple step (or left, push, left), ball-change

Timing Cues

4/4 time signature:	Four beats to a measure, each beat gets one count
Total counts:	Six (accents on even counts)
Rhythmic counts:	1-&-2; 3-&-4; 5, 6
Weight changes:	Eight (on each whole count and on two "&" counts)
Duration of steps:	Quick-quick-slow; quick-quick-slow; slow, slow
Direction of steps:	a. Two-hands-joined position: Side-together-side; side-together-side; backward, forward (to replace)
	b. Semiopen position: Triple step forward; triple step backward; backward, forward (to replace)
Length of steps:	Small, small, large; small, small, large, in-place

SWING BASIC STEP PATTERN

DRILLS

1. Single-Time Swing Execution Challenge

Review the Keys to Success (see figures 7.2 and 7.3) for the single-time swing basic. Try this basic step pattern by yourself, then try it with a partner. Start in a two-hands-joined position, then try the basic step from a semiopen position.

Success Goal = 10 consecutive repetitions of the basic step pattern without a partner, then two minutes with a partner to swing music (use track 11)___

Success Check
- Basic step uses six counts___
- Step on count 1 and slightly bend that knee on count 2___
- Step on count 3 and slightly bend that knee on count 4___
- Ball-change steps on counts 5, 6___

To Increase Difficulty
- Repeat basic to any fast-tempo swing music.
- Add torso leans on the "slow" cues (review figure 7.4).

To Decrease Difficulty
- Without a partner, use verbal counts and match your actions to each count (i.e., do something on each whole count, including non-weight actions such as slightly bending your knee on the second half of each "slow" cue).
- Start with a slow tempo and gradually increase the tempo to match the music.

2. Double-Time Swing Execution Challenge

Review the Keys to Success (see figure 7.5) for the double-time swing basic step pattern. Try this basic step pattern by yourself to get the rhythm, then try it with a partner. Start in a two-hands-joined position, then try it from a semiopen position.

Success Goal = 10 consecutive repetitions of the basic step pattern without a partner, then two minutes with a partner to swing music (use track 9)___

Success Check
- Basic pattern uses a total of six counts___
- Toe dig (or touch) on count 1 and heel drop (or step) on count 2___
- Toe dig (or touch) on count 3 and heel drop (or step) on count 4___
- Ball-change steps on counts 5, 6___

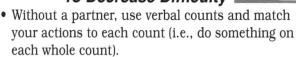

To Increase Difficulty
- Repeat basic to any moderate-tempo swing music.
- Vary the non-weight action (e.g., substitute a small kick, step for each touch, step).

To Decrease Difficulty
- Without a partner, use verbal counts and match your actions to each count (i.e., do something on each whole count).
- Face a partner without touching hands and slowly repeat the basic step, as if facing a mirror.

3. Triple-Time (or Triple-Step) Swing Execution Challenge

Review the Keys to Success (see figure 7.6) for the triple-step swing basic step pattern. Try this basic step pattern by yourself to get the rhythm. Then try it with a partner from a two-hands-joined position. Last, try it from a semiopen position with your partner.

Success Goal = 10 consecutive repetitions of the basic step pattern without a partner, then two minutes with a partner to swing music (use track 10)___

Success Check
- Basic pattern uses a total of six counts___
- Three steps (triple step) to correspond with counts 1-&-2___
- Three steps (triple step) to correspond with counts 3-&-4___
- Ball-change steps on counts 5, 6___

To Increase Difficulty
- Repeat basic pattern to any slow swing music.

To Decrease Difficulty
- Without a partner, use verbal counts and make a weight change not only on each count, but also on each "&" count.
- Face a partner without touching hands and slowly repeat the basic step and mirror actions in reverse such that one partner's left foot moves left (left, right, left) while the other partner's right foot moves right (right, left, right).

4. Match the Basic Step Patterns to the Tempo

Ask a partner to play swing music for you without telling you the tempo ahead of time. Listen to the underlying beats and identify the tempo. Without a partner, try each of the three swing basic step patterns (single-time, double-time, triple-time) to the music selected, then decide which one best fits the music's tempo (i.e., slow, moderate, or fast). Remember that there is no one answer; rather, it is a matter of what feels most comfortable for you. Generally, each of the swing basic step patterns fits a slightly different tempo.

Success Goal = Two minutes of continuous repetition of any of the three optional swing basic step patterns (use tracks 9 through 11)___

Success Check

- With a slow tempo, try the triple-time swing basic pattern___
- With a moderate tempo, try the double-time swing basic pattern___
- With a fast tempo, try the single-time swing basic pattern___

To Increase Difficulty

- Repeat this drill with a variety of swing music selections (including three different tempos).
- Start in a two-hands-joined position with a partner.
- Start in a semiopen position with a partner.
- With a fast tempo, experiment with using either a swing basic step or a foxtrot basic step to see which works best for the particular music selection played.

To Decrease Difficulty

- Ask a partner to announce the type of music being played and/or the tempo, as possible.
- Start in a two-hands-joined position facing a partner to mirror each others' actions.

SWING TRANSITION

DRILLS

1. Leads From a Semiopen Position to a One-Hand-Joined Position and Back to a Semiopen Position

There are two transition options for connecting these two partner positions: an arch-out/arch-in or a roll-out/roll-in. Both transitions are effective in moving from a semiopen position to a one-hand-joined position (i.e., the leader's left hand and the follower's right hand) and in returning to the semiopen position. One major difference in the roll-out and roll-in leads is to keep the hands at approximately waist height rather than lifting them high, as in the arch-out and arch-in leads. In both transitions, each partner rotates either counterclockwise or clockwise along an imaginary triangle on the floor.

a. *Arch-out/arch-in:* To lead the arch-out, begin in a semiopen position with a partner and repeat the appropriate swing basic at least twice. Then, at the end of any ball-change portion, the leader lifts his outside hand and arm, bringing both partners' outside arms up to form an arch (see figure 7.7, a and b). This indicates that a CW turn (an arch-out) for the follower is coming during the next basic step. Both partners do the forward half of their basic while the follower moves forward under the arch. On count 2, the leader presses with the heel of his right hand to guide the follower's CW 180-degree turn on her outside (right) foot (see figure 7.7c). Both partners continue their backward half of the basic (counts 3-&-4) while facing each other in a one-hand-joined position; notice that the leader needs to move counterclockwise into the spot that the follower vacated. On count 5 (see figure 7.7d), both partners pull their elbows and joined hands back in opposition (as if pulling on a rein). On count 6, the leader brings his left hand across his midline to his right side, lifting it high to form an arch (see figure 7.7e). The leader can then loop his left hand over the head of the follower (see figure 7.7f), who does a CCW turn (arch-in) under the raised hands during the next basic step. Notice that the leader must now move clockwise back into his initial starting spot (on the left side of the imaginary triangle) on the first "slow." This opens up the follower's initial starting spot (on the right side of the imaginary triangle) for her to move into during the second "slow" of the swing basic step pattern. Both partners are side by side in the semiopen position during the ball-change steps (see figure 7.7g).

a Start arch-out after a ball-change

b Counts 1-&

c Counts 2 (turn), then 3-&-4

d Count 5

e Count 6 (start arch-in)

f Counts 1-&-2 (turn)

g Counts 3-&-4, then 5, 6

Figure 7.7 Arch-out/arch-in transitions.

b. *Roll-out/roll-in:* To lead the roll-out, begin in a semiopen position with your partner. Repeat the appropriate basic at least twice. At the end of the ball-change portion, the leader gently rotates his entire upper torso counterclockwise (by twisting at the waist) to gently lead the follower along a curved path out toward the leader's left-front diagonal (see figure 7.8a). The leader can then move into the spot that the follower vacated (i.e., go to the right side of the imaginary triangle; see figure 7.8b).

Then, at the end of any ball-change (see figure 7.8c), the leader may signal the roll-in by gently pulling his left hand horizontally toward his right side as he begins to move clockwise back to his initial starting position (left side of the imaginary triangle). At the end of the first "slow," the leader uses his left hand to trace a large "J" horizontally in the air at approximately waist height (starting at the top of the "J"). A cue word is "J-stroke" to signal that the follower should move toward the leader, then swivel on her right foot at the end of the first "slow" (see figure 7.8d) to move into her starting position beside the leader (i.e., with the leader on the left side and the follower on the right side of the imaginary triangle; see figure 7.8e). Both partners execute both the second "slow" and the ball-change while stationary and in the semiopen position.

a Slow   b Slow   c Ball-change

d Slow   e Slow, then ball-change

Figure 7.8   Roll-out/roll-in transitions.

Success Goal = Eight consecutive repetitions of each of the following combinations:

   a. two repetitions of the swing basic step pattern followed by an arch-out/arch-in transition__

   b. two repetitions of the swing basic step pattern followed by a roll-out/roll-in transition__

Success Check

• Four repetitions of the appropriate swing basic step pattern are needed to complete this practice combination__

• The follower executes the turn (either clockwise or counterclockwise) at the end of count 2 by swiveling on the ball of her right foot. Leaders need to avoid any tendency to signal the follower to go under the arch or to roll any earlier__

To Increase Difficulty

• Repeat this drill using the appropriate swing basic step pattern to match at least three different tempos (slow, moderate, or fast).

• Experiment to mix and match these transitions; for example, try a roll-out and an arch-in, or an arch-out and a roll-in.

To Decrease Difficulty

• Practice your role (whether leader or follower) separately without a partner until you can repeat the basic step pattern appropriate for at least one of the three different tempos.

• Practice only one transition with a partner and use the same tempo.

2. Leads From a One-Hand- to a Two-Hands-Joined Position and Back to a One-Hand-Joined Position

The easiest way to move from a one-hand- to a two-hands-joined position, and vice versa, is to either release one hand or to grasp both hands. However, there are ways to execute these simple transitions with more finesse. One option for getting to a two-hands-joined position in the swing is to take advantage of the natural rotation of the basic step pattern by executing a half-rotation turn. An option for returning to a one-hand-joined position is to execute an inside left turn. Both transition options require partners to exchange locations, approximately 180 degrees. Thus, the leader will be moving more on these transitions.

   a. *Half-rotation turn:* Start in a one-hand-joined position (leader's left and follower's right). Create a tempo by executing at least one basic step in place. At the end of the ball-change within the next basic step, the leader can cross his right foot slightly in front of his left foot (to move slightly to his left). The leader can then step forward along this circular path with his left foot on the first "slow" as he cups his right hand and places it in front of and slightly to the side of his right hip (see figure 7.9). These actions indicate that he wants to connect with the follower's left hand when both partners move closer together. They also bring both partners' right shoulders inward toward the center of the small circle and provide a space for the follower to step forward with her right foot (to stay within a small circle on the floor).

      At the end of count 2, the follower needs to place her left hand in the leader's right hand as both partners swivel on the ball of their lead foot (his left foot and her right foot) in order to face each other. Avoid grasping your partner's hand until the end of count 2. Take your time; there is no need to rush. Now, holding two hands, both partners step slightly to the side (on the second "slow") while still facing, then execute their ball-change steps. Ideally, this CW partner rotation involves at least a 180-degree rotation, although the amount of rotation may be either slightly more or slightly less. It is up to the leader and the momentum established.

■ **Figure 7.9** Present hand and transition to a two-hands-joined position when bodies come closer on the turn.

b. *Inside left turn:* From a two-hands-joined position, the lead is given at the end of any ball-change. The leader brings his left hand toward his right shoulder on the first "slow," then loops a small CCW circle over the follower's head as she turns counterclockwise. This is the same lead (and follower's turn) as for an arch-in (review figures 7.8, e and f), with two major differences for the leader. First, as the follower goes under the arch, the leader releases his right hand grasp (to be in a one-hand-joined position again). Second, on an inside left turn for the follower, the leader is also rotating clockwise at the end of count 2 in order to exchange partner locations on the floor, ideally making a 180-degree switch.

Success Goal = 10 repetitions of alternating the transition from a half-rotation turn to a two-hands-joined position with the transition from an inside left turn to a one-hand-joined position___

Success Check

a. *Half-rotation turn*
• Partners camouflage the transition to two hands by grasping when their right shoulders are close together___
• Following an imaginary small CW circular floor path, the basic step pattern is executed forward, half turn, either side or backward, then with a ball-change while stationary___

b. *Inside left turn*
• The leader and follower exchange locations, ideally making a 180-degree switch___
• The follower's turn camouflages the release of one hand by the leader___

To Increase Difficulty

a. *Half-rotation turn*
- Continue with two or more repetitions of the half-rotation turn while holding two hands.
- Practice using three different tempos and the appropriate swing basic steps.

b. *Inside left turn*
- Experiment with the leader rotating 180 degrees to repeat two or more repetitions of the inside left turn.
- Randomly alternate between an inside left turn and an arch-in transition back to closed position.
- Practice to a variety of tempos and use the appropriate basic for the tempo of the music.

To Decrease Difficulty

- Practice each transition separately, then combined.
- Do any number of repetitions of the appropriate basic step patterns before executing these transitions.

SWING VARIATIONS AND COMBINATIONS

DRILLS

1. CW and CCW Turning Basic

The fun of swing is to revolve, or rotate, while executing the basic step. The leader may rotate either counterclockwise or clockwise. The degree of rotation on each swing basic step may vary.

a. *Rotate counterclockwise:* Start in a semiopen position and execute the appropriate basic step for a slow tempo. Just prior to the ball-change steps, the leader may open his left shoulder in order to rotate his chest and upper torso counterclockwise. This CCW rotation can be as minimal as one-eighth of a turn (see figure 7.10). Facing this new direction, execute the ball-change steps. Repeat until you've rotated 360 degrees back to where you started.

b. *Rotate clockwise:* Start in a semiopen position. Prior to the ball-change portion of the swing basic, the leader may bring his right shoulder back or rotate his chest and upper torso clockwise (see figure 7.11). Once facing the new direction, execute the ball-change steps. Continue making these slight angle adjustments until you have rotated 360 degrees back to your starting location.

Once you can execute each option separately, it is time to challenge yourself by putting them into a short combination. Start in a semiopen position with your partner and experiment with the following selected combinations:

- In-place basic, basic with CCW rotation, arch-out, and arch-in
- In-place basic, basic with CW rotation, arch-out, and arch-in
- In-place basic, basic with CCW rotation, roll-out, and roll-in
- In-place basic, basic with CW rotation, roll-out, and roll-in

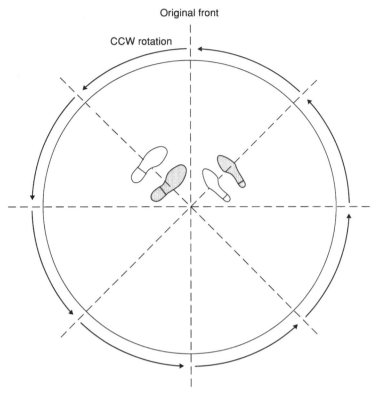

Figure 7.10 Counterclockwise rotation in the swing may rotate either more or less than one-eighth of a turn with each basic step.

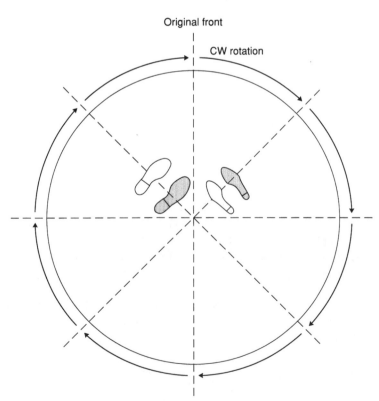

Figure 7.11 Clockwise rotation in the swing may rotate either more or less than one-eighth of a turn with each basic step.

Success Goal = Two 360-degree rotations, either counterclockwise or clockwise, within any three of the selected combinations, using the appropriate swing basic for the tempo selected___

✔ Success Check

• Keep the upper torso and frame firm___
• Think of moving your center (or sternum) to face the new direction___

To Increase Difficulty

• Try to rotate on each portion of the swing basic step versus just prior to the ball-change steps.
• Experiment with the number of basics (e.g., try to complete a 360-degree rotation using only four basics). What is the minimum number needed for you and your partner to rotate completely back to your starting location?
• Repeat this drill using the appropriate basic step for three different tempos: slow, moderate, and fast.
• Vary the order to create your own combination using the variations and transitions that you know so far; for example, try putting the rotation options at the end of the suggested combinations.

To Decrease Difficulty

• Do multiple repetitions to gradually complete a 360-degree rotation.
• Select only one tempo and its appropriate basic step.
• Add as many in-place basics as you like before and after each 360-degree rotation.
• Reduce the number of options in the combination; for example, alternate in-place basics with basics using either CW or CCW rotations (i.e., leave out the transitions at the end of each of the combination examples).

2. Single Under

Start in a one-hand-joined position facing your partner. The lead for the single under is the same as for the arch-in transition with one exception—the leader must exchange places, in a 180-degree switch, with the follower (versus remaining stationary for the arch-in transition).

a. *For the leader:* After any ball-change, bring your left hand across your midline toward your right shoulder (see figure 7.12a). Then lift it high to make a small CCW loop over the follower's head (see figure 7.12b). To end the turn, lower your hand and keep your elbow bent approximately 90 degrees (see figure 7.12c). Throughout the follower's left inside turn, face your partner and rotate 180 degrees clockwise at the end of count 2. Face each other to execute the second "slow" and the ball-change. During the turn, the leader keeps his fingers pointing downward, and the follower loosely cups her hand around the leader's fingers (maintaining contact without gripping tightly).

b. *For the follower:* The follower's footwork for the single under is the same as that used with the arch-in transition. On the first "slow," travel forward and spin 180 degrees counterclockwise on the ball of your right foot at the end of count 2. Face your partner to execute the second "slow" and the ball-change steps.

a Ball-change   b Slow   c Slow, then ball-change

Figure 7.12   Single under.

Once you can execute the single under and distinguish it from the arch-in transition, it is helpful to combine what you know so far. Start in a semiopen position and do the following three-lead combination: an arch-out transition, a single under, and an arch-in transition. You should end in a semiopen position. The leader must be ready to either switch places with his partner and remain in a one-hand-joined position or remain stationary and bring his partner back to the semiopen position.

Success Goal = Eight repetitions of this three-lead combination with correct timing___

Success Check
• Continuously repeat the basic step appropriate for the selected tempo___
• Avoid getting too far apart___

To Increase Difficulty
• Vary the number of consecutive single under repetitions (e.g., try two, three, four, or more consecutive leads).
• Vary the tempo and use the appropriate swing basic for the tempo selected, whether slow, moderate, or fast.
• Lengthen the combination by adding either CCW or CW rotation prior to the arch-out.

To Decrease Difficulty
• Use only one tempo and the corresponding basic until the combination becomes more automatic.
• Repeat each part in isolation, gradually linking them.

3. Double Under

This variation has sometimes been called a "she, he" turn because of the timing of the turns—she goes, then he goes. To execute the double under, proceed as if you are doing a single under, except that the leader turns counterclockwise under the arched hands and arms during the second "slow" (see figure 7.13). The follower's part remains the same whether she is doing the arch-in, inside left turn, single under, or double under. To avoid hitting heads in the middle, make sure that the follower's turn is completed (on counts 1 and 2) before the leader turns under his left arm (on counts 3 and 4). Both partners end up switching positions 180 degrees and facing each other for the ball-change steps.

Follower's CCW underarm turn on counts 1-&-2

Leader's CCW underarm turn on counts 3-&-4

Figure 7.13 Double under.

Again, you can challenge yourself by putting the double under in a practice combination. Start with the combination from the previous drill and add any number of repetitions of the double under after the single under. After leading the double under, the leader has at least three options: (1) to immediately lead another double under, (2) to lead a single under, or (3) to lead the arch-in transition back into the semiopen position. Do each of the three options after a double under with your partner at least four times to slow music.

Success Goal = Four repetitions of each of the three options after a double under___

Success Check
• Timing order should be "she, he" for the double under turns corresponding to the first two "slows"___
• Face your partner on the ball-change steps and initiate the next lead by pulling back, then directing the follower toward the intended direction___

To Increase Difficulty
• Vary the tempo and use the appropriate swing basic for the tempo selected, whether slow, moderate, or fast.
• Create your own combinations to include the double under.

To Decrease Difficulty
• Practice each of the three options after a double under separately, then add the first part of the combination from the previous drill.

4. Brush

The brush is a fancy, behind-the-back pass for the leader from a one-hand-joined position. It ends up with an awkward hand grasp that is easily adjusted by leading immediately into either a single or a double under. This adjustment will soon become automatic.

a. *For the leader:* To set up the brush, the leader needs to transfer the follower's right hand from his left to his right hand on any second "slow" (counts 3 and 4). Both partners continue the basic on count 5. On count 6, as the leader finishes the ball-change and shifts his weight forward, he also rotates his wrist counterclockwise, as if turning a doorknob. During the "slow" forward, the leader passes the follower on her right side (see figure 7.14a) as he lowers his right hand to pass her hand from his right to his left hand. The leader's pass needs to be low, approximately at hip level, to avoid bending the elbows and hitting the follower on his turn (see figure 7.14b). Then both partners face each other for the second "slow" and the ball-change steps with a different hand grasp (see figure 7.14c). To return to a normal grasp, the leader has two immediate options—to lead either a single under or a double under.

b. *For the follower:* The follower uses the same footwork as with the half-rotation turn. She needs to face her partner throughout the brush step.

a Brush right shoulders to lead

b Follower turns CW; leader turns CCW

c Ball-change

Figure 7.14 Brush step.

Success Goal = Four repetitions of each option (i.e., either a single or a double under) immediately after a brush___

✔ **Success Check**
• Set up with a right-to-right handshake grip___
• The leader must keep his behind-the-back hand pass low (without bending his elbows)___
• Avoid getting too far apart___
• Switch positions approximately 180 degrees with your partner during the brush step___

To Increase Difficulty
• Vary the tempo and use the appropriate swing basic for the tempo selected, whether slow, moderate, or fast.
• At the end of a single under, the leader may switch to a right-to-right hand grasp so as to go immediately into the brush without another basic step.
• Include the brush in a longer combination; for example, starting in semiopen position, do either a CCW or a CW rotation, an arch-out, a single under, a brush step, a double under, and a roll-in.

To Decrease Difficulty
• Use only one selected tempo and corresponding basic step.

5. Belt Loop

The belt loop is sometimes called a waist slide. It starts from a one-hand-joined position. As in the brush step, this variation also ends with the hands in an awkward position, yet it is easily adjusted by immediately leading either a single or a double under.

a. *For the leader:* After any ball-change, the leader may bring his right hand and arm over the top of the grasped hands. On the "slow," the leader turns counterclockwise, placing his left hand at his belt loop on the right side of his waist and releasing his partner's hand. On the next "slow," he regrasps her right hand on the left side of his waist with his left hand. Thus, the leader's left hand is used throughout this variation. The ball-change is executed in a one-hand-joined position. The leader then immediately leads either a single or a double under to adjust the hand position.

b. *For the follower:* On the two "slow" cues, the follower remains facing the leader while switching locations 180 degrees. What is different is that the leader places the follower's right hand at his left side and then releases it. The follower lightly slides her right hand across the leader's back at his waist, or at belt level. The leader then picks up the follower's right hand on the left side of his waist, after which the partners face each other to do the ball-change.

Success Goal = Four repetitions of each option (i.e., either a single or a double under) immediately after a belt loop (or waist slide)___

✔ **Success Check**
• The leader turns counterclockwise, initially rolling into his own left arm, releases, then regrasps with his left hand___
• Remember to switch places with your partner___

To Increase Difficulty
• In random order, substitute the belt loop for the brush step.
• Vary the tempo and use the appropriate swing basic for the tempo selected, whether slow, moderate, or fast.

To Decrease Difficulty
• Practice the waist slide portion without footwork.

6. Alternating Shoulder Touches

This variation is sometimes called a sprinkler, as it resembles a revolving lawn sprinkler that alternates the flow of the water. In this case, one shoulder is touched or tapped for one partner, then for the other partner. Both partners rotate CW.

a. *For the leader:* This variation starts from a right-to-right hand grasp. Either execute a basic step and pass (her right hand to your right hand) or lead a single under and pass (her right hand to your right hand). Travel forward and rotate your shoulders clockwise on your first "slow" until you are standing behind your partner. Extend both your right hands to almost shoulder level at your right side, and touch the follower's left shoulder with your left hand. On your second "slow," rotate your shoulders counterclockwise and bring both your right hands to your right shoulder, then forward, in order to have your back toward your partner so that she can touch or tap your left shoulder. Both partners continue rotating clockwise during their "slow" steps and repeat for at least two more shoulder touches.

   To end these alternating shoulder touches, the leader modifies the ball change to two walking steps (rotating clockwise) and signals a CCW turn for the follower by lifting his right hand and making a CCW loop over her head. At the end of the follower's turn, the leader may either switch her right hand immediately back into his left hand or do so on the follower's next turn (e.g., at the end of either a single or a double under lead).

b. *For the follower:* On the first "slow," the leader's actions cause you to open your left shoulder beyond normal, and he will touch your left shoulder. On the second "slow," the leader's actions will rotate you clockwise such that you will be standing behind him and able to touch his left shoulder with your left hand. These alternating shoulder touches may be repeated any even number of times, which repeats the "slow" cues until the leader signals something else. Take two steps on your CCW turn to end this variation.

Success Goal = Four repetitions of the alternating shoulder touches followed by a CCW turn for the follower___

Success Check
• Rotate to stand behind your partner for the shoulder touches or taps___
• One repetition of this variation (as described earlier) extends and modifies the basic for a total number of 10 counts___

To Increase Difficulty
• The leader may do two shoulder touches, then two walks, as he leads the follower into a CCW turn. Repeat this option at least twice (i.e., 12 total counts, or 6 counts per repetition).
• The leader may lead any even number of shoulder touches prior to the CCW turn. For example, try six or eight "slow" steps prior to the CCW turn.
• Vary the tempo and use the appropriate swing basic for the tempo selected, whether slow, moderate, or fast.

To Decrease Difficulty
• Position yourself with a partner to try alternating shoulder touches without any footwork. Freeze each position for clarity.
• Use more repetitions of the alternating shoulder touches (i.e., any even number).

7. Tuck and Spin

The tuck and spin, or tuck turn, includes a turn either for only the follower or for both partners. It is a fun variation that requires a firm arm position for both the leader and the follower.

a. *For the leader:* Again, this variation starts from a modified right-to-right hand grasp. So, after a single under or on a basic step, pass the follower's right hand into your right hand with your palm facing upward. Finish your basic step. On the first "slow," tuck or bring your right elbow in close to your right side, keep the elbow bent 90 degrees, and hold it firmly in place. Think of pulling your right elbow back until your right hand is by your waist, then push your forearm and hand forward and release your grasp to lead the spin. Grasp the follower's right hand with your left hand at the end of the turn. Both of you do the ball-change facing each other in a one-hand-joined position. As an option, the leader may also spin counterclockwise on the ball of his left foot on count 2 (at the same time as the follower's spin).

b. *For the follower:* The different hand position that the leader uses will prompt you to have your right palm downward. On the tuck, keep your elbow bent 90 degrees and lean your weight into the leader's hand. On the spin, keep your weight on the ball of your right foot and turn clockwise on count 2. Make sure that your entire body turns, rather than just your right arm moving backward. Then face your partner to finish the basic step.

Success Goal = Four repetitions of the tuck and spin, either with only the follower spinning or with both spinning___

Success Check

- On the tuck, the leader keeps his right hand firmly at or slightly in front of his waist___
- Both partners keep their elbows bent 90 degrees on the tuck___
- On the spin, the follower needs to have a firm right arm and to transfer the momentum to her body for the CW spin on the ball of her right foot___
- The leader may spin counterclockwise on the ball of his left foot simultaneously with the follower's spin___

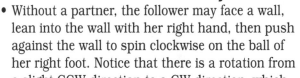

To Increase Difficulty

- Do two consecutive repetitions.
- Vary the tempo and use the appropriate swing basic for the tempo selected, whether slow, moderate, or fast.

To Decrease Difficulty

- Without a partner, the follower may face a wall, lean into the wall with her right hand, then push against the wall to spin clockwise on the ball of her right foot. Notice that there is a rotation from a slight CCW direction to a CW direction, which is an example of Newton's law of action and reaction.
- Without a partner, the leader may practice rotating his shoulders slightly clockwise as he steps onto his left foot, then rotate counterclockwise for his spin on the ball of his left foot.

8. Wrap and Unwrap

The wrap and unwrap basically reverses the order of the arch-out and arch-in transitions, except that two hands are held throughout. Begin in a two-hands-joined position facing your partner. The leader remains stationary and brings the follower to his right side (for the wrap), then back to the facing position again (for the unwrap). It takes a minimum of one swing basic to get into the wrap position and one swing basic to unwrap. The number of basics executed in the wrap position is optional.

a. *For the leader:* From a two-hands-joined position, the lead for the wrap is given on any ball-change and is twofold. While keeping his right hand low at his right side, the leader also lifts his left hand toward his right shoulder and circles counterclockwise above the follower's head (see figure 7.15a). These actions both turn the follower 180 degrees counterclockwise and place her on the leader's right side, yet slightly in front (see figure 7.15b). Finish with the second "slow" and ball-change steps in the wrap position.

   The lead to unwrap is given on any ball-change. The leader needs to lift his left hand to form an arch for the follower to go under (see figure 7.15c). He may also gently press on his partner's right side with the inside wrist of his right hand to guide her under the arch. Continue to hold both hands with your partner to end up in a two-hands-joined position. Finish the second "slow" and ball-change steps in this facing position.

b. *For the follower:* The follower's footwork is the same as for a single under, except that both hands are held and she ends up standing on the right side of the leader (review figure 7.15b). Both partners remain in the wrap position to execute the second "slow" and the ball-change steps.

To unwrap, the follower goes under the arch, turning clockwise 180 degrees on the first "slow" of the next basic step forward. Remain facing your partner to finish the swing basic step.

a Slow   b Slow (to wrap)   c Ball-change (arch to unwrap)

Figure 7.15 Wrap and unwrap.

Success Goal = Eight repetitions of the wrap and unwrap___

✔ Success Check

- Both of partner's hands are held throughout___
- The follower is on the right side and slightly in front of the leader when in the wrap position___

To Increase Difficulty

- Add basics when in the wrap position.
- Experiment with either a CCW or a CW basic step rotation while in the wrap position.
- Repeat this entire drill with a faster tempo and using the appropriate swing basic.

To Decrease Difficulty

- Take as many basics prior to leading the wrap as needed to establish a tempo with your partner.
- It is easier to use only one swing basic to wrap, then one swing basic to unwrap.
- An easy transition to a one-hand-joined position is for the leader to release his right hand during the unwrap.

9. Row Step

The row step is a fun variation that takes advantage of centrifugal force and uses a two-hands-joined position. Because this step involves spinning first on one foot and then the other, it is typically done with a single-time swing basic, even if you are dancing to slow or moderate tempos. Once the row step is over, resume whatever swing basic step is most appropriate for the music's tempo.

Stand facing your partner and imagine a small circle on the floor that connects your feet. Label this circle like a clock (notice that each partner's 12 o'clock is in the direction that the partner's midline is facing). Imagine that you are standing at 6 o'clock and your partner is positioned at 12 o'clock. Grasp both hands with your partner.

a. *Footwork:* At the end of any ball-change, the leader may rotate counterclockwise approximately 45 degrees. With both partners facing a diagonal, step forward toward your partner's right side, yet still on the imaginary circle connecting your feet. Spin on the ball of that foot approximately 180 degrees to face your partner's left side and make a weight change either by bringing your feet together or by stepping behind your other foot. Continue the rotation to face your partner with your shoulder square to execute the ball-change.

b. *Arm actions:* The hands and arms are positioned at shoulder level for the two "slow" steps, then back to a two-hands-joined position for the ball-change. If you imagine a bow-and-arrow-type pull, then the leader pulls his left hand back with his right arm extended during the first "slow" (see figure 7.16a). For the second "slow," the leader pulls his right hand back with his left arm extended (see figure 7.16b). Resume a two-hands-joined position for the ball-change (see figure 7.16c).

Notice that the "bow-and-arrow" lead for the row step is executed at shoulder height, which distinguishes it from a half-rotation turn (executed at waist height). Both partners need to keep both arms flexible yet firm enough to provide sufficient resistance for the proper lead. Avoid "spaghetti" arms here! Your arms and shoulders need to act together, so that a gentle push or pull on your hand will cause your entire upper torso (and not just your arms) to rotate.

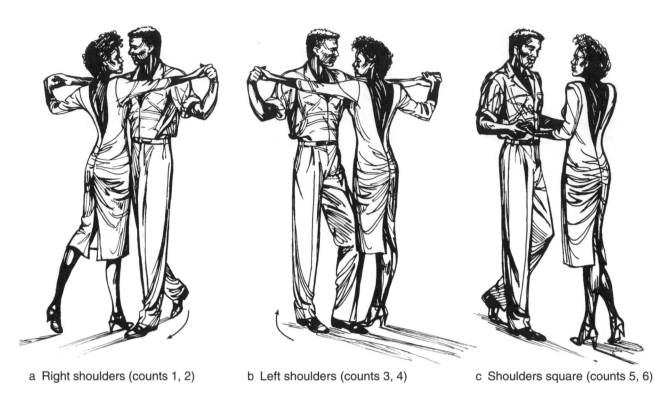

a Right shoulders (counts 1, 2)   b Left shoulders (counts 3, 4)   c Shoulders square (counts 5, 6)

Figure 7.16   Row step.

Success Goal = Two consecutive repetitions of the row step___

Success Check
- Right shoulders in, left shoulders in, then shoulders square___
- Step diagonally, bring feet together (or step behind), and ball-change___
- Experience some momentum or revolution with your partner___

 To Increase Difficulty
- Add more consecutive repetitions of the row step.
- Experiment with more rotation during the row step by the leader crossing his right foot behind his left foot on the second "slow."
- Alternate the row step with a wrap and unwrap.

To Decrease Difficulty
- Bring feet together on the second "slow."
- Isolate just the footwork, then just the arms, then put them together.

10. Double Cross

The double cross can be done by itself or immediately after any number of row steps. It is executed from a two-hands-joined position. The double cross ends in and thus becomes a transition to get into a handshake grip (i.e., right-to-right hand position).

a. *Body positions:* On the first "slow," make a CCW quarter turn to face your left side. On the second "slow," make a CW quarter turn back to face your partner. Execute the ball-change facing your partner.

b. *Arm positions:* Start in a two-hands-joined position. At the end of any ball-change, the leader may lift both hands high to form two arches (see figure 7.17a). The leader keeps the hands high as both partners make a CCW quarter turn (see figure 7.17b), then the leader lowers his right hand behind his partner's head and his left hand behind his own head (see figure 7.17c). On the CW quarter turn back to face each other, the leader releases both hands, yet keeps his right arm parallel and on top of the follower's right shoulder (see figure 7.17d). The leader then slides his hands down to regrasp right hand to right hand on the ball-change (see figure 7.17e).

After you finish a double cross, you are in a perfect position for the leader to lead a brush step, which is typically followed by either a single or a double under.

a Lift arms

b Quarter turn left

c Face left side to lower arms

d Face partner (quarter turn right)

e Ball-change

Figure 7.17   Double cross step.

Success Goal = Four repetitions of the double cross in isolation, then four repetitions of the double cross immediately combined with a brush step and either a single or a double under___

✔**Success Check**
- Move in unison with your partner into each position___
- Face left side on first "slow" cue___
- Face partner on second "slow" cue___
- Slide slightly apart to right-to-right hand grasp on the ball-change___

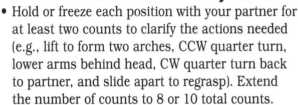

To Increase Difficulty
- Combine the row step with the double cross.
- Create a longer combination that includes the double cross.
- Use the appropriate swing basic for three swing tempos.

To Decrease Difficulty
- Hold or freeze each position with your partner for at least two counts to clarify the actions needed (e.g., lift to form two arches, CCW quarter turn, lower arms behind head, CW quarter turn back to partner, and slide apart to regrasp). Extend the number of counts to 8 or 10 total counts.
- Eliminate footwork on the first two "slow" portions; instead, focus on positioning your body to face to your left side, then toward your partner. Continue with your ball-change.
- Use a single-time swing basic step, regardless of the tempo of the music.

11. Three-Position Combinations

You may have noticed that the swing variations can be categorized according to the dance position from which they are executed. Three dance positions have been used: semiopen position, one-hand-joined position, and two-hands-joined position. Thus, grouping by position is one way of helping you recall the swing variations covered in this book.

Challenge yourself by creating swing combinations that include any two or more variations from each of the three positions with appropriate transitions (see the following chart). You can place them in any order and use any number of repetitions of each. Select the variations that you do best, and remember to add styling. Practice your sequence to the tempo of your choice. Repeat your selected sequence three times in a row. Rehearse with your partner until you feel comfortable enough either to imagine that you are performing before an audience or to demonstrate your selected sequence for others to watch.

Swing Variation Summary

A. Semiopen Position Variations
    1. Basic step in place
    2. Basic step turning or rotating counterclockwise
    3. Basic step turning or rotating clockwise
B. One-Hand-Joined Position Variations
    1. Single under
    2. Double under
    3. Brush step
    4. Belt loop
    5. Alternating shoulder touches
    6. Tuck and spin

C. Two-Hands-Joined Position Variations
1. Wrap and unwrap
2. Row step
3. Double cross

D. Transitions
1. Arch-out and arch-in
2. Roll-out and roll-in
3. Half-rotation transition
4. Inside left turn
5. Release one hand during unwrap

Success Goal = Eight different combinations that link any six or more variations___

Success Check
• Keep transitions and variations smoothly connected___
• Make a list of your favorite eight combinations for future reference___

To Increase Difficulty
• Vary the tempo and use the appropriate swing basic for the tempo selected, whether slow, moderate, or fast.
• Practice with a variety of partners.

To Decrease Difficulty
• Start in the order listed (i.e., from semiopen position), and add variations from both one-hand- and two-hands-joined positions, then end up in the semiopen position again.

SWING SUCCESS SUMMARY

The swing is a popular, energetic dance. It offers three different basic step patterns to choose from that are based on the tempo of the music (i.e., fast, moderate, or slow). Either or both partners may elect to do any one particular basic, depending on your preference. Each of the three basic six-count rhythmic patterns may be executed from a number of partner positions. The swing has many transition options that can connect, for example, (a) the semiopen to a one-hand-joined position and back to the semiopen position again, and (b) a one-hand-joined to a two-hands-joined position and back to the one-hand-joined position again. The variations for the swing are categorized according to the specific partner position in which they occur (i.e., semiopen, one-hand-joined, or two-hands-joined position). Multiple combinations are possible with the swing.

STEP 8 WALTZ: MOVING STATELY

The waltz is a smooth, graceful dance that became popular after two Austrian composers, Johann Strauss and Franz Lanner, created beautiful waltz music in the 1800s. Waltz music accentuates the first count and uses a 3/4 time signature. Dancers take a longer step to also accent the first count of the music. The waltz is recognizable by its stately posture and a wavelike rise-and-fall motion.

Although there are three different tempos of waltz music, only the slow-tempo American waltz will be described in this book for two reasons: It is the easiest to learn, and it is the version you are most likely to encounter on the social dance floor. The fast tempo is appropriate for the Viennese waltz, which alternates multiple left-then-right turns. The moderate tempo is appropriate for the International waltz, which began in England in the 1800s and incorporates very complicated movements at a moderate tempo.

The basic step pattern for the waltz uses three counts, with the first count accented. Thus, the rhythm cues are slow, quick, quick (SQQ). This rhythmic pattern is used within two foundational waltz variations: the box step and the half-box progression. The waltz uses primarily a closed dance position.

The slow, quick, quick rhythmic pattern is repeated twice to create the waltz box step. Just like the box step in the foxtrot, the box step in the waltz is composed of two half boxes in two directions, either forward or backward. Initially, the leader starts with the left foot and executes one half-box basic forward, then one half-box basic backward. The follower starts with the right foot and executes one half-box basic backward, then one half-box basic forward.

Forward half-box basic: To execute the forward half-box basic, stand with your weight more on your right foot. Bend your right knee, then push backward against the floor to take a long stride forward onto your left foot. Move your right foot diagonally to the right-front corner of an imaginary rectangle on the floor and step onto your right foot. Bring your left foot beside your right foot and change weight (onto your left foot) as your feet come together. These three weight changes comprise the forward half box.

Backward half-box basic: To execute the backward half-box basic, stand with your weight more on your left foot. Bend your left knee, then push forward against the floor to take a long stride backward onto your right foot. Move your left foot diagonally to the left-back corner of an imaginary rectangle on the floor and step onto your left foot. Bring your right foot beside your left foot and change weight (onto your right foot) as your feet come together. These three weight changes comprise the backward half-box basic.

Notice that the half-box basic uses the following foot positions: start in parallel first position, step forward (or backward) into parallel fourth position, step sideways into second position, then bring the feet together to return to parallel first position.

As in the foxtrot, an alternative in the waltz is to continue to travel forward (or backward) on the second half-box basic. In doing so, you are executing a series of forward (or backward) half-box progressions.

Figure 8.1 shows the various ways you might organize the counts and footwork for the two basic waltz steps. Some cues may be more helpful than others. Select those cues that most help you retain how to execute the basic waltz steps.

FIGURE 8.1 KEYS TO SUCCESS: WALTZ BASIC THREE-COUNT RHYTHM (SQQ)

Footwork Cues

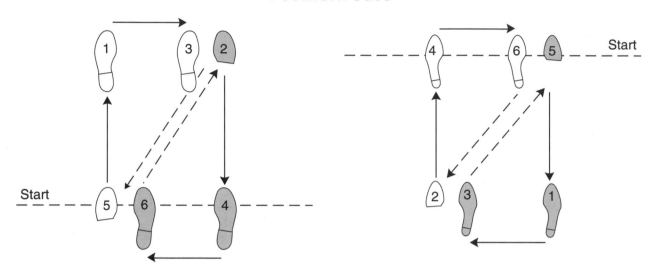

a Leader's box step

b Follower's box step

Box Step

a. Leader: Forward, side, together; backward, side, together
b. Follower: Backward, side, together; forward, side, together

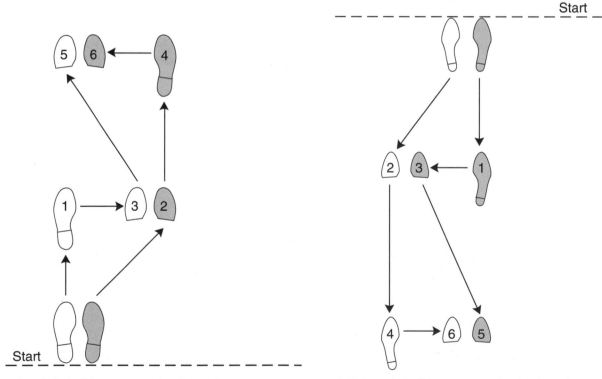

c Leader's half-box progression forward

d Follower's half-box progression backward

Half-Box Progression

a. Leader: Forward, side, together; forward, side, together
b. Follower: Backward, side, together; backward, side, together

Timing Cues

3/4 time signature:	Three beats to a measure, each beat gets one count (accent on counts 1 and 4)
Total counts:	Six
Rhythmic counts:	**1**-2-3; **4**-5-6 or **1**-2-3; **2**-2-3
Weight changes:	Six (in two measures; on each whole count)
Duration of steps:	Slow, quick, quick (both halves)
Direction of steps:	a. Box step: Forward half box, then backward half box (leader); or backward half box, then forward half box (follower) b. Half-box progression: Forward half box, forward half box (leader); backward half box, backward half box (follower)

WALTZ BASIC STEP PATTERN

DRILLS

1. Box Step Execution Challenge

Review figure 8.1, a and b, for the box step footwork and timing cues. Imagine a rectangular-shaped box on the floor that is longer than it is wide. The width should be approximately the width of your own shoulders. The first step is taken along the length of this rectangle, whereas the two "side, together" steps are executed along the width of the rectangle. Repeat your three weight changes in the opposite direction such that you step along the length, then take two steps in the corner (either right front or left back). After you can easily repeat the basic box step alone, try it with a partner in closed dance position.

Success Goal = Two consecutive minutes of the waltz box step___

Success Check
- Take one count for the "slow" (along the length of the rectangle)___
- Take one count for the "quick" (either in the right-front or left-back corner)___
- Take one count for the "quick" (bring feet together)___
- Lower your center of gravity and push off prior to taking your first step (within each set of three counts)___
- Blend both half-box basics into a fluid box step___

To Increase Difficulty
- Use a variety of slow waltz music (use track 13).
- Change partners frequently.
- Add rise-and-fall motion (i.e., bend on count 1, rise on count 2, and lower on count 3).

To Decrease Difficulty
- Prepare yourself to move by using extra cues. For example, in a race, the contestants hear "ready, set, go." The equivalent cues in waltz might be "&-a-1." The "&" alerts you to be ready, the "a" signals you to bend your standing knee and push off to stride forward (or backward), and the "1" is the first count or first weight change.
- Face a partner and match both palms (like a stop signal). Repeating the drill using this alternative dance position is an easy way to see how the bending of your standing knee can connect you with a partner, as well as initiate the rise-and-fall motion characteristic of the waltz.

2. Half-Box Progression Execution Challenge

The half-box progression is a good option when there is room to travel. Repeat the previous drill, except continue in the initial direction. Leaders start with the left foot and travel forward on each half-box basic. Followers start with the right foot and travel backward on each half-box basic. Review figure 8.1, c and d, as necessary, to identify each partner's basic execution.

Success Goals = Two consecutive minutes of half-box progressions___

Success Check
- Lower your center of gravity and push off prior to taking your first step (within each set of three counts)___
- "Slow" steps should be long steps to accent counts 1 and 4___
- Diagonally move your foot directly into a corner (either right front or left back) prior to counts 2 and 5___
- Side steps should be no wider than the width of your own shoulders___

To Increase Difficulty
- Use a variety of slow waltz music.
- Switch partners frequently.

To Decrease Difficulty
- Use slow verbal counts until you can make six weight changes in six counts (or two measures of music).
- Modify the starting position to face a partner and match facing palms. Once in motion, continue moving at the same pace, especially at the end of the first half-box basic. If the momentum stops, then the follower thinks that a box step (versus a half-box progression) is being executed.

3. Alternate Two Basics

It is very helpful for both the leader and the follower if you follow the rule of executing at least two repetitions of any one basic step before switching to the other one. For example, you might try alternating two box steps (four half boxes, or 12 total counts), then four forward half-box progression steps (four half boxes, or 12 total counts). Then reverse this order. Which order is easier for you?

Success Goal = Two consecutive minutes of alternating two waltz basic steps using two different orders___

Success Check
- Keep your head and eyes up___
- Lower your center of gravity and push off prior to taking your first step (within each set of three counts)___

To Increase Difficulty
- Use a variety of waltz songs (from slow to moderate tempo).
- Repeat this drill with different partners.
- Select any multiple of two repetitions of each basic to create your own sequence (i.e., try four, six, or eight repetitions before switching to the other basic step).

To Decrease Difficulty
- Practice alone until you are comfortable with each order.
- Gradually increase the tempo, first using counts, then slow waltz music.

WALTZ TRANSITION

DRILL

1. Leads From a Closed Position to a Promenade Position and Back to Closed

Using box rhythm, the cross step may be executed in either the foxtrot or the waltz. It uses two half-box basics (within two measures of music) and creates the transition between a closed partner position and a promenade position. What makes this transition more challenging is that it requires isolation such that your hands, torso, and arms remain stationary while your lower body angles 45 degrees. To get an idea of what this rotation entails, stand facing a wall without a partner. Place your hands against the wall at about shoulder height. Position your weight over the balls of your feet and twist your feet such that your toes face either your right hand (for followers) or your left hand (for leaders).

You don't need to be extremely flexible, as you'll only need to rotate your hips 45 degrees to either side (or 90 degrees total). The most common error is to move your arms. The second most common error is to rotate/twist too far to the side (beyond 45 degrees). Practice this subtle lower body rotation separately, then with a partner.

For the waltz, the box rhythm uses three weight changes, with each weight change getting one count (or beat in the measure). The cross step includes one half-box basic to move into a promenade position, then another half-box basic to move back to a closed position.

    a. *Transition to promenade:* From a closed partner position, start to execute a half-box basic. Both partners take a normal step on the first slow, followed by a regular side step. At the end of the side step, the leader needs to swivel on the ball of his right foot so as to twist or rotate his lower body counterclockwise approximately 45 degrees and to gently press with the heel of his right hand on the follower's left shoulder blade. Thus, in the waltz, the lead occurs at the end of count 2 and prior to count 3. Both partners look toward their extended hands, then bring their feet together on the third weight change to be in a promenade position (see figure 8.2).

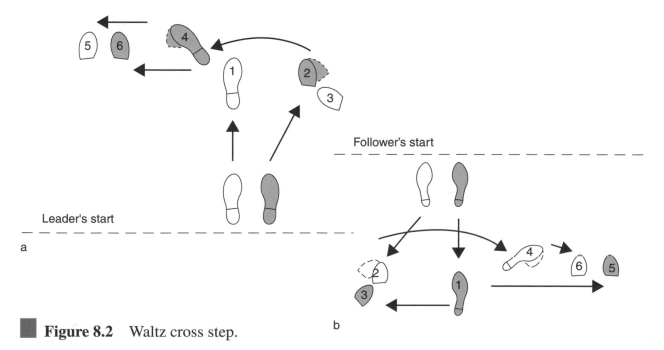

Leader's start

a

Follower's start

b

Figure 8.2 Waltz cross step.

b. *Transition to closed:* In the promenade position, both partners' inside feet should be free (his right foot and her left foot) to start the second half-box basic step. On the first weight change, the leader crosses his right foot over his left foot while the follower crosses her left foot over her right foot. At the end of this step, both partners swivel on the ball of their weighted foot in order to face each other in closed position again. Then both partners execute their "side, close" steps (i.e., their second and third weight changes) in the closed dance position (see counts 4 through 6 in figure 8.2 a and b).

Success Goal = 10 correct hip rotation leads of the cross step from a closed partner position to a promenade position, then back to a closed position___

Success Check

a. *First half-box basic*
- Leader: Forward (left foot), side (right foot and CCW swivel), together (left foot)___
- Follower: Backward (right foot), side (left foot and CW swivel), together (right foot)___
- Angle lower body 45 degrees from partner when in the promenade position___

b. *Second half-box basic*
- Inside feet cross on first weight change, then swivel___
- Square up hips (to be parallel) with partner when in the closed dance position___

To Increase Difficulty
- Repeat this transition only once, then alternate it with the waltz box step.
- Practice to a variety of tempos.

To Decrease Difficulty
- Place your hands on a wall at approximately shoulder height. Keep your weight on the balls of your feet as you practice the entire cross step in place without a partner.
- Repeat at least twice before changing to something different.

WALTZ VARIATIONS AND COMBINATIONS

DRILLS

1. Left Box Turn

The left box turn is a variation of the box step. It is composed of four CCW quarter turns. Alternately, a forward quarter turn is combined with a backward quarter turn, or vice versa. The leader initiates the left box turn by rotating his upper body counterclockwise until his midline is facing (i.e., perpendicular to) his left-front diagonal direction. The leader starts with the forward direction while the follower starts with the backward direction. Visually, a diagram of the complete left box turn gets complicated. Thus, if you think about breaking it down into a quarter turn that faces each wall of the room using alternating directions for each half-box basic, it is easier to conceptualize. Or, if you start facing the LOD, your quarter turn orientation is as follows: center, reverse LOD, outside wall, and LOD.

a. *Forward CCW quarter turn:* From a closed dance position, imagine a 45-degree diagonal line on the floor extending from your left foot along your left-front diagonal direction. After the leader's upper body CCW rotation toward the left-front diagonal, step forward with your left foot along this left-front diagonal for the first "slow" (using a toes-angled-outward placement). Take the next two weight changes while remaining in place: step to the right with your right foot (feet in parallel second position), then bring your feet together (left foot beside right foot) and change weight onto the left foot with feet in parallel first position. At the end of this half-box basic (three counts), notice that you have made a quarter turn and are facing a new wall (or the center).

b. *Backward CCW quarter turn:* From a closed dance position, imagine a 45-degree diagonal line on the floor extending backward from your right heel. The leader's upper body rotation lead facilitates your right foot's step backward (using a toes-angled-inward placement) along this right-back diagonal path. Step to your left side with your left foot, then bring your feet together (shifting your weight onto your right foot).

The third and fourth half-box steps repeat these movements. After the fourth quarter turn, the leader may end the turn by firmly keeping his frame (upper torso and arms) facing the LOD (see figure 8.3, a and b).

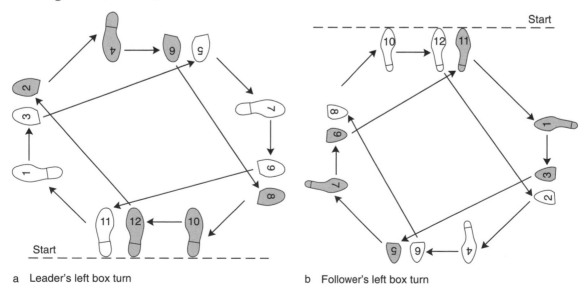

a   Leader's left box turn   b   Follower's left box turn

Figure 8.3 Left box turn footwork for the waltz (12 total counts).

Success Goal = Four waltz left box turns in correct position and with proper leads___

Success Check
- Face a new wall on each quarter turn___
- Four CCW quarter turns (using four half-box basic steps) comprise a left box turn___
- Toes angle outward on forward quarter turns, then angle inward on backward quarter turns___

To Increase Difficulty
- Experiment with a right box turn, which adds two more half-box basic steps and also reverses directions. From the leader's point of view, execute a half-box progression forward to free your right foot. Make a CW quarter turn (toward the outside wall) by stepping forward with your right foot along your right-front diagonal. For the second CW quarter turn, step backward with your left foot along your left-back diagonal. Alternately repeat these directions for two more CW quarter turns. Finish with another half-box progression forward to free your left foot again.
- Try combining two left quarter turns with two right quarter turns. Notice that this combination moves in the LOD.

To Decrease Difficulty
- Practice footwork and upper torso rotation without a partner.
- Use less than a 45-degree angle on each half-box basic and take as many basics as you want to revolve 360 degrees.

2. Balance

The balance is a variation that permits you to remain relatively in place, which is especially useful for fast-tempo waltz music or any time that you want to slow down a bit. The balance step uses three actions: a step, a touch, and a hold. It may be executed forward, backward, or sideways. The leader starts with the forward balance and his left foot while the follower starts with the backward balance and her right foot.

a. *Forward balance:* Step forward onto your left foot (count 1) and touch the ball of your right foot beside the instep of your left foot (count 2). Hold this touch position on count 3.

b. *Backward balance:* Step backward onto your right foot (count 1) and touch the ball of your left foot beside the instep of your right foot (count 2). Hold this touch position on count 3.

c. *Sideways balance:* The leader steps to his left side (count 1) and touches the ball of his right foot beside the instep of his left foot (count 2). At the same time, the follower steps to her right side (count 1) and touches the ball of her left foot beside the instep of her right foot (count 2). Both partners hold this touch position on count 3. Both partners then repeat the entire balance step to the opposite side on counts 4, 5, and 6.

Success Goal = Eight repetitions of the balance step combining at least two directions each time: (a) forward and backward or (b) side to side___

Success Check

• Touch the ball of one foot beside the inside edge of the ball of the opposite foot___
• Use any multiple of two repetitions (as there are two sides to the waltz before you get your starting foot free again)___

To Increase Difficulty

• Alternately bend and straighten knees to lower on count 1, add a rise on count 2, then remain level on count 3.
• Experiment with adding an outside (right) underarm turn on the third balance to the side. The leader lifts grasped hands to form an arch at the end of count 6 then guides the follower's turn with his right hand on her back.

To Decrease Difficulty

• Step (change weight) on each count while taking tiny steps in place during counts 2 and 3. A hold is sometimes more difficult than making a weight change on each count/beat of the music.
• Repeat each combination option at least twice. For example, try forward, backward, forward, backward balance steps. There is no need to rush.

3. Combine Two Variations

Using the appropriate waltz leads with your partner, try each of the following combinations to slow waltz music:

- Two boxes and a left box turn
- Two boxes and four half-box progressions forward
- Four half-box progressions forward and a left box turn
- Two boxes and four balances (forward and backward)
- Two boxes and four balances (side to side)
- Two boxes and two cross steps

Success Goal = Continuously repeat each combination listed, then alternate any two variations of your choice for the length of one song___

Success Check

- Use a smooth transition when alternating variations___
- Maintain the waltz tempo and styling___

To Increase Difficulty

- Repeat each of the combinations listed in drill 3 in reverse order.
- Experiment with a different number of repetitions for each combination. For example, try half-box progressions forward along the length of the room. In the corners of the room, execute only one CCW quarter turn, then continue with half-box progressions forward again. Or try to do fewer repetitions of each variation, as space allows.
- Add an underarm turn during the second half of a box step. Thus, on the leader's backward half-box basic (count 4), he lifts his left hand and arm to form an arch, then gently directs or guides the follower to move forward under the arch on counts 5 and 6. The follower may either turn quickly to face the leader, or continue forward in a circular path for two more half-box basics (as the leader does the box step in place). This variation option adds a total of four half-box basics to give the follower time to face her partner again. The leader needs to notice when the follower's left foot is free to execute her forward half-box basic; then he may connect with the follower to resume a box step in closed dance position.

To Decrease Difficulty

- Add more repetitions to each combination listed in drill 3 (e.g., four, six, or eight consecutive repetitions of any one variation).

4. Weave

The weave is a modification of the cross step that is used as a transition from closed to promenade position. It introduces an open (side-by-side) position with the outside hands (furthermost from your partner) released when facing each side. After a half-box basic, the cross step is repeated three times, alternating from side to side in an open position. The weave is also a foxtrot variation (review figure 6.7, a-d).

a. *For the leader:* During the transition to promenade position, the leader does a swivel at the end of count 2 of his forward half-box basic to face his left side. On count 3, he releases and extends his left hand while facing his left side. The first cross step starts with the leader's right foot. On count 5, the leader places his left hand on the follower's right shoulder blade and releases his right hand. On count 6, the leader faces his right side. On the second cross step, the leader crosses with his left foot, places his right hand on the follower's left shoulder blade, then faces his left side again with his left arm extended. The third cross step is done with the leader's right foot, after which he faces his partner to resume a closed dance position.

b. *For the follower:* The follower's footwork consists of a backward half-box basic with a swivel at the end of count 2 to face her right side. As the follower's right hand is now released, she may open her right arm in a curved position as she faces her right side. The follower crosses her left foot, then swivels to face her left side and extends her left arm. She continues to cross with the right foot and swivel to face her right side with her right arm extended. The third cross is done by stepping with the left foot back to a closed dance position.

Success Goal = Eight repetitions of the weave step to slow waltz music___

Success Check
- The weave is composed of four half-box basics___
- In open position, partners should have symmetrical arm positions on each side___
- Keep your extended arm curved with the elbow and hand in front of your shoulder___
- Followers need to keep elbows up and in frame throughout so that the leader can locate her shoulder blade when facing each side___

To Increase Difficulty
- Use a variety of tempos.
- Practice with a variety of partners.

To Decrease Difficulty
- Use a slow tempo.
- Practice without a partner, then with a partner.

5. Combine Three Variations

The purpose of this drill is to combine three waltz variations. The advantage of combining or clustering moves is that once you start any particular cluster, the rest of the moves seem to flow automatically without your having to think about them. Try each of the following three-variation combinations with a partner to waltz music, then experiment with combining any three variations:

- Two boxes, four half-box progressions forward, two left box turns
- Two boxes, a left box turn, four half-box progressions forward
- A left box turn, four half-box progressions forward, two boxes
- Two left box turns, two boxes, six half-box progressions forward
- Two balances (forward and backward twice), a cross step, a weave step
- Two CCW quarter turns, four half-box progressions backward, two CW quarter turns

Success Goal = Consecutive repetition of each of the combinations listed in drill 5, then select and link any three variations into a combination for the length of one song___

Success Check
- Maintain the slow, quick, quick rhythm___
- Write down at least four of your favorite combinations to trigger your memory later___

To Increase Difficulty
- Vary the number of repetitions of each of the variations within the combinations listed in drill 5.
- Create your own combinations.

To Decrease Difficulty
- Repeat each variation at least twice to give you more time to prepare for the next lead and to get in sync with your partner.

6. Rollovers

Rollovers are similar to the weave, but both partners are facing the LOD in an open position, and any multiple of two repetitions may be executed. A rollover results when the partner on the inside (left side) rolls in front of (faces) and moves across to the opposite side (right side) while the other partner does the basic in place. As in the leads used with the weave step, the leader will alternately hold the follower's left shoulder blade with his right hand, then hold the follower's right shoulder blade with his left hand, keeping the opposite arm extended in a curved and open position. The rollovers progress in the LOD.

a. *For the leader:* From a closed dance position, make a transition to a semiopen position with both partners facing the LOD, which is sometimes called an open twinkle. Execute the open twinkle as follows: step forward with your left foot, step diagonally forward with your right foot, then bring your feet together (step onto your left foot). At the end of count 1, rotate your upper torso and frame 45 degrees CW to lead the open twinkle and to bring the follower to your right side. At the end of count 2, release your left hand so that both partners' free hands and arms may extend or open in a rounded position (facing the LOD on count 3). On the next half-box basic, execute the rollover as follows: step with the right foot on a right-front diagonal path to cross in front of the follower, turn clockwise to face your partner, then continue turning to face the LOD again (using three beats of music). The leader does the next three waltz steps in place as the follower does a rollover. Continue alternating. To end the rollovers, the leader resumes a closed dance position when the follower is facing him during her rollover. The leader finishes with a half-box progression forward.

b. *For the follower:* From a closed position, execute an open twinkle as follows: step backward with your right foot, step diagonally backward with your left foot and pivot clockwise to face the LOD, then step in place with your right foot. As the leader releases your right hand, extend that arm and hand to a curved position. You should be on the right-hand side of the leader, both facing the LOD. Execute the next three steps in place as the leader does his rollover. Repeat the leader's actions for your rollover. Continue alternating until the leader resumes a closed dance position at the end of any of your rollovers. The follower finishes with a half-box progression backward.

Success Goal = Eight repetitions of the rollovers to slow waltz music___

Success Check
- Keep your extended arm in a curved shape, symmetrical with your partner's extended arm___
- Keep your arms in frame throughout___

To Increase Difficulty
- Do fewer repetitions of the rollovers.

To Decrease Difficulty
- Do multiple repetitions of the rollovers (in groups of two half-box basics).
- Imagine a triangle with the leader on the left, the follower on the right, and the LOD at the point of the triangle. Thus, the rollovers move in the LOD while the inside person rolls across.

7. Scissors

The scissors variation may also be called spirals, serpentines, or zigzags because it follows a diagonal floor path that alternates toward the center, then toward the outside wall (see figure 8.4). Start in a closed dance position for the scissors. It takes at least four half-box basic steps to execute the scissors variation. Both the first and the fourth half-box basics are transitions into and out of the zigzag floor path that is characteristic of the scissors step. The scissors starts in a closed position, which gets modified by rotating 45 degrees to move into a right parallel position with the right shoulders together (to travel toward the center of the room), then by rotating 45 degrees to move to a left parallel position with the left shoulders together (to travel toward the outside wall).

a. *For the leader:* On the transition to a right parallel position with your partner, the first step is to move forward with your left foot. The second step is to move diagonally to your right with your right foot, then swivel (on the ball of your right foot) to face your left-front diagonal. The third step brings your feet together (as you shift your weight onto your left foot). This transition to a right parallel position (with the follower on your right diagonal) is sometimes called a closed twinkle.

On the second half-box basic, the leader steps diagonally with his right foot toward his left-front diagonal. On the second step in this direction, pivot with your left foot 90 degrees to face your right-front diagonal direction. Then bring your feet together (as you step onto your right foot).

On the third half-box basic, the leader steps (with his left foot) on the diagonal toward his right-front diagonal direction (see figure 8.5). He then continues forward along this diagonal with his right foot and pivots 90 degrees to face his left-front diagonal direction. Next, he brings his feet together to step onto his left foot, then

Figure 8.4 Zigzag floor path used in the scissors variation.

Figure 8.5 Diagonal reach from left parallel position.

continues alternating sides. To end the scissors, the leader reduces the degree of rotation to remain facing the LOD on any second basic (after his right foot steps diagonally toward his left-front diagonal direction).

On the fourth half-box basic, the leader may either end the scissors variation by doing a half-box progression forward or rotate 90 degrees to face the center to continue the zigzag floor path.

b. *For the follower:* Use the first half-box basic to make the transition to the right parallel position (using the closed twinkle transition) as follows. Step backward with your right foot. Step slightly to your left-back diagonal for your second step, and pivot counter-clockwise 45 degrees to face your left-back diagonal direction. Bring your feet together on your third step in place.

On the second half-box basic, reach backward with your left foot, then your right foot. At the end of your second backward step, pivot clockwise 90 degrees and bring your feet together on the third step.

On the third half-box basic, reach backward with your right foot (see figure 8.5), then your left foot. At the end of your second backward step, pivot counterclockwise (either 90 degrees or 45 degrees, depending on the amount of rotation given by the leader), then bring your feet together on the third step. If the former, then continue to repeat the zigzag floor path. If the latter, then execute a half-box progression backward.

Success Goal = Eight repetitions of the scissors to slow waltz music___

✔ **Success Check**

- The scissors' long, reaching step (first beat of the second and third measures) is taken with the leg closest to the LOD, or the leg opposite the diagonal direction of travel (i.e., the leader's right foot moves toward his left-front diagonal; the follower's left foot moves toward her right-back diagonal)___
- Footwork cues for the scissors: diagonal, pivot, together___
- Leader moves forward while follower moves backward during the scissors___
- Alternate a right- then left-parallel partner position___

To Increase Difficulty

- Repeat the zigzag floor path multiple times.
- Lead a right underarm turn on the last diagonal zigzag to come out of the scissors. The follower's turn should occur on count 5.
- Slide apart to use an open two-hand position (extend arms to sides at shoulder level) during the scissors.

To Decrease Difficulty

- Place your hands on your partner's shoulders to become aware of the diagonals and to keep the follower in front of the leader with a clear right (or left) parallel position.
- Without a partner, practice pivoting no more than 90 degrees to face each diagonal direction and to travel in the LOD.

8. Combine Four Variations

The next challenge is to link at least four variations into longer combinations. Try each of the following sample practice combinations involving at least four different variations:

- Two boxes, four half-box progressions forward, two left quarter turns and two right quarter turns, a left box turn
- Two boxes, two left quarter turns and two right quarter turns, a left box turn, eight scissors
- Two boxes, four balances forward and backward, a left box turn, a weave step
- Four half-box progressions forward, two box steps, two weave steps, six rollovers
- Two boxes, two cross steps, eight half-box progressions, a weave step, six scissors

Now either modify these combinations or create your own combinations that include any four or more waltz variations. Use the following summary chart to reference the variations covered in this book.

Waltz Variation Summary

A. Variations
1. Box step
2. Half-box progressions
   a. Forward
   b. Backward
3. Box turn
   a. Left (CCW)
   b. Right (CW)
4. Cross step
5. Balance
   a. Forward and backward
   b. Side to side

6. Weave
7. Rollovers
8. Scissors
B. Transitions
  1. Cross step
  2. Open twinkle
  3. Closed twinkle

Success Goal = Consecutive repetition of each of the practice combinations listed, then select and link any four or more variations into a combination for the length of one song___

Success Check
• Keep all transitions smooth___
• Practice proper partner etiquette___

To Increase Difficulty
• Reverse the order of the variations used in the practice combinations.
• Link more than four variations together.

To Decrease Difficulty
• Use a slow tempo.
• Link at least three different variations.

WALTZ SUCCESS SUMMARY

The waltz is a graceful, stately dance. It has a three-count rhythmic pattern with an accent on the first count of each measure. The closed dance position is used primarily; however, it is helpful to be able to make the transition to a promenade, or semiopen position, then back to closed again. Two advanced transitions are the open twinkle (used in the rollovers variation) and the closed twinkle (used in the scissors variation). The selected variations for the waltz are listed for your convenience (in the last drill). If you get the opportunity to join a mixer that uses the waltz basic step pattern, try it out!

STEP 9

POLKA: HAVING FUN

The polka basic step originated as a folk-dance step found in English country dances and German and Polish folk dances. However, the styling of each varies—from a light, springy quality to a heavy, forceful quality. The polka uses the versatile triple step and adds a modified hop prior to the downbeat. At first, the polka may seem difficult, because you must perform more actions than with any other basic step and you must do them very quickly. Because the polka is so vigorous, you will need to build up your stamina to last the entire length of a song—and ultimately an evening's worth of polkas and other dances!

The polka basic step pattern uses two counts, or one measure of 2/4 time music. However, you need to repeat the polka step on both sides, so there are a total of four counts until your starting foot is free again. Thus, many dancers find it helpful to count the basic step in sets of four counts (merging two measures) and to treat the music as 4/4 time.

The polka basic footwork actions start as a "hop, step, ball, step"—all within two beats of music. Then, on the second repetition, the hop actually blends with the end of the triple step to take on the timing of a skip (i.e., becoming a step, hop). If it is too difficult for you to hop on the first execution of the polka basic, you may want to start with the triple step and then add the modified hop on the "&-a" count prior to your next triple step. Once started, these actions become continuous movements combining a skip with a triple step. From a stationary start, the timing of the skip corresponds to "&-e-a" because three actions need to be executed prior to the downbeat: a knee bend, a push off the floor to rise in the air, and a landing on that same foot. Then the triple step is executed on "1-&-2" with the other foot. Now, the last triple step may be used to start the next hop, if you bend that knee. This knee bend is the first action needed to execute a hop. The remaining two ac-

tions may be cued as "&-a" to correspond with the rise in the air and the landing on that same foot.

For the leader: From an inside-hands-joined position, start with your weight on your right foot. To execute the hop, bend your right knee, push off the floor to rise in the air (high enough to bring the ball of your right foot off the floor), and land on your right foot. Keep these actions in a vertical plane—avoid traveling forward. To start the triple step, step forward onto your left foot on count 1. Position the ball of your right foot beside the instep of your left foot and push downward and backward on the "&" count. Step forward onto your left foot again on count 2. Repeat these actions starting the hop with your left foot.

For the follower: From an inside-hands-joined position, start with your weight on your left foot. To execute the hop, bend your left knee, push off the floor to rise in the air (high enough to bring the ball of your left foot off the floor), and land on your left foot. Keep these actions in a vertical plane—avoid traveling forward; rather, use a "down, up, down" motion. To start the triple step, step forward with your right foot on count 1. Position the ball of your left foot beside the instep of your right foot and push downward and backward on the "&" count. Step forward onto your right foot again on count 2. Repeat these actions starting the hop with your right foot.

Notice that one foot is always in front of the other foot during the triple step. With a partner, start with your feet in first position. Both of you hop on your inside standing leg prior to executing the triple step. Keep your feet in a parallel fourth position on each step, then in a parallel third position on the "ball" or push step. Figure 9.1 shows the various ways that you might organize the counts and footwork cues for the polka basic step pattern. Some cues may be more helpful than others. Select those cues that most help you retain how to execute the polka basic step.

FIGURE 9.1	BASIC STEP PATTERN

Footwork Cues

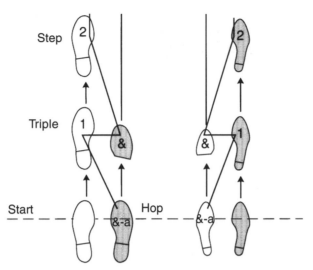

a Leader's left side   b Follower's right side

Leader

Hop (bend, rise, land on right), triple step (left, right, left); repeat on opposite side

Follower

Hop (bend, rise, land on left), triple step (right, left, right); repeat on opposite side

Timing Cues

2/4 time signature:	Two beats to a measure, each beat gets one count
Total counts:	Four (two counts per side)
Rhythmic counts:	Hop, 1-&-2; hop, 3-&-4; or &-a, 1-&-2, &-a, 3-&-4
Duration of steps:	"&-a," quick, quick, slow (both sides)
Direction of steps:	a. *Inside-hands-joined position:* In place, forward, forward, forward (keep the same foot in the lead during execution of the triple step on any one side of the body; leaders step onto left, push, left, while followers step onto right, push, right)
	b. *Closed position:* Leader travels forward starting with left foot on the triple step while the follower starts traveling backward with the right foot (again, both partners keep the same foot in the lead during execution of the triple steps)

POLKA BASIC STEP PATTERN

DRILLS

1. Polka Basic Execution Challenge

Because you combine a hop and a triple step in the polka basic step, it is helpful to practice each part separately, then put them together. The number of weight changes in only two beats of music makes this basic more difficult. Thus, use slow counts to give yourself enough time to execute each part. Try each of the following parts, then repeat the polka basic without a partner or music until it becomes automatic.

a. A hop begins and lands on the same foot. It is executed in a vertical plane—you should not travel forward, or you'll lose your balance. To execute a hop safely, you need to apply Newton's law of action and reaction. Stand with your weight all on one leg. Bend that knee, then push off the floor to spring into the air (just high enough that the ball of your foot comes slightly off the floor). The rise into the air does not need to be very high. Land on the same leg and foot that you started with, and bend that knee to absorb the force of your landing. Thus, one knee should bend, straighten, and bend again during the execution of each hop. Try executing only a hop on one foot. Then combine a step and a hop. On each hop, you should remain in one location; that is, keep the hop in a vertical plane (using down, up, down actions). On each step, move forward (or backward).

b. You've used a triple step (i.e., combining three weight changes) in the waltz. However, the foot positions are modified in the polka basic to be executed from either a parallel third or an extended third foot position. Try executing a series of triple steps. Notice that after executing the first triple step with one foot, your other foot is free to start the second triple step. It takes two repetitions of the triple step before your starting foot is free to begin again. On the triple steps, you'll travel forward (or backward).

c. Without a partner or music, combine a hop with a triple step to do consecutive polka basic steps in the LOD (counterclockwise around the room). Make sure that you are blending each part into one continuous motion (review figure 9.1). Notice that the second step of each triple step becomes the foot that you hop on. Also, notice that the timing of the hop now becomes more like a skip (review figure 3.4).

Success Goal =

a. 16 correctly executed combinations of a step and a hop___

b. 16 correctly executed triple steps___

c. 16 correctly executed polka basic steps___

Success Check

- Use a "down, up, down" motion to both initiate and absorb the landing force with each hop___
- On counts "1-&-2," one foot alternately stays in the lead on any one side of the body with each triple step___
- Bring your free foot forward after the hop to be ready to execute the triple step___

To Increase Difficulty

- Use slow polka music (use track 15).
- Try the polka basic step while traveling backward.
- Join inside hands with your partner and repeat the polka basic step. The partner on the left side starts the triple step with the left foot and the partner on the right side starts the triple step with the right foot.

To Decrease Difficulty

- Use separate cues for each action of the hop (i.e., "bend, push/rise, land" might correspond to "down-up-down" or "&-e-a," using cues to correspond to the actions needed). Gradually speed up the tempo until you can land on one foot and bring your free foot forward to step on count 1 (combining a hop and a step and using the timing of a skip).
- Eliminate the hop on the very first basic and start with the triple step on the downbeat. Then add the hop at the end of each triple step thereafter.

2. Promenade, or Semiopen, Position

The polka basic step may be executed from a semiopen position with a partner. Stand beside a partner with the leader on the left and the follower on the right. Rotate your upper torso by bringing your outside shoulder forward approximately 45 degrees toward your partner. Place your hands in the promenade, or semiopen, position. Shift your weight onto your inside foot. Execute the polka basic step while maintaining this position. Both partners repeat the polka basic step pattern first with their outside foot (see figure 9.2a), then with their inside foot (see figure 9.2b). Notice how the promenade position facilitates the use of an extended third foot position, a third foot position, then an extended third foot position on the triple step.

a Basic with outside feet   b Basic with inside feet

Figure 9.2 Polka basic step executed from a promenade, or semiopen, position.

Success Goal = 16 polka basic steps in unison with a partner__

Success Check
• Take small steps on the triple steps__
• Keep your upper torso and arms stationary__

To Increase Difficulty
• Add slow polka music.
• Follow a CCW path around the perimeter of the room.

To Decrease Difficulty
• Gradually increase the tempo from counts to slow polka music.
• Stand beside a partner and repeat the drill without touching.

3. Inside-Hands-Joined Position

Stand beside a partner such that the leader is on the left side and the follower is on the right, both facing the same direction. Join inside hands and put your free hand on your hip. Stand with your weight on your inside leg; that is, the one closest to your partner. Slowly go through each part of the polka basic step. In unison, hop on your inside foot, bring your outside foot forward, and execute a triple step starting with your outside leg (the one farther away from your partner). Reverse these actions starting with your outside foot (to hop), then execute a triple step forward starting with your inside foot.

It is fun to relate to your partner by rotating your outside shoulder forward 45 degrees during your triple step with your outside foot, then rotating your inside shoulder forward 45 degrees during your triple step with your inside foot. You'll be looking at your partner, then away from your partner (see figure 9.3, a and b). The inside-joined hands naturally swing back as you face inward, then swing forward as you face outward. The hands swing to waist or shoulder height only. Also be aware of a tendency to overrotate your shoulders to literally face or turn your back to your partner. Try to align your shoulders perpendicular to a forward diagonal direction, either left or right.

a Basic with outside feet   b Basic with inside feet

Figure 9.3 Polka inside arm swing *(a)* backward, then *(b)* forward.

**Success Goal =** 16 polka basic steps in unison with a partner___

✔ Success Check
- Partners use either their inside or their outside feet in unison___
- Rotate the outside shoulder 45 degrees forward with the outside foot's forward triple step, then the inside shoulder forward for the inside foot's forward triple step___

To Increase Difficulty
- Add slow polka music.
- Gradually increase the tempo (use track 16).

To Decrease Difficulty
- Place both hands on your hips and twist or rotate your upper body without moving your lower body. This isolation drill is good practice for the styling needed in doing the polka basic step from an inside-hands-joined position.
- Imagine you are moving in slow motion as you bring your outside shoulder forward during the hop on your inside foot. Freeze this position and check your relationship with your partner (i.e., shoulders perpendicular to a front diagonal, weight on inside foot, and outside foot ready). Keep your outside shoulder forward during the triple step with your outside foot. Then check positioning with inside feet.

4. Closed Position

An alternative position for executing the polka basic step is from a closed dance position. The leader faces in the intended direction and the follower faces the leader. Thus, the leader moves in a forward direction while the follower moves backward. It is a bit more difficult to travel backward when executing the polka basic step. The main difference occurs on the triple steps. When moving backward, the follower's right foot is still in front, but the reference point becomes the heel of the foot (versus the toe). You can identify the direction of travel by extending an imaginary line from the heel.

The shoulders rotate slightly to face either a front diagonal (left, then right, for the leader) or a back diagonal (right, then left, for the follower). Thus, each triple step is taken along a diagonal.

Success Goal = 16 polka basic steps in unison with a partner___

Success Check
- Either align left shoulder forward with left foot, or right shoulder forward with right foot, on the triples___
- Avoid rotating shoulders beyond the diagonals (i.e., rotate only 45 degrees)___

To Increase Difficulty
- Add slow polka music.
- Repeat the polka basic step for the length of one song.

To Decrease Difficulty
- Gradually increase the tempo from slow counts to slow music.
- Modify the dance position to a two-hands-joined position, which will give each partner more room to move.

DRILLS

1. Leads From an Inside-Hands-Joined Position to Promenade and Back to Inside-Hands-Joined

If you start the polka basic step pattern from an inside-hands-joined position, how do you lead into the semiopen, or promenade, position? One easy transition takes advantage of the natural swinging motion of the inside-joined hands. It is described by its actions such that the leader places the joined hands onto his shoulder to make the transition to a promenade position. From the promenade position, an easy way to make the transition back to the inside-hands-joined position is to slide apart.

a. *Hand-to-shoulder transition:* Technically, any time the inside hands and arms swing back (and you step with your outside foot), the lead may be given for this transition. For example, take two polka basics with a partner and let your inside arms swing back and forward. On your third polka basic, swing back as usual, except the leader now places the follower's joined hand on top of his right shoulder (see figure 9.4a). On the fourth polka basic, the leader releases his right hand, places it just below the follower's left shoulder blade (see figure 9.4b), and extends his outside (left) arm and hand forward so that the follower can put her right hand on top (see figure 9.4c).

a Basic with outside feet   b Basic with inside feet   c Basic with outside feet

Figure 9.4 Hand-to-shoulder transition.

b. *Slide-apart transition:* Once in the promenade position, the leader may make the transition back to the inside-hands-joined position whenever both partners' outside feet are executing the basic step. For example, take two polka basics to establish a tempo with your partner. On the third polka basic, the leader releases his left hand grasp (see figure 9.5a). On the fourth polka basic, the leader begins to move apart as he slides his right hand with the palm up under the follower's arm until both can grasp inside hands (see figure 9.5b). Then both partners may again place their outside hands on their hips and let their joined hands swing back (see figure 9.5c).

a Basic with outside feet   b Basic with inside feet   c Basic with outside feet

Figure 9.5   Slide-apart transition.

Success Goal = Four correct transitions from an inside-hands-joined position to a semiopen position and back to an inside-hands-joined position___

Success Check
• When swinging inside hands, keep outside hands on hips___
• On any odd-numbered repetition of the polka basic, the leader may place the follower's joined hand on his right shoulder to make the transition to promenade (i.e., when hands swing back)___
• Keep extended arms firm when in the promenade position to establish a frame with your partner___
• On any odd-numbered polka basic, the leader may make the transition back to an inside-hands-joined position___

To Increase Difficulty
• Continuously repeat a combination of four polka basics into promenade, then four polka basics to inside-hands-joined position.
• Practice with different partners and different tempos.

To Decrease Difficulty
• Practice each transition separately, then combined, without music.
• Practice to a slow count, gradually increasing the tempo until you can move to slow polka music.

2. Leads From Closed to Promenade Position and Back to Closed Position

To make smooth transitions from a closed to a promenade position and back again, it is helpful to group at least eight polka basic steps. The leader remains facing the LOD throughout these transitions. The follower starts with her back to the LOD, then rotates to face the LOD, then turns to face her partner again.

a. *Rotation to face LOD:* From a closed position, the leader may signal a transition to promenade at the end of any even-numbered polka basic. For example, partners take two polka basics, and on the second basic, the leader gradually rotates his entire upper torso and arms clockwise until his left hand is pointed toward the LOD, which brings the follower to the leader's right side. There is no need to rush this transition. The follower should be ready to pivot clockwise 180 degrees on the ball of her left foot (at the end of count 4) until she faces the LOD. Now both partners are in a promenade position to repeat the polka basic step.

b. *Rotation to face partner:* From a promenade position, the leader may signal a transition to closed position at the end of any even-numbered polka basic. For example, partners take two polka basics, and at the end of the second basic, the leader gradually rotates his entire upper torso and arms counterclockwise to bring the follower into closed position again. The follower should be ready to pivot counterclockwise (180 degrees) on the ball of her left foot (on count 4 or 8) to face her partner again.

Success Goal = Four correct transitions from a closed position to a promenade position and back to a closed position___

Success Check
- The lead may be given at the end of any even-numbered polka basic___
- The follower pivots on the ball of her left foot, either clockwise or counterclockwise___

To Increase Difficulty
- Do any even number of polka basics before leading these transitions.
- Practice to different tempos.
- From the promenade position, the leader may randomly lead into an inside-hands-joined position.
- Connect any three partner positions. For example, start in an inside-hands-joined position, make the transition to a promenade position, then move to a closed position. Or start in a promenade position, make the transition to a closed position, then to a promenade position again.

To Decrease Difficulty
- Practice your part separately from your partner until you can demonstrate it competently.
- With a partner, isolate each combination of transitions, gradually adding another partner position.
- Practice to counts, then to slow polka music.

3. Leads From Closed to Sweetheart Position and Back to Closed

From a closed position, group six polka basics (two counts each, or a total of 12 counts) to make the transition to the sweetheart position. The leader remains facing the LOD while the follower makes 1 1/2 turns to face the LOD.

a. *Arch-under with hand change and 1 1/2 turns:* Take at least two polka basics to establish a tempo with your partner. At the end of any second polka basic, the leader may lift his left hand and arm to form an arch while keeping his right hand on the follower's upper back. This signals the follower to pivot 180 degrees clockwise to face the LOD at the end of any count 4 (see figure 9.6, a and b). The leader needs to maintain contact with the follower (right hand on her back) as she executes a third polka basic (starting with her right foot) while facing the LOD. At the end of the third polka basic, the follower pivots 180 degrees clockwise on the ball of her right foot to face her partner as the leader transfers her hand from his left to his right hand (see figure 9.6c). Traveling backward, the follower executes her fourth polka basic. At the end of the fourth polka basic, the leader continues with a small, CW, circular motion above the follower's head to signal her to do another 180-degree CW pivot on the ball of her left foot to face the LOD again (see figure 9.6d). As the follower's left hand passes the leader's left hand, he may grasp it. Remember to position your hands just in front of the follower's shoulders and equidistant from her shoulders. Continue with polka basics five and six in the sweetheart position.

b. *Arch-over with hand change:* The transition back to closed is similar to that used from the promenade position in the previous drill. Take at least two polka basics in the sweetheart position. At the end of any second polka basic (count 4), the follower's weight is on her left foot. The leader needs to time the lift of his right hand over the top of the follower's head to coincide with count 4, when the follower may pivot counterclockwise on the ball of her left foot to face the leader again. The leader finishes the transition by placing the follower's right hand into his left hand and resuming a closed position.

a Closed position   b Counts 1-&-2, first half turn to face LOD   c Counts 3-&-4, second half turn to face partner   d Sweetheart position, third half turn to face LOD

Figure 9.6 Polka transition from the closed to the sweetheart position.

Success Goal = 10 smoothly executed transitions from closed to sweetheart position, then back to closed position again___

Success Check
- The follower is approximately a half step in front of the leader when in the sweetheart position___
- On the transition into the sweetheart position, the follower makes three CW turns, or pivots: to face the LOD and execute a forward basic, to face her partner and execute a backward basic, then to face the LOD and execute a forward basic___
- The leader makes a hand change both into and out of the sweetheart position___

To Increase Difficulty
- Practice to a variety of tempos.
- Practice with a variety of partners.

To Decrease Difficulty
- Use a slow tempo, gradually moving from counts without music to practicing with music.
- Practice without a partner.

POLKA VARIATIONS AND COMBINATIONS

DRILLS

1. Underarm Turn

An underarm turn is a variation that permits the follower to rotate 360 degrees. The amount of rotation involved depends on which dance position is being used. From a closed position, it is easier to lead either two CW half turns (to yield one full turn as used in the transition to sweetheart position, except without a hand change) or two CW full turns. Remember that the polka basic is executed on both sides of the body. Thus, it is an advantage to both partners when the leads are grouped in multiples of two basics, or a minimum of four counts. From an inside-hands-joined position, it is easy to lead a full turn.

a. *From a closed dance position:* Do two polka basics. Prior to the third polka basic, the leader simultaneously lifts his left hand to make an arch and gently presses with the heel of his right hand. The leader maintains contact with the follower's upper back to guide the follower's CW pivot (half turn) to face the LOD. The follower looks toward the LOD as she executes her third polka basic (review figure 9.6b). Prior to the fourth polka basic, the follower pivots another CW half turn to face the leader. Both do the fourth polka basic and resume a closed dance position.

   If the follower likes to turn, a full turn for each of two basics may be executed. After two basics, the leader makes an arch and keeps his left hand above the follower's head. He ends the turns by lowering his left hand. His right hand doesn't maintain contact during the two turns. The follower turns 360 degrees twice (for a total of four counts).

b. *From an inside-hands-joined position:* Do three polka basics, letting your inside hands naturally swing backward, forward, then backward, respectively (see figure 9.7a). On the fourth polka basic, as the hands swing forward (see figure 9.7b), the leader lifts his hand above the follower's head, extends two fingers for the follower to cup her hand around, and makes a small circular CW motion above her head (see figure 9.7c). These actions lead the follower into a full turn on any second polka basic.

a Counts 1-&-2   b Arm lift lead   c Counts 3-&-4 (underarm turn)

Figure 9.7 Underarm turn from inside-hands-joined position.

Success Goal = Eight repetitions of each underarm turn to slow polka music___

Success Check
• The follower's pivots (half turns) occur at the end of either count 2 or 4___
• Take your time to match either a half turn or a full turn with a basic step. There is no need to rush___

To Increase Difficulty
• Do continuous polka basics and make the transition from a closed position to an inside-hands-joined position and back to a closed position again, including the appropriate underarm turn variations in each position.
• From a closed position, try CCW half turns. This move takes four basics. At the end of the first basic, lead the follower to pivot counterclockwise on her right foot (left inside turn) to face the LOD. The follower does the second basic facing the LOD, then pivots CCW a half turn on her left foot prior to the third basic to face her partner. Resume a closed dance position on the fourth basic.

To Decrease Difficulty
• Practice pivots without a partner.
• With a partner in closed position, the follower can imagine looking through a window (formed by the arch) to execute one basic, then pivot to face her partner to execute the next basic.

2. Partner Turn

The clockwise partner turn is extremely fun to do and represents one of the most popular polka variations. It may be executed from either a closed partner position or from a semiopen, or promenade, position. The following descriptions will be from a closed position. Do at least two polka basics to set the tempo and connect with your partner.

At the end of any second basic and on the next hop, the leader transitions to a semiopen position and lowers his extended left hand and arm below his waist and raises his right elbow above his shoulder. At the same time, he can keep his right hand firmly on his partner's left shoulder blade to signal that she should execute her basic in place. The leader then moves slightly ahead of the follower until he is facing his right-front diagonal direction (see figure 9.8a). On the hop prior to the fourth basic, both partners rotate clockwise a half turn. Now it is the leader's turn to execute the basic in place. He signals the follower to move ahead toward the LOD by angling the arms from high to low toward the LOD (see figure 9.8b). Execute at least two more polka basics to resume a closed position.

a Counts 1-&-2
(leader moves in front)

b Counts 3-&-4
(follower moves in front)

Figure 9.8 Clockwise partner turn.

Success Goal = Eight repetitions of the CW turn (alternating two basics forward and two basics turning) to slow polka music___

✔ Success Check

- Alternately during the polka turn, first the follower, then the leader, marks time or executes the triple step portion of the polka basic in place while the other partner moves ahead___
- The 180-degree rotations occur on the hop portion of the polka basic during the partner turn___

To Increase Difficulty

- Experiment with two or more consecutive partner turns without any basics between them.
- Create a combination involving underarm turns and a partner turn.

To Decrease Difficulty

- Without a partner, stand with either shoulder toward the LOD and your weight on your back foot. Do a polka basic. Prior to your next polka basic, simultaneously do a half turn on your hop so that you have your opposite shoulder pointed toward the LOD, then do a triple step. Continue to alternate sides by turning during the hop portion of the polka basic.
- Focus your eyes toward the LOD during the triple step portion of the polka basic.

3. Gallop Combination

Another variation from a promenade, or semiopen, position involves gallops or slides within eight counts. The rhythm for the gallops is "1-&, 2-&, 3-&, 4-&, 5-&, 6-&, 7-&-8." Start with the leader's left foot and the follower's right foot. For the first six whole counts, step onto your lead foot, then bring your feet together (with a weight change) on the "&" cues. To end the gallops, hop on your outside foot on the sixth "&" cue, then do a regular polka basic with your inside foot (i.e., the leader's right foot and the follower's left foot).

Success Goal = Two consecutive gallop combinations to slow polka music___

✔Success Check

• Step, together (gallop) six times, then polka basic___
• Make a weight change on each rhythm cue___
• Make sure that there is enough room to execute the gallop combination___

To Increase Difficulty

• Separate the eight counts into two halves and try a modified partner turn with gallops. Thus, gallop four times, rotate clockwise a half turn on the hop, then continue with four more gallops and rotate clockwise a half turn at the end so that you are back in promenade position to continue your basics.
• Execute the gallop combination with at least one other variation that you know so far.

To Decrease Difficulty

• Use a slow tempo.

4. Twist Combination

The twist combination is a variation that combines two polka basics with four twist actions (each twist getting one count) for a total of eight counts. The twists result from a swiveling action on the ball of the back foot.

a. *For the leader:* From a promenade position, execute at least two polka basics. At the end of the second polka basic, the leader holds his upper torso and arms (frame) very firm as he swivels on the ball of his right foot to face his partner. This allows him to bring his left foot in front (see figure 9.9a). Then he swivels on the left foot and brings the right foot in front (see figure 9.9b). These two swivel-and-forward actions are repeated for a total of four swivels or twists (or counts).

b. *For the follower:* After any two polka basics, swivel on the ball of your left foot to face your partner. This allows you to bring your right foot in front (review figure 9.9a). Swivel on your right foot and bring your left foot in front (review figure 9.9b). Repeat these two swivel-and-forward actions for a total of four swivels or twists (or counts).

a Swivel with outside feet forward

b Swivel with inside feet forward

Figure 9.9 Twist combination includes four swivels or twists.

Success Goal = Eight repetitions of the twist combination to slow polka music___

Success Check
- Keep your knees slightly bent during the swivels or twists___
- Arms and upper torsos remain stationary while the lower body twists___
- Maintain a promenade position for two polka basics and four twists___

To Increase Difficulty
- Experiment with either four or eight twists.
- Execute the twist combination with at least one other variation that you know so far.

To Decrease Difficulty
- Without a partner, place your hands against a wall, lean into the wall, and practice swiveling your back foot and bringing the other foot in front, or crossing, on each whole count.
- Do four polka basics before executing the twist combination.

5. Around-the-World

In this variation, the leader is considered the "world" and the follower moves around him. Thus, it is called "around-the-world." For practice, this drill uses eight polka basics, or four basics to set up and four basics to complete the around-the-world. The drill starts and ends in a sweetheart position. Both partners hold both hands throughout.

Execute three polka basics from the sweetheart position. On the fourth polka basic, the leader lowers his right hand and lifts his left hand over the follower's head to signal a half turn such that the follower is facing the reverse LOD (see figure 9.10a). The leader continues to bring his left hand over his own head and his right hand up by his right shoulder (on the fifth basic), then places the follower's right arm behind his own head (on the sixth basic). At this point, the follower should be halfway around and on the leader's left-hand side (see figure 9.10b).

The leader continues to pull gently with his left hand and lift his right hand over his own head (see figure 9.10c) in order to bring the follower in front of him (on the seventh basic). His right hand forms an arch for the follower to turn under and move back to sweetheart position (see figure 9.10d).

a Fourth polka basic   b Sixth polka basic   c Seventh polka basic   d Eighth polka basic

Figure 9.10 Around-the-world executed within eight polka basics from a sweetheart position.

Success Goal = Eight repetitions of the around-the-world variation to slow polka music___

✔ **Success Check**
• The leader executes the polka basic in place, taking small steps___
• The follower moves clockwise around the leader___
• On the sixth basic, the follower should be on the leader's left side___

To Increase Difficulty
• Combine the around-the-world variation with any other variation that you know in a closed dance position.

To Decrease Difficulty
• Practice the leads without any footwork. Freeze and check each position.
• The leader may move slightly to one side or the other to decrease the distance that the follower needs to travel around him.

6. Reverse Around-the-World

This variation of the previous drill differs in that the direction of travel is counterclockwise. The reverse around-the-world takes four polka basics.

From the sweetheart position, the leader gently pulls in a CCW direction with both hands as he brings his right hand over the follower's head (on the first polka basic) and slightly lowers his left hand (see figure 9.11a). Then he continues his gentle CCW pull, placing his right hand (and the follower's right arm) over and behind his own head. His left arm extends from his left shoulder, with the follower now on his left-hand side (on the second polka basic, which is shown in figure 9.11b). As the leader continues to pull counterclockwise with his right hand, his left hand lifts up over both his own head and the follower's (on the third polka basic, as shown in figure 9.11c). Finish the follower's turn back to the sweetheart position (on the fourth polka basic).

a First polka basic   b Second polka basic   c Third polka basic

Figure 9.11   Reverse around-the-world.

Success Goal = Eight repetitions of the reverse around-the-world variation to slow polka music___

Success Check
• The leader needs to take small steps in place___
• The follower needs to be on the leader's left side after two polka basics___

To Increase Difficulty
• Vary the number of basics prior to leading this variation.
• Create a combination that links both the around-the-world and the reverse around-the-world.

To Decrease Difficulty
• Practice the arm leads without any footwork. Freeze and check your positions.
• Use a set number of polka basics prior to the reverse around-the-world (e.g., four).

7. Front-to-Front and Back-to-Back Turns

This variation is executed from an inside-hands-joined position and is similar to the partner turn, except it is executed in a different position.

Take two polka basics to get connected with your partner and to let your inside hands swing naturally to the back, then to the front. On the next basic, the leader faces the follower and grasps her right hand with his left hand, which modifies the basic to be side, together, side (and in a front-to-front position). Pivot a half turn on the next hop (the leader turns clockwise while the follower turns counterclockwise). Do a side, together, side polka basic in this back-to-back position and reach back toward your partner with your free hand to grasp hands (i.e., the leader's right hand grasps the follower's left hand). Pivot a half turn on the next hop to return to the inside-hands-joined position again.

Success Goal = Eight repetitions of the front-to-front and back-to-back turns to slow polka music___

Success Check
• Pivot a half turn on the hop___
• Modify the triple steps to be more of a slide or gallop___
• Make a hand change on each basic, first when facing your partner, then when facing away from your partner___

To Increase Difficulty
• Try two or more consecutive repetitions of this variation.
• Create a combination linking this variation with at least one other variation that you know so far.

To Decrease Difficulty
• Practice without a partner.
• Review drill 2.

8. Combine Three Variations

Now it is time to review the polka variations and link any three or more into a longer combination. In addition, one challenge with the polka is to select one variation from at least three different partner positions when creating your combinations. The following is a list of the variations covered in this book.

Polka Variation Summary

A. Variations
   1. Basic step
   2. Underarm turns
      a. Half
      b. Full
   3. Partner turn
   4. Gallop combination
   5. Twist combination
   6. Around-the-world
   7. Reverse around-the-world
   8. Front-to-front and back-to-back turns

B. Transitions
1. Hand-to-shoulder
2. Slide-apart
3. Rotation to face LOD
4. Rotation to face partner
5. Arch-under with hand change and 1 1/2 turns
6. Arch-over with hand change

Success Goal = Eight different combinations linking any three or more variations from at least three different partner positions___

Success Check
- Make transitions smooth and fluid___
- Maintain a constant tempo as appropriate to the music selected___

To Increase Difficulty
- Use a faster tempo.
- Practice with a variety of partners.

To Decrease Difficulty
- Reduce the Success Goal to less than eight different combinations (e.g., try four).
- Write down your combinations and refer to them as needed.

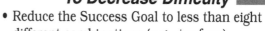

POLKA SUCCESS SUMMARY

The polka is a lively dance that is just plain fun to do. The basic step pattern is challenging because it must be executed quickly to match the music tempo. There are many transition options, and several different partner positions may be used. One transition option is from an inside-hands-joined position to a promenade and back to an inside-hands-joined position. Another transition option is from a closed position to a promenade position and back to closed position again. A third transition option is from a closed position to a sweetheart position and back to closed position again. The variations for the polka are listed for your reference, along with the challenge of selecting combination variations that include at least three different partner positions.

STEP
10
CHA-CHA: BEING FLIRTATIOUS

One of the most popular Latin dances is the cha-cha, which was originally called the cha-cha-cha in Cuba during the mid-1950s to reflect the three quick steps used in the footwork and the calypso sounds heard in the music. Finding "cha-cha-cha" cumbersome, however, Americans shortened the name to "cha-cha." Due to its Latin influence, the cha-cha alternately uses smooth and staccato movements, which requires coordination and control and a blending of other dances. In particular, it slows down the timing yet still breaks on count 2, as in the mambo, and it adds a modified triple step from the swing. Some even refer to the cha-cha as a triple mambo because of the combining of the break step with a triple step. The cha-cha is also characterized by Cuban motion in that the upper body remains level while the lower body moves. Cuban motion results from alternately bending one knee as you straighten the other—the hips only *appear* to do all the work! The leg bearing the weight has a straight knee, whereas the non-weight-bearing leg is positioned with a bent knee, which results in a delayed weight change. It takes a lot of practice to achieve proper Cuban motion.

The styling for the cha-cha is flirtatious. For instance, on turns you might look at your partner out of the corners of your eyes as you turn your head slightly to tease and challenge your partner to follow or look at you. Another way to give the illusion of a challenge is to alternately follow your partner's forward and backward movements—one advances and the other retreats. Thus, you seem to be connected, but you are actually approximately two feet apart and facing each other (in the shine position).

Another styling uniqueness of the cha-cha is the addition of hand movements or "talking" with your hands. Initially, you can "talk" with your hands by keeping your elbows bent 90 degrees and fairly close to your sides, but allowing them to move approximately 45 degrees either forward or backward from your shoulder joints. Then let your forearms, wrists, and hands rotate freely with the flow of your movements.

The cha-cha uses a slow, slow, quick, quick, slow (SSQQS) rhythm. The "slow, slow" portion corresponds to a break step. A break step may be initiated starting either in a forward or a backward direction on the first "slow," then reversing the direction on the second "slow." Each break step takes two counts and is composed of two weight changes. The forward break step shifts weight forward onto the left foot, then rocks or shifts weight backward onto the ball of the right foot (see figure 10.1a). The backward break step shifts weight backward onto the ball of the right foot, then rocks or shifts weight forward onto the left foot (see figure 10.1b). Alternating between each break step is a triple step, which corresponds to the "cha-cha-cha" (quick, quick, slow) in the music. The cha-cha-cha steps may be executed either alternating forward and backward directions or alternating left and right side directions.

How you start the cha-cha basic step pattern is optional. Some dancers like to take a preparatory side step on the downbeat, then do a break step. If the side step is taken with your normal starting foot, then the leader steps to his left side with his left foot (and the follower steps to her right side with her right foot). The leader's right foot is then free, and he can break backward from this position. At the same time, the follower's left foot is free (thus, she can break forward from this position).

Or, a preparatory side step on the downbeat may be taken with the opposite foot (leader's right, and follower's left). Then on count 2, the leader breaks forward with his left foot, while the follower breaks backward with her right foot.

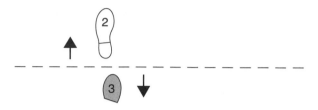

a Forward break (weight shifts forward, then backward)

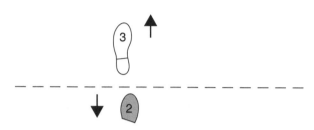

b Backward break (weight shifts backward, then forward)

Figure 10.1   Break steps *(a)* forward and *(b)* backward.

Another option is to hold (not move) on the downbeat, so that the leader's left foot is free to do a forward break (and the follower's right foot is free to do a backward break). Regardless of the starting option selected, the break steps should be timed to coincide with counts 2, 3. Notice that once you get started, the last triple step occurs on the downbeat, so it may help to imagine that the preparatory side step (or weight shift or hold) coincides with the end of a triple step.

Forward half basic: To execute a forward break, your left foot should be free. For the first weight change, place your left foot forward and shift your weight onto that foot. For the second weight change, place the ball of your right foot slightly behind the heel of your left foot and shift your weight onto that foot. Throughout the break step's weight changes, keep your center of gravity between both feet, rather than letting your upper torso move beyond your base

of support (i.e., your feet). Your left foot is now free to execute a triple step backward (stepping left, right, left for the "cha-cha-cha"). This is one half of the basic cha-cha step pattern.

Backward half basic: To execute a backward break, your right foot should be free. For the first weight change, place the ball of your right foot slightly behind the heel of your left foot and transfer your weight onto *only* the ball of your right foot as you slightly lift your left foot off the floor. On the second weight change, transfer your weight forward onto your left foot (replacing your weight and keeping that foot in its original location). As you execute the backward break, you need to keep your upper torso centered above both feet—much like an agility drill so that you can quickly shift your weight, or like marching in place. Now your right foot is free to execute a triple step forward (for the cha-cha-cha steps). These actions complete one half of the basic cha-cha step pattern.

Notice that the following foot positions are used: Starting in first position with feet together, the break steps may be executed either in parallel fourth or in fifth foot position. The triple step may be executed using three foot positions: parallel fourth, modified first (without passing feet), and parallel fourth. Or you may opt to use either an extended third or fifth, either a third or fifth, and either an extended third or fifth foot position on the forward and backward triple step. Any of these foot position options work; the choice depends on how dramatic you want your styling to be. When the triple step is executed to the side, the foot positions would alternate as follows: parallel second, parallel first, and parallel second.

The cha-cha basic step pattern may be initiated from a shine position, a two-hands-joined position, or a closed position. Figure 10.2 shows various ways that you might use to organize the counts and footwork for the cha-cha. Some cues will be more helpful to you than others. Select those cues that most help you retain how to execute the cha-cha basic step pattern.

FIGURE 10.2   KEYS TO SUCCESS: CHA-CHA BASIC STEP PATTERN

Footwork Cues

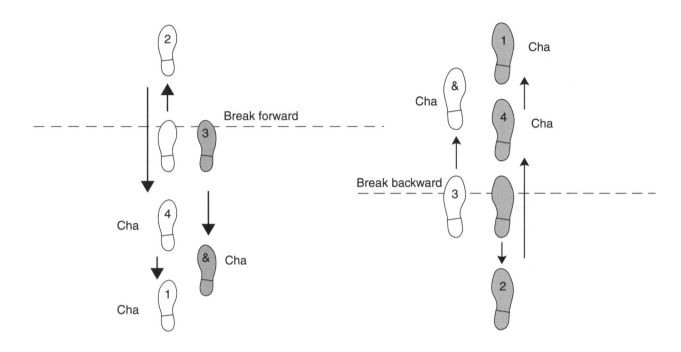

Forward Half Basic

Break step (left, right), triple step (left, right, left)

Backward Half Basic

Break step (right, left), triple step (right, left, right)

Timing Cues

4/4 time signature:	Four beats to a measure, each beat gets one count
Total counts:	Eight (two measures)
Rhythmic counts:	2, 3, 4-&-1 (break occurs on counts 2, 3 for each half); or 2, 3, 4-&-5, 6, 7, 8-&-1 (breaks occur on counts 2, 3 and on counts 6, 7)
Weight changes:	10 (on each rhythmic count)
Duration of steps:	Slow, slow, quick, quick, slow (both halves)
Direction of steps:	a. Forward half basic: break forward, backward; backward triple step
	b. Backward half basic: break backward, forward; forward triple step
Starting options:	a. Hold first count (downbeat), then forward break (for leader) and backward break (for follower).
	b. Step to side (normal start foot) on first count (downbeat), then backward break (for leader) and forward break (for follower).
	c. Step to side (opposite foot starts) on first count (downbeat), then forward break (for leader) and backward break (for follower).

CHA-CHA BASIC STEP PATTERN

DRILLS

1. Basic Forward and Backward

Face your partner in shine position and hold (don't move) on the downbeat (count 1). The leader may then execute a forward half basic while the follower mirrors by executing a backward half basic. Then complete the other half basic while still facing your partner in shine position.

Success Goal = 16 consecutive repetitions of the cha-cha basic step pattern, traveling forward and backward (use track 14)___

Success Check

- A forward break shifts weight forward onto the left foot, then back onto the ball of the right foot___
- A backward break shifts weight backward onto the ball of the right foot, then forward onto the left foot___
- Triple step uses "step, push, step" actions (with the "push" foot always behind the "step" foot)___

To Increase Difficulty

- Review foot positions for more precise execution.
- Repeat drill using a closed dance position.

To Decrease Difficulty

- Face a partner with fingertips and palms touching (halfway between the two of you) and repeat drill.
- Select or imagine a straight line on the floor that you can follow while repeating this drill.

2. Add Styling

In the shine position, imagine that horizontal strings are connecting the two of you at your shoulders, hips, and ankles. As one moves either forward or backward, the other automatically follows in unison. This invisible connection helps you to move fluidly with your partner and also presents you both with the challenge of following the other's directional changes.

Once you can move as a unit with a partner, experiment with "talking" with your hands. Keep your elbows at approximately 90-degree angles, but let them move forward and backward approximately 45 degrees in either direction from your shoulder joints. It is natural for one arm to swing forward as the other swings backward. Notice that these arm actions are opposite of the leg or foot actions—your right elbow and forearm swing forward when your left foot is forward and your left elbow and forearm swing forward when your right foot is forward. As you become more comfortable with repeating the basic cha-cha step pattern, you'll soon find that your forearms, wrists, and hands rotate freely as you execute your movements. Have fun with it.

Success Goal = 16 consecutive repetitions with at least two different partners using slow cha-cha music___

Success Check

- Elbows bend approximately 90 degrees___
- Let wrists, hands, and forearms rotate freely to "talk" or gesture as you move___

To Increase Difficulty

- Use a variety of cha-cha music selections with different tempos.
- Repeat with a variety of partners.

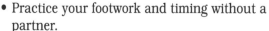

To Decrease Difficulty

- Practice your footwork and timing without a partner.
- Mentally count the rhythm (i.e., 2, 3, 4-&-1) throughout a song to match your actions to the tempo of the music.

3. Basic Side to Side

Even though the timing of the break step receives a lot of attention, to match the music, you also need to be aware of the timing of the triple step. Repeat a triple step (side, together, side) to each side while mentally (or verbally) counting "4-&-1" and make a weight change on each cue (for three weight changes to each side). Notice that the third "cha" is taken on count 1, or the downbeat of a measure. Thus, if you prefer to start with a preparatory side step, then the third "cha" step is the equivalent of a preparatory side step that is an option to use only when starting the basic cha-cha step pattern.

Now execute a break step prior to a side triple step. Remember that the break step is a way to change directions quickly, shifting weight either forward to backward or backward to forward. After each forward break (starting with your left foot), your left foot is free to do a triple step to your left side. After each backward break (starting with your right foot), your right foot is free to do a triple step to your right side. Try this alone without music, then with music. When you are comfortable, try the basic using a side triple step with a partner in closed position.

To understand the four direction changes, it helps to imagine an H painted on the floor. This image does not work out to be a true H, yet the image helps, as you will alternately use the vertical right-front bar on forward breaks (when your left foot is free), the horizontal bar on the triple step to your left side, the left-back vertical bar on backward breaks (when your right foot is free), and the horizontal bar on the triple step to your right side. Figure 10.3 shows the basic H floor path, which will help remind you to keep the break steps alternating in the forward-backward directions and the triple steps alternating to either side.

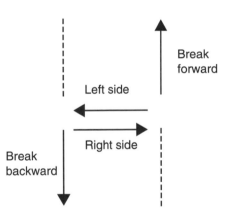

Figure 10.3 Basic H floor path.

Success Goal = Two consecutive minutes of the cha-cha basic step pattern, traveling to alternating sides on each triple step___

Success Check
• Break step occurs on counts 2, 3___
• Each side triple step occurs on counts 4-&-1___

To Increase Difficulty

- Use a variety of slow cha-cha music.
- Face a partner in shine position to repeat this drill.
- Do four repetitions of the forward and backward half basics, then four repetitions of the basic cha-cha step pattern following the basic H floor path.

To Decrease Difficulty

- Either verbally or mentally cue the counts using a slow tempo.
- Ask an observer to give you feedback on how precisely you move in the four different directions. It should be easy for an observer to identify in which direction you are traveling. Avoid traveling on a diagonal at this point.

CHA-CHA TRANSITION

DRILLS

1. Leads From Closed to One-Hand-Joined Position and Back to Closed Position

In the cha-cha, the closed position may be modified slightly for styling. If you choose to add this modification, then bend the arms of your joined hands at the elbow and bring them closer together in the center space between you until your forearms almost touch. Even if you don't elect to use this modification, notice the distance between you and your partner when in a closed position. Imagine that there is a centerline or fence separating you. Most of the leads in the cha-cha initiate from this centerline. Each partner has one half of the shared space.

a. *Float away:* Following the basic H floor path, take some basic steps to establish a tempo with your partner. After any backward break step with the right foot, as the leader shifts his weight forward onto his left foot, he may press gently through the palm of his left hand into the follower's right hand. If the center hands are kept in the same location, then the follower is signaled to take a larger back step (at the end of her forward break step). At the same time, the leader also needs to release his right hand. These actions signal the follower to move or "float" away as both continue with the basic step in a one-hand-joined position.

b. *Close up:* To resume a closed position, the leader may use the same backward break step and hand pressure to presignal that he is going to move closer to the follower during his sideways cha-cha-cha steps. This signals the follower to lift her left elbow to put her hand on the leader's right shoulder, and it permits the leader to bring his right hand under the follower's left elbow and position it on her left shoulder blade again. Both continue the basic in a closed dance position.

Success Goal = 10 smoothly executed transitions from closed position to a one-hand-joined position and back to closed position again___

Success Check

- Keep your elbows bent approximately 90 degrees in the one-hand-joined position___
- Keep your hands on the imaginary centerline when in the one-hand-joined position___

To Increase Difficulty

• Add an underarm turn during the close up. The leader may lift his left hand to make an arch during his backward break so that the follower can execute an underarm turn (see figure 10.4). The follower does a pivot turn (left foot to side, pivot/shift weight onto right foot to face the opposite side), then continues the CW turn to face her partner as both execute the sideways steps and move into closed position.

To Decrease Difficulty

• Practice keeping your elbows and hands in front of your shoulders so that you can take advantage of your body's weight shift from backward to forward during any backward break step. Avoid moving your hands either beyond or behind the centerline that indicates your half of the partner position.

Figure 10.4 Underarm turn during the leader's backward break step.

2. Leads From One-Hand- to Two-Hands-Joined Position and Back to a One-Hand-Joined Position

You have practiced the break step both forward and backward. The break step may also be executed to each side from a cross-body lead. From a one-hand-joined position, the leader brings his left hand across his midline, then opens to the side to do a cross-body break. The leader must then repeat the cross-body break on the opposite side before he can make the transition to another dance position. The cross-body breaks alternate between a two-hands-joined and a one-hand-joined position.

Notice that the cha-cha also modifies the hand grasp when in a two-hands-joined position. The leader's thumb and fingers are separated (so they can open and close much like a bird's beak), with his fingers on top of the follower's hand (see figure 10.5).

Figure 10.5   Modified two-hands-joined position hand grasp for the cha-cha.

a. *Grasp both hands:* Once you are in a one-hand-joined position, it is easy to make the transition to two hands. After any backward break, the leader may grasp the follower's other hand when traveling either forward or to his right side on the cha-cha-cha steps. When in a two-hands-joined position, the leader has the option of leading the basic cha-cha step pattern in either an H floor path or in the forward and backward directions. To make the transition back to a one-hand-joined position, the leader may release his right hand grasp of the follower's left hand at the end of any backward break.

b. *Cross-body lead:* From either a one-hand- or a two-hands-joined position and after any backward break, the leader may release his right hand grasp and bring his left hand across his midline during the triple step to his right side. As his left hand continues to the side, both partners open to face the leader's right side so that they can initiate a cross-body break (see figure 10.6a) with their inside feet (his left and her right). During the triple step to the leader's left side, the leader can grasp both hands (see figure 10.6b). The leader may now release his left hand grasp and bring his right hand across the midline of his body to open to his left side. Both partners execute the cross-body break with their inside feet (his right and her left) while facing the leader's left side (see figure 10.6c). The leader may grasp both hands again when executing the triple step to the leader's right side (see figure 10.6d).

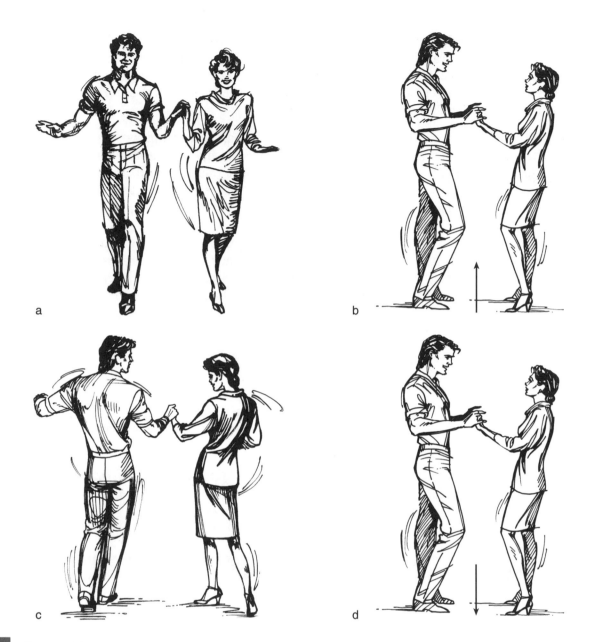

Figure 10.6 Cross-body leads to cross-body breaks.

Success Goal = 10 smoothly executed transitions from a one-hand-joined to a two-hands-joined position and back to a one-hand-joined position___

Success Check
• Grasp a hand when coming closer to your partner, instead of reaching___
• Keep your hands on the centerline that separates and defines both your own and your partner's space___

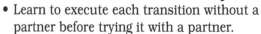 **To Increase Difficulty**
• Randomly practice transitions, connecting at least three different partner positions (closed, one-hand, and two-hands joined).
• Use a variety of tempos.

To Decrease Difficulty
• Learn to execute each transition without a partner before trying it with a partner.
• Practice only one transition at a time.

3. Leads Into and From Shine Position

The shine position is a featured position in the cha-cha as it lets each partner "shine" or express their personality when not holding hands. The elbows are primarily in a 90-degree angle, which places the hands in front of the body. Thus, whenever the leader chooses to close up and resume another dance position, he can find the follower's hands.

a. *Release both hands:* From a two-hands-joined position, the leader may release both hands to get into a shine position. It is easy to take advantage of the momentum during your forward and backward direction changes to make your transition. Thus, after any backward break, the leader can release both hands and take smaller steps on his forward triple step to let the follower get farther away (or open up the space between them) to be in a shine position.

b. *Resume partner contact:* The leader also has many options for resuming contact with the follower from a shine position. For example, after any backward break, the leader can simply travel farther on his forward triple step to close up the space between him and his partner and resume a one-hand-joined, a two-hands-joined, or a closed position.

Success Goal = 10 smoothly executed transitions into and from a shine position___

Success Check
- Take advantage of resuming a position when moving closer to your partner___
- Keep elbows at about a 90-degree angle when separated from your partner and not holding hands (in shine position)___

To Increase Difficulty
- Execute an underarm turn from a one-hand-joined position, then move to a shine position.
- Randomly practice different partner positions alternated with a shine position.

To Decrease Difficulty
- Practice each position option separately.
- Use a slow tempo.

CHA-CHA VARIATIONS AND COMBINATIONS

DRILLS

1. Chase

Both of the following variations in the shine position exemplify the "teasing" and flirting with the eyes that are characteristic of the cha-cha, because you continue to look over your shoulder toward your partner as long as you can on each turn. The first variation involves a half turn, and the second involves a full turn. Each variation takes four counts.

Both variations involve a follow-the-leader challenge such that the leader does a variation and then the follower must repeat that same variation. Both partners do the same footwork, except the follower executes the variation four counts later. This alternating process continues until the leader stops turning and faces his partner, which nonverbally signals that the "chase" is over.

a. *Half chase:* As its name implies, the half chase involves a half turn. The half chase starts with the leader's forward break step. As usual, he steps forward onto his left foot on count 2. Prior to count 3, he pivots clockwise 180 degrees on the balls of his feet before transferring his weight onto his right foot (see figure 10.7, a and b). With the leader's back to his partner, he travels forward to execute the cha-cha-cha steps on counts 4-&-1.

To face his partner again, the leader steps forward with his right foot on count 2 to start a CCW pivot. Prior to count 3, he pivots 180 degrees counterclockwise on the balls of both feet and shifts his weight forward onto the ball of his left foot on count 3 (see figure 10.7, c and d). The leader then continues traveling forward with his triple step on counts 4-&-1. Figure 10.7, c through f, shows how the follower is four counts behind the leader before starting to do the half chase variation.

Whenever the leader's left foot is free again, he has two options: to continue the half chase or to end it. If the leader decides to continue the half chase, the follower will see his back. If he decides to end the variation, the follower will be facing her partner again.

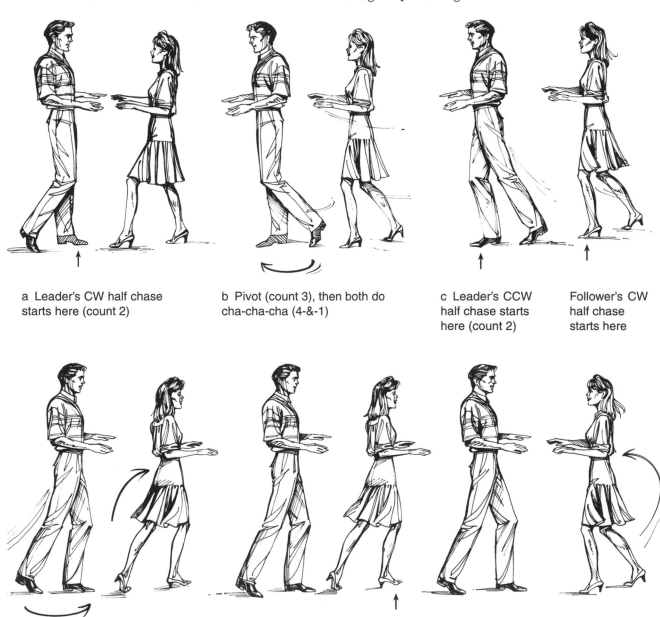

a Leader's CW half chase starts here (count 2)

b Pivot (count 3), then both do cha-cha-cha (4-&-1)

c Leader's CCW half chase starts here (count 2)

Follower's CW half chase starts here

d Both pivot (count 3), then do cha-cha-cha (4-&-1)

e Follower's CCW half chase starts here (count 2)

f At the end of leader's forward break, follower faces in shine position again (count 3)

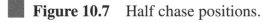

Figure 10.7 Half chase positions.

b. *Full chase:* The full chase is similar to the half chase, except that a full turn occurs. To execute the full turn, repeat the half chase directions on counts 2 and 3. However, on counts 4-&-1, continue to rotate clockwise during your small cha-cha-cha steps by rotating your toes slightly clockwise with each step to complete another 180-degree turn (see figure 10.8). The leader completes his full turn, after which it is the follower's turn to complete her full turn.

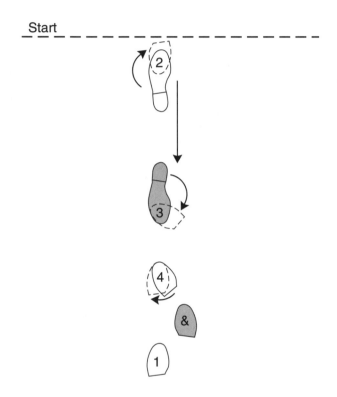

Figure 10.8   Full chase positions.

Success Goal = Eight repetitions of the half turn and the full turn to slow cha-cha music___

Success Check
• Shift your weight on each break step whether executing a half or a full chase___
• Orient the directions of the half turns according to your own midline. Imagine that your midline initially faces 12 o'clock. Thus, during the half chase, alternately turn clockwise (from 12 o'clock to 6 o'clock) and counterclockwise (from 6 o'clock back to 12 o'clock)___

To Increase Difficulty
• The leader may randomly alternate half and full chases.
• Experiment with a double chase or a double turn. Do your regular half turn on counts 2 and 3, then complete a 1 1/2 turn on counts 4-&-1 so as to face your partner again.

To Decrease Difficulty
• Execute the turns without a partner. On the half chase, imagine opening and shutting a door to help you remember which way to turn. On the full chase, continue all the way around.

2. Cross and Hop

From a shine position, this variation may be executed on any forward basic. Either partner may initiate this variation while the other does the backward basic. Thus, when your left foot is free, cross it over your right foot and shift weight onto your left foot during the first "slow," or count 2. Cross your right foot over your left foot and shift weight onto your right foot during the second "slow," or count 3. On the "&" before count 4, add a hop in the backward direction with your right foot. Then continue traveling backward with your cha-cha-cha steps (left, right, left).

Success Goal = Eight repetitions of the cross and hop to slow cha-cha music___

Success Check

• To execute the hop, bend your knee, push off, and land on your right foot___
• This variation takes four total counts___

 To Increase Difficulty

• During the hop, accent it by lifting your arms to form a diagonal line, with your left arm placed high above your head and your right arm placed below your waist.
• Randomly alternate any of the chase variations with the cross and hop variation.

To Decrease Difficulty

• Match each position with a cue, "cross left, cross right, hop, cha-cha-cha," giving the hop a half beat, or an "&" cue.

3. Figure-Eight Turns

From a closed dance position, this variation is a modification of the underarm turn. It alternates CW and CCW underarms turns off the cross-body breaks for the follower while the leader does the basic in the H floor path. After the leader makes an arch with his left hand on his backward break, the follower does a pivot turn under the arch (review figure 10.4). To continue another pivot turn on the other side, the leader must keep his left hand above the follower's head during the side triple step and gently direct the next pivot turn as he circles his left hand in a horizontal figure eight. When he wants the turns to end, the leader simply lowers his left hand. Try to do three pivot turns before stopping.

Success Goal = Eight repetitions of figure-eight turns to slow cha-cha music___

Success Check

• The leader's left hand traces a horizontal figure-eight path in the air above the follower's head___
• The follower faces each side prior to the pivot, then pivots to face the opposite side, replaces her foot (without moving it from its original location) then continues her turn to face the leader so both can do a triple step to the side___

To Increase Difficulty

• Lead more than three consecutive underarm turns during the figure-eight turns.
• Randomly alternate the figure-eight turns with any one other variation that you know so far (e.g., cross-body breaks).

To Decrease Difficulty

• The follower should practice consecutive break turns without a partner.

4. Parallel Breaks

When in a closed position, this variation permits two options: either to break forward or to break backward. The direction is determined by the leader's position. Using the basic H floor path, the leader may substitute parallel breaks during the regular breaks. Both partners' shoulders and feet should be parallel (angling 45 degrees), with the feet in a forward-backward stride position.

a. *Forward parallel breaks:* For both sides of this variation, the leader parallel breaks forward. On the last of the cha-cha-cha steps to the leader's right side, he slightly angles his right foot outward, which slightly rotates his upper torso to face his right-front diagonal direction. This angle facilitates a forward parallel break step with the leader's left foot to step forward in this new direction, keeping his feet parallel with his partner (see figure 10.9). The leader continues with the cha-cha-cha steps to his left side and repeats the variation on the other side by angling 45 degrees to face his left-front diagonal and parallel break forward with his right foot. To resume a closed dance position and the basic H floor path, the leader needs to keep his shoulders parallel with his partner without angling.

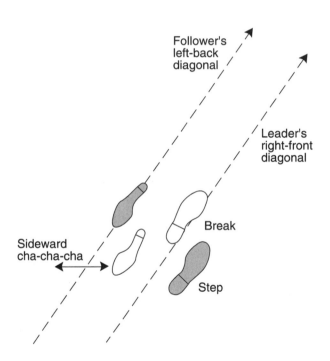

Figure 10.9 Forward parallel breaks on leader's right side.

b. *Backward parallel breaks:* For both sides of this variation, the leader parallel breaks backward. On the last of the right sideways cha-cha-cha steps, he slightly angles his right foot inward and rotates his upper torso to face his left-front diagonal direction. This facilitates a backward parallel break with his left foot. The leader repeats the cha-cha-cha steps to his left side and rotates his shoulders and upper body to face his right-front diagonal, then parallel breaks backward with the right foot. The leader resumes a closed position by not rotating, but rather remaining squared up, parallel shoulders to his partner.

Success Goal = Eight repetitions of both forward and backward parallel breaks off the basic H floor path to slow cha-cha music___

✔ **Success Check**

- If a proper closed dance connection is maintained, the follower will be aware of whether or not the leader's shoulders are angling 45 degrees prior to the break steps___
- On the last of the leader's right sideways cha-cha-cha steps, his shoulders may angle 45 degrees either clockwise (to parallel break forward) or counterclockwise (to parallel break backward)___
- Square up (keep shoulders parallel) with your partner's shoulders on the sideways cha-cha-cha steps (between the parallel breaks)___

To Increase Difficulty

- Alternate forward parallel breaks with backward parallel breaks using any multiple of two repetitions of each.
- Combine either parallel break with any one other variation, such as an underarm turn at the end (when back to the basic H floor path).

To Decrease Difficulty

- Practice foot positions to clearly distinguish between regular and parallel break foot and body placements. Ask an observer to provide feedback, or use tape on the floor or select other reference points that help show forward-backward versus parallel breaks.

5. Fifth-Position Breaks

From a closed position, another variation using backward breaks by both partners at the same time is called fifth-position breaks. In this modification of the backward parallel breaks, a fifth position angles the heel of one foot beside the big toe of the other foot.

Start with the basic step in an H floor path. At the end of the leader's left sideways cha-cha-cha steps (see figure 10.10a), he needs to indicate to the follower to break backward as well. His leads include gentle pressure with the fingers of his right hand on the follower's left shoulder blade and a CW rotation of his upper torso and frame. He can then break backward with his right foot (see figure 10.10b). The reverse occurs at the end of the leader's right sideways cha-cha-cha steps onto his right foot (see figure 10.10c). He presses with the heel of his right hand on the follower's left shoulder blade, and he rotates counterclockwise with his upper torso and frame. He can then break backward with his left foot (see figure 10.10d).

a   b   c   d

■ **Figure 10.10** Fifth-position breaks.

Success Goal = Eight repetitions of the fifth-position breaks to slow cha-cha music___

✔ Success Check
• Both partners break backward at the same time___
• Both partners break with a toe-to-heel foot placement___

To Increase Difficulty
• Release outside hands (toward the direction you are facing on the breaks); that is, the leader opens or extends his right hand when breaking back with his right foot, then opens or extends his left hand when breaking back with his left foot. The open arm positions on each side are similar to those used with the weave step in the waltz.
• Combine the fifth-position breaks with any two other variations that you know so far.

To Decrease Difficulty
• Without a partner, check that your foot placement is in the proper position.
• Use any multiple of two repetitions before changing to another variation. Do at least four repetitions when first learning this variation.

6. Butterfly

The butterfly is a variation used during the cross-body breaks. It alternately combines one cross-body break with a triple step to the side, then one fifth-position break with a triple step to the side. This variation is called a "butterfly" because both partners alternately close (face each other) and open up (face the side) like an emerging butterfly's wings. The butterfly may be led on either side. The following describes how to execute this variation off the leader's left cross-body break. Simply reverse the directions to lead off the leader's right cross-body break.

After the leader's left cross-body break (with his left foot), he faces his partner as usual to do the sideways cha-cha-cha steps with one exception. If he opens his right palm like a stop sign, this signals the follower to place her left hand in the same position. Both let their palms touch during the triple step to his left side, then the leader releases his pressure and rotates 45 degrees clockwise to open his right shoulder (and the follower's left shoulder opens). Both partners do a fifth-position break (his right foot back and her left foot back), then a triple step to his right side. The leader continues to show his right palm until he wants to end this variation and continue with regular side breaks. To end this variation, the leader can grasp both hands on the triple step to the side, then release one hand to make the transition into a cross-body break on the other side.

Success Goal = Eight repetitions of the butterfly from both sides to slow cha-cha music___

✔ Success Check
• The leader's stop sign with open palm signals that the butterfly is coming next___
• The follower needs to bring her hands back to the center for either a cross-body break or to match the leader's open palm position___

To Increase Difficulty
• Alternate the butterfly with figure-eight turns.
• Combine the butterfly with any two other variations that you know so far.

To Decrease Difficulty
• Isolate each part to the counts (without music).

7. Push-Away Turns

A fun variation of the cross-body break is a push-away turn. This turn is similar to the half chase turns, except that both partners turn at the same time and the pivot is side to side, then another quarter turn is added at the end to face your partner again. The leader has a lot of options on this turn. The turn may be executed on only one side or on both sides, using either single or multiple repetitions.

During a cross-body break on the leader's right side, the leader's left foot (and the follower's right foot) begins the cross-body break. The leader needs to keep his left hand and forearm horizontal, releasing and gently pushing away the follower's right hand (see figure 10.11a). Both partners need to keep their feet in a forward-backward stride (notice the extended fifth foot position) as they pivot away from each other (clockwise for the leader, counterclockwise for the follower). Think of facing each side wall. On count 3 of the pivot, notice that your inside forearms may be close or slightly touching (see figure 10.11b). This helps you know where your partner is at the end of the pivot. Then continue rotating to face your partner for the side cha-cha-cha steps (see figure 10.11c). The leader may signal the next push-away turn on either side, or on both sides, or may execute cross-body breaks in between.

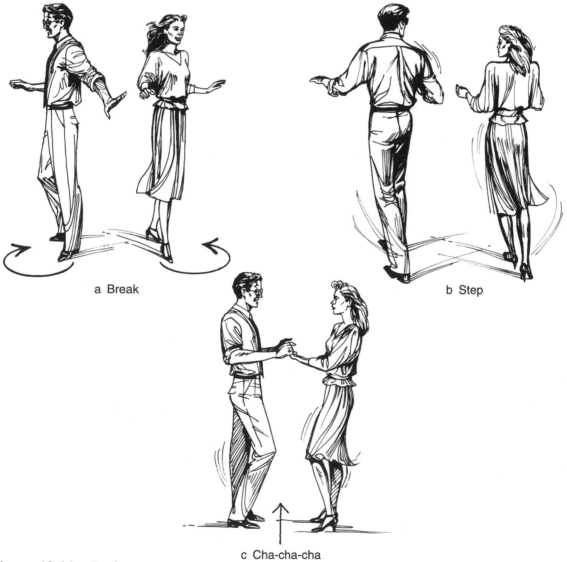

a Break

b Step

c Cha-cha-cha

Figure 10.11 Push-away turns.

Success Goal = Eight repetitions of the push-away turns on either side, then on both sides, to slow cha-cha music___

✔ **Success Check**
- Keep your feet in a forward-backward stride on the pivot, using a "pivot, replace" so you don't move your foot from its original position on count 3___
- Remember to meet in the middle with your hands when facing your partner___

To Increase Difficulty
- Randomly lead the push-away turns to one side, to the other side, or to both sides.
- Combine the push-away turns with any two other variations that you know so far (e.g., try four consecutive push-away turns, then transition to a shine position for half and full chases).

To Decrease Difficulty
- Lead the push-away turn using a set order (e.g., only on the fourth side break, only on the third side break, or on both the third and fourth side breaks).

8. Freeze

The freeze is a variation that adds two extra counts to each cross-body break. Because the freeze adds two extra counts, it is important to repeat this variation on both sides. As the music is in 4/4 time, this adds four counts total, which equals one measure.

During the freeze, a cross-body break is repeated twice. On the first cross-body break, the leader keeps his inside hand and forearm firm to signal both partners to rock their weight forward and backward twice. At the end of the second cross-body break, the leader continues with a triple step. He may then repeat the freeze on the opposite side.

Success Goal = Eight repetitions of the freeze on both sides of the body to slow cha-cha music___

✔ **Success Check**
- Both partners position their feet in a forward-backward stride during the freeze___
- The leader's inside hand firmly remains at waist level to initiate the freeze___
- Remember to lead the freeze on both sides (i.e., in multiples of two repetitions)___

To Increase Difficulty
- Alternate the freeze with push-away turns, using any number of cross-body breaks between them.
- Combine the freeze with any two other variations that you know so far.

To Decrease Difficulty
- Check that you are making four weight changes or rocking your weight from one foot to the other four times prior to a triple step.

9. Combine Four Variations

The next challenge is to link at least four different variations into longer combinations. Try each of the following sample practice combinations:

- Fifth-position breaks, cross-body breaks, push-away turns, freeze
- Basic H floor path, butterfly, push-away turns, figure-eight turns
- Half chase, full chase, cross-body breaks, push-away turns
- Parallel forward breaks, underarm turn, cross-body breaks, freeze, butterfly
- Full chase, cross and hop, cross-body breaks, push-away turns

Now either modify the above combinations or create your own combinations that include any four or more cha-cha variations. Use the following summary chart to reference the variations covered in this book:

Cha-Cha Variation Summary

A. Shine Position Variations
   1. Basic forward and backward
   2. Chase
      a. Half chase
      b. Full chase
   3. Cross and hop
B. One- or Two-Hands-Joined Positions
   1. Cross-body breaks
   2. Figure-eight turns
   3. Butterfly
   4. Push-away turns
   5. Freeze
C. Closed Position
   1. Basic H floor path
   2. Parallel breaks
   3. Fifth-position breaks
D. Transitions
   1. Float away
   2. Close up
   3. Grasp both hands
   4. Cross-body leads
   5. Release both hands
   6. Resume partner contact

Success Goal = Consecutive repetition of each of the cha-cha practice combinations listed above, then select and link any four or more variations into a combination for the length of one song___

Success Check
- Keep all transitions smooth___
- Practice proper partner etiquette___

To Increase Difficulty
- Repeat with different partners.
- Use a faster tempo.

To Decrease Difficulty
- Use as many basics as you need between each variation to prepare for the next lead.
- Use a slow tempo.

CHA-CHA SUCCESS SUMMARY

The cha-cha is an interactive, flirtatious dance with styling that can be either very smooth or very staccato. The styling depends on how dramatic you want to be in your execution of the basic step pattern, which alternates a break step with a triple step. One of the transition options will help you start in closed position, move to a one-hand-joined position, then back to a closed position again. Another transition will help you move from a one-hand-joined to a two-hands-joined position, then back to a one-hand-joined position. A third transition will help you move into and from a shine position. The variations for the cha-cha are categorized according to the dance position from which they are executed.

STEP 11

RUMBA: REFLECTING ROMANCE

The rumba has been called the "dance of love" because of its sultry and romantic styling. The rumba is African in origin and was originally a courtship, marriage, and street dance with suggestive body and exaggerated hip movements. A slower and more refined version gradually evolved. Rumba music is a blend of Latin and African music with a staccato beat. Accompanying instruments typically include the maracas (originally dried gourds with seeds inside), the claves (two sticks), and the drums.

The rumba was introduced in the United States around 1913, but it did not catch on until the late 1920s. At that time, a major influence was Xavier Cugat, a famous musician, who formed an orchestra specializing in Latin music. His orchestra opened at the Coconut Grove in Los Angeles, California, and his music was featured in early sound movies such as *In Gay Madrid*. The American version of the rumba uses a box rhythm with footwork similar to that used in the waltz box step, yet with the timing of the foxtrot (4/4 time).

The rumba was introduced in Europe in the 1930s by Monsieur Pierre, a leading dance teacher. He and his partner, Doris Lavelle, popularized Latin American dancing in London. Their "Cuban rumba" became the officially recognized version in 1955 and paralleled the American version. However, soon after this, Pierre visited Havana and discovered that the rumba was danced with a rhythm and timing similar to that used in the cha-cha. He shared this discovery, which evolved into the standard International Cuban rumba that is used in competition today. Either version is appropriate on the dance floor. However, the American rumba is a bit easier for beginning dancers and is more often seen on the social dance floor. Both versions may use Cuban motion. Cuban motion gives the illusion of taking a step without initially placing weight on that step. Cuban motion does not result from thrusting the hips sideways, but rather from alternately keeping one knee straight while the other knee is bent with each weight change. With Cuban motion, keep your feet flat on the floor and avoid lifting your heel higher off the floor than your toes. If you have trouble with the Cuban motion, don't worry about it, as it takes time to master it.

The two basic steps used in the American rumba are the box step and the half-box progression. These basic rumba steps start from a closed dance position and use a four-count rhythmic pattern. A "slow, quick, quick" rhythm is repeated twice to create a box step similar to the box step used in the foxtrot (and in the waltz, except for the timing). A box step is composed of two half boxes in two directions, alternating forward and backward (or backward and forward). The leader starts on the forward half with his left foot while the follower starts on the backward half with her right foot. Each partner then executes a half-box basic in the opposite direction. Detailed descriptions for adding Cuban motion in each direction are as follows. If you choose to execute the half-box basics without Cuban motion, then your footwork execution is similar to the waltz box step except that the "slow" gets two counts in rumba.

Forward half-box basic: To execute the forward half-box basic *using Cuban motion*, shift your weight onto your right foot and place (or extend) your left foot forward on counts 1, 2. On count 3, shift your weight onto your left foot and place (or extend) your right foot to your right side (if you take a small step, your right knee will be bent). Keep your steps very small. On count 4, shift your weight onto your right foot as you bring your left foot beside your right foot to close your feet (left knee is bent).

Notice that the foot positions for the half-box basic are as follows: start in parallel first position, extend forward (or backward) into parallel fourth position, step sideways into second position, then bring the feet together to return to parallel first position.

As in the foxtrot and the waltz, an alternative is to continue traveling forward on the second half-box basic. This option becomes the forward half-box progression. It is very versatile in the rumba, especially with more advanced moves. Or you may also execute a backward half-box progression by continuing to travel backward on the second half-box basic.

Backward half-box basic: To execute the backward half-box basic *using Cuban motion,* shift your weight onto your left foot as you place (or extend) the heel of your right foot two to three inches backward, beyond the heel of your left foot on counts 1, 2. On count 3, shift your weight onto your right foot and place or extend your left foot to your left side (with your left knee slightly bent if a small step is taken). On count 4, shift your weight onto your left foot as you close your feet (bringing your right foot with a bent knee beside your left foot without a weight change).

Figure 11.1 shows the various ways you might organize the counts and the footwork (without adding Cuban motion) for the rumba basic step patterns.

FIGURE 11.1	**KEYS TO SUCCESS: RUMBA BASIC FOUR-COUNT RHYTHM (SQQ)**

Footwork Cues

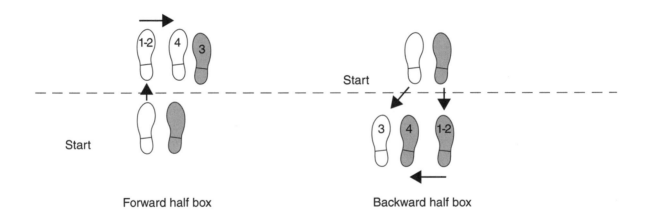

Forward half box   Backward half box

Box Step

a. Leader: Forward, side, together; backward, side, together

b. Follower: Backward, side, together; forward, side, together

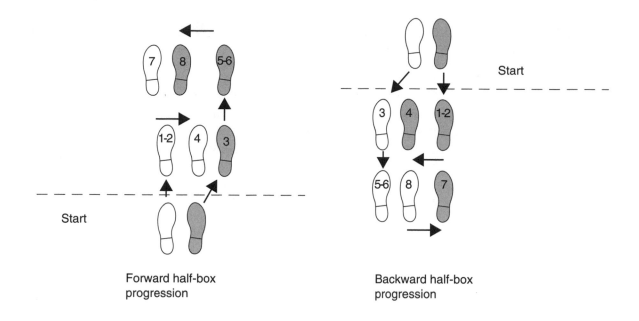

Forward half-box
progression

Backward half-box
progression

Half-Box Progression

a. Leader: Forward, side, together; forward, side,
   together
b. Follower: Backward, side, together; backward,
   side, together

Timing Cues

4/4 time signature:	Four beats to a measure, each beat gets one count
Total counts:	Eight (in two measures)
Rhythmic counts:	1-2, 3, 4; 5-6, 7-8, or 1-2, 3, 4; 2-2, 3-4
Weight changes:	Six (in two measures)
Duration of steps:	Slow, quick, quick (both halves)
Direction of steps:	a. Box step: Forward (or backward), side, then in place
	b. Half-box progression: Forward (or backward), side, then in place

RUMBA BASIC STEP PATTERN

DRILLS

1. Cuban Motion Execution Challenge

One of the distinguishing characteristics of the rumba is Cuban motion. It takes practice to be able to appear to take a step without actually shifting weight on that step. One way to think about this task is to consider two simultaneous actions—a weight shift onto a straight leg and a foot placement with the opposite knee bent (and no weight change onto that foot). A weight shift from one straight leg to the other happens automatically when you are standing and waiting for someone who is late. Your weight shifts naturally from one leg to the other as you get tired of waiting. Try this and notice that the leg without weight is bent at the knee. It is easier to bend at the knee if you take small steps and place only the inside edge of the foot on the floor.

The next challenge is to coincide two actions: shift your weight onto a straight leg *and* place the opposite foot. Where might you "place" the opposite nonweighted foot? There are four options: sideways left, sideways right, forward, or backward. Practice each option. Notice that the sideways steps alternate the free foot's position, first to the side, then close (feet together). However, when you position the free foot forward, extend the toe of the free foot beyond the toe of the standing leg. Or when you position the free foot backward, extend the heel of that foot slightly behind the heel of your standing leg. Thus, the nonweighted foot indicates the direction you are traveling.

Success Goal = Eight "shift and position" repetitions in any direction___

Success Check
- The straight leg has the weight___
- The bent knee indicates no weight on that leg___
- Shift your weight and position your opposite foot simultaneously___
- The nonweighted (free) foot indicates the direction of travel___

To Increase Difficulty
- Repeat this drill alternating any two directions, for example, eight "shift and position" steps forward, then eight backward. Then try eight "shift and position" steps to the left side and eight to the right side. Which combination flows best? The alternating side steps are a bit more awkward, as you'll need to extend the right foot when traveling to the right, then the left foot when traveling to the left. The forward and backward transition is easier, as it is only a matter of positioning the free foot either forward or backward.
- Position the nonweighted foot using a rhythmic pattern; that is, on each "slow, quick, quick" cue.

To Decrease Difficulty
- Break down each action to the cues "shift and position" such that by the time you have fully shifted your weight onto a straight leg, you've also positioned your opposite free foot. This is somewhat like rubbing your stomach and patting your head in that you need to slow down the weight shift and speed up the foot positioning until they coincide.
- Don't worry if you can't do Cuban motion right away. It takes practice, practice, and more practice!

2. Box Step Execution Challenge

If you've practiced the box step in the waltz and the foxtrot, then you already know it. However, in the rumba, you eventually need to add Cuban motion, as well as follow a box shape on the floor (review figure 11.1, a and b). Repeat the basic rumba box step until you are comfortable without a partner, with slow music, and then with a partner.

Success Goal = Two consecutive minutes of the rumba box step (use track 17)___

Success Check
- Maintain a "slow, quick, quick" rhythmic pattern___
- Take small steps___

To Increase Difficulty
- Use a variety of slow rumba music.
- Change partners frequently.
- Simultaneously "shift and place" on each cue to add Cuban motion.

To Decrease Difficulty
- Face a partner without touching and repeat the drill to see how your actions mirror your partner's in reverse.
- Master the basic alone to counts until you can match the tempo of slow rumba music.

3. Half-Box Progression Execution Challenge

The main advantage of the half-box progression is that it permits you to travel whenever there is room to travel (review figure 11.1, c and d). Try it to slow rumba music without and then with a partner. Once you get comfortable with the basic half-box progression execution, experiment with a practice combination such as eight basics forward, then eight basics backward.

Success Goal = Two consecutive minutes of the half-box progression alternating eight basics forward, then eight basics backward___

Success Check
- Maintain the rhythmic pattern to the tempo of the music___
- Make direction changes smooth transitions___
- Take small steps___

To Increase Difficulty
- Vary the number of repetitions, keeping the "rule of two" in mind. Thus, try six basics forward and six basics backward, or try four basics forward and four basics backward or two basics forward and two basics backward. Which combination is easiest for you and your partner?
- Add Cuban motion.

To Decrease Difficulty
- Use more than two repetitions of the basic in any one direction to have more time to prepare for the next direction.

4. Alternate Two Basics

When the dance floor is very crowded with no room to travel forward, then selecting the box step is an ideal way to start. Try four box steps, then assume that there is room to travel. Try four half-box progressions forward, then assume that there is no room to travel. Repeat this combination with a partner to slow rumba music.

Success Goal = Two consecutive minutes alternating four box steps, then four half-box progressions___

Success Check
• Match the tempo of the music___
• Make a smooth transition between these two steps___

To Increase Difficulty
• Randomly alternate these two basic rumba steps, keeping the rule of two repetitions in mind.
• Add backward half-box progressions to your combination.

To Decrease Difficulty
• Use more than two repetitions before changing to a different step.

RUMBA TRANSITION

DRILLS

1. Leads From Closed to One-Hand-Joined Position and Back to Closed Position

An underarm turn for the follower makes this transition fun to do. The leader continues to execute two box steps while the follower moves under the arch and follows a small circular path until facing her partner again.

a. *Underarm turn and circle:* From a closed dance position and executing a box step, the leader may signal an underarm turn by lifting his left hand and arm to make an arch during the second half-box basic or on any backward half-box basic. With his right hand on the follower's left shoulder blade, the leader gently guides the follower to move under the arch created by their raised arms and hands (review figure 10.4). Since the steps are smaller in the rumba than in other dances, the follower may take at least two more forward half-box progressions to circle clockwise to face the leader.

b. *Close up:* After moving under the arch, the follower gradually moves along a small, circular floor path until facing her partner again. Then, the leader may close up the space between them and resume a closed dance position. The timing needs to mesh such that the follower's fourth half-box basic is forward, while the leader is doing a backward half-box basic.

Success Goal = 10 smoothly executed transitions from closed to one-hand-joined position, then back to closed position___

Success Check
• Keep your free arm curved and slightly in front of your body___
• Take your time on the underarm turn and circle to avoid rushing it___

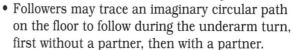

To Increase Difficulty

- The leader may rotate slightly counterclockwise on his backward half-box basic to leave more space for the follower to move under the arch.
- The leader may continue to rotate counterclockwise to face his partner after the follower moves under the arch in order to complete the underarm turn in two half-box basics. This splits the distance that the follower has to travel, allowing the turn to be executed in fewer half-box basics (i.e., two).
- The leader may randomly select any of three dance positions after the follower's underarm turn and circle.

To Decrease Difficulty

- Followers may trace an imaginary circular path on the floor to follow during the underarm turn, first without a partner, then with a partner.

2. Leads Alternating From One Hand to Two Hands, and Back to a One-Hand-Joined Position

Many transitions from the cha-cha also work with the rumba. For example, you may move from one to two hands, alternate from two to one hand, and add cross-body leads to cross-body breaks in the rumba.

   a. *Grasp both hands:* At the end of the underarm turn and circle transition, the leader may grasp the follower's other hand on the fourth half-box basic. While holding both hands, continue with the box step.
   b. *Cross-body leads:* From a two-hands-joined position, the leader may step to his left side with his left foot and release his left-hand grasp (on the "slow"). The leader may bring his right hand across his midline to lead into cross-body breaks (on the "quick, quick" cues). Repeat on the other side to grasp both hands when parallel and facing your partner, then the leader releases one hand (his right), brings the left hand across his midline, and does a cross-body break to his right side. Review figure 10.6 as necessary.

Success Goal = 10 smoothly executed transitions alternating from one to two hands and back to a one-hand-joined position___

✔ Success Check

- Maintain SQQ rhythmic pattern___
- Maintain your arm positions, rather than letting your arms hang freely___

To Increase Difficulty

- Connect all partner positions together and finish in a closed position. Experiment with a right underarm (pivot) turn (see figure 10.4) for the follower off the leader's left side cross-body breaks. The leader breaks backward with his right foot while the follower pivots with her left foot. Then both resume a box step.

To Decrease Difficulty

- Practice each part separately, gradually linking more parts together.

DRILLS

1. Left Box Turn

The left box turn is a variation of the box step, which is executed from a closed position. The box step is composed of both a forward half box and a backward half box. The box step takes eight beats of music before your starting foot is free again (i.e., the leader's left foot and the follower's right foot). The upper-torso lead for the left box turn occurs prior to the forward half-box portion.

In rumba, there is no hurry to complete the left box turn in any specific number of half-box steps, as four quarter turns are often used in both the waltz and the foxtrot left box turn variations. Start with the box step to establish a tempo. Prior to any forward half-box step, the leader rotates, or turns, his upper torso and frame counterclockwise approximately 45 degrees. Repeat the box step while facing this new direction. Continue to rotate slightly prior to each forward half-box step, slowly turning counterclockwise until you've turned 360 degrees.

Success Goal = Eight repetitions of the left box turn to slow rumba music___

Success Check
- Upper torso and frame move as one unit___
- The left foot angles outward (and forward) prior to each forward half-box step___
- The right foot angles inward (and backward) prior to each backward half-box step___
- Rotate in small increments on each half-box basic___

To Increase Difficulty
- Vary the tempo.
- Rotate prior to both the forward and backward half-box portions.

To Decrease Difficulty
- Take small steps.
- Use any number of box step basics prior to the left box turn.

2. Fifth-Position Breaks

This variation is similar to the cha-cha variation of the same name. The fifth-position breaks occur off the box step from a closed dance position (review figure 10.10, a-d). The lead is signaled by the leader stepping sideways on his left foot instead of forward (which initiates a box step). The leader opens his right shoulder (to reverse promenade position) and gently presses with the fingers of his right hand on the follower's left shoulder blade. This signals both partners to break back (with his right foot and her left foot).

Repeat the movement on the other side with the leader taking a side step to his right with his right foot. The leader gently presses with the heel of his right hand on the follower's left shoulder blade to rotate to a promenade position. Both partners break backward (his left foot and her right foot). Continue to repeat on both sides for any multiple of two repetitions. Just resume a forward half-box basic to go back to the box step.

Success Goal = Eight repetitions of the fifth-position breaks to slow rumba music___

Success Check
- Place feet toe-to-heel (and angled 45 degrees) during the fifth-position breaks___
- Maintain frame with your partner___

Let

To Increase Difficulty
- Alternate the fifth-position breaks with a left box turn.
- The leader may release one hand and open both partners to each side during each fifth-position break (i.e., the right arm opens when the right foot breaks back and the left arm opens when the left foot breaks back). Avoid opening your arms either straight to the side or behind your body; rather, keep your free hand in front of your shoulder at approximately 45 degrees.

To Decrease Difficulty
- Practice without a partner to clarify your foot placements.
- Practice facing a partner without touching; instead, mirror your actions to review the fifth-position breaks.

3. Second-Position Breaks

The second-position breaks occur off the box step from a closed dance position. The second-position break starts with a modification of the forward half-box basic. The leader takes the normal forward "slow" step with his left foot. On the "quick, quick" steps, the leader shifts his weight onto his right foot to his right side, then shifts his weight back to replace (lift and lower) his left foot's position (see figure 11.2 a).

The leader repeats the break on the other side by stepping onto his right foot and closing the left foot on the first "slow." He shifts weight onto his left foot to his left side on the "quick," then replaces his right foot on the second "quick" (see figure 11.2b). End the second-position breaks after any multiple of two repetitions.

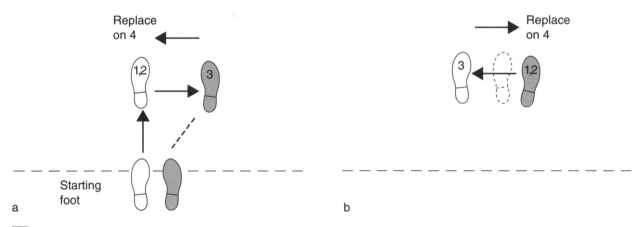

Figure 11.2 Second-position breaks for the leader.

Success Goal = Eight repetitions of the second-position breaks to slow rumba music___

Success Check
- Keep side steps approximately shoulder-width apart___
- Remember to replace (lift and lower in the same location) the foot position used for each "slow"___

To Increase Difficulty
- Randomly combine the second-position breaks, box steps, and fifth-position breaks.

To Decrease Difficulty
- Alternate the second-position breaks with the box step using at least four repetitions of the second-position breaks.

4. Walk-Around

The walk-around is a variation of the underarm turn and circle transition that lets both partners rotate around a central axis, much like a wheel. Start in closed dance position and execute a box step. On the leader's backward half-box basic, he lifts his left arm on the "slow" to form an arch. On the "quick, quick," the leader guides the follower under the arch by putting gentle pressure on her back with his right hand (review figure 10.4). She continues to move forward under the arch with half-box progressions, following a circular path. When the follower gets approximately a third of the way around, the leader bends his left elbow until both partners' forearms are touching and then rotates to do backward half-box progressions (see figure 11.3). Continue to rotate with your elbows as the central axis to make at least a 360-degree revolution with your partner. When the leader is executing a backward half-box progression with his right foot, he can release his left elbow connection with the follower and let her face him. The leader can then go back to executing a box step.

■ **Figure 11.3** Walk-around forearm position.

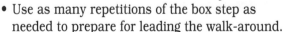

Success Goal = Eight repetitions of the walk-around to slow rumba music___

Success Check
• During the walk-around, the leader backs up to do backward half-box progressions while the follower does forward half-box progressions___
• Rotate at least 360 degrees with your forearms as the central axis___

To Increase Difficulty
• Randomly combine the walk-around, the box step, and a left box turn.

To Decrease Difficulty
• Use as many repetitions of the box step as needed to prepare for leading the walk-around.

5. Around-the-World

In this variation, the leader is the "world" and the follower moves "around the world." Like the walk-around, it starts with an underarm turn and circle transition, except the leader brings his left hand over his head to guide the follower completely around his body. The follower does forward half-box progressions in a small circle around the leader. The around-the-world variation takes eight half-box basics.

The leader starts the same as for the walk-around, except he places his right hand on the follower's back as she goes under the arch and maintains contact as he continues to guide her in a small CW circle (see figure 11.4). To maintain the momentum, the leader keeps his left hand high and brings the follower to his right side, then guides her behind him as his left hand goes over his own head as if looping a rope. On the seventh half-box basic, the leader does a left quarter turn to face his partner, then resumes closed position again on the eighth half-box basic.

a   b   c   d

Figure 11.4   Around-the-world leads after an underarm turn and circle.

Success Goal = Eight repetitions of the around-the-world variation to slow rumba music___

Success Check
- Simultaneously, after the leader's left-hand arch, his right hand guides the follower as he brings his left hand to his right side and over his own head___
- The follower moves in a circular path clockwise around the leader___

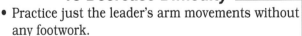

To Increase Difficulty
- Randomly alternate the walk-around and the around-the-world variations.
- Vary the total number of basics used.

To Decrease Difficulty
- Practice just the leader's arm movements without any footwork.

6. Combine Three Variations

The next challenge is to link at least three different rumba variations into a combination. For practice, try the following sample combinations using any number of repetitions of each:

- Box step, walk-around, fifth-position breaks
- Box step, fifth-position breaks, around-the-world
- Box step, second-position breaks, walk-around
- Box step, forward half-box progressions, left box turn, backward half-box progressions
- Box step, underarm turn and circle, cross-body breaks, right underarm (pivot) turn

Now it's your turn to link any three or more rumba variations to create your own combinations.

Rumba Variation Summary

A. Variation Options
1. Half-box basic
   a. Forward
   b. Backward
2. Half-box progressions
   a. Forward
   b. Backward
3. Left box turn
4. Fifth-position breaks
5. Second-position breaks
6. Walk-around
7. Cross-body breaks
8. Around-the-world

B. Transitions
1. Underarm turn and circle
2. Close up
3. Grasp both hands
4. Cross-body leads
5. Right underarm (pivot) turn

Success Goal = Four different combinations linking any three or more rumba variations___

Success Check
- Keep transitions smooth.
- Maintain frame.
- Maintain rhythmic pattern.

To Increase Difficulty
- Practice with a variety of partners.
- Vary the tempo.

To Decrease Difficulty
- Write down your combinations and refer to them as needed.
- Use as many basics between the different variations as needed to prepare for the next lead.

RUMBA SUCCESS SUMMARY

The rumba is a Latin dance that uses a slow tempo. The rumba basic step pattern uses box rhythm timing, as in the foxtrot, for the box step and for the half-box progression. The transition options will help you to start in closed position, move to a one-hand-joined position, then move into a two-hands-joined position. Many of the American rumba variations typically both start and end in a closed position.

STEP 12

TANGO: EXPRESSING ATTITUDE

The tango is a smooth dance that has three common styles—each executed with a dramatic flair. The American tango is slow and slinky with open positions, fans, and dips. It progresses counterclockwise in the line of dance and uses catlike walks and staccato foot movements. The International tango, which originated in Buenos Aires, Argentina, has a different hold with the follower's arm lower. It is characterized by staccato head snaps, with the couple moving as a unit within a closed position. The Argentine tango is also danced only in closed position, yet it is more of a spot dance and uses a lot of leg and foot actions. Of these three styles, the American tango is the most popular in social dance settings and is described here in more detail.

The American tango basic step uses the following rhythmic pattern: slow, slow, quick, quick, slow. It is executed in the line of dance, or counterclockwise around the perimeter of the room. The tango basic step will be described using a closed dance position and traveling both forward and sideways (from the leader's perspective, as the follower does the mirror reverse).

For the leader: To execute the tango basic step pattern in a forward direction, the leader starts with his left foot and takes two long steps forward. The long steps get two counts each and correspond to the "slow, slow" rhythmic cues. The leader then takes two short steps, one forward and one slightly to his right side (leaving the toe of his left foot on the floor). The short steps get one count each and correspond to the "quick, quick" rhythmic cues. On counts 7-8, the leader can slowly drag the inside edge of his left foot (toe) along the floor to close his feet (without making a weight change). This "close" corresponds to the "slow" rhythmic cue. At the end of the tango basic step pattern, the leader's left foot is free to repeat the tango basic step pattern.

For the follower: To execute the tango basic step pattern in a forward direction, the follower starts with her right foot and takes two long steps backward. The long steps get two counts each and correspond to the "slow, slow" rhythmic cues. The follower then takes two short steps, one backward and one slightly to her left side (leaving the toe of her right foot on the floor). The short steps get one count each and correspond to the "quick, quick" rhythmic cues. On counts 7-8, the follower can slowly drag the inside edge of her right foot (toe) along the floor to close her feet (without making a weight change). This "close" corresponds to the "slow" rhythmic cue. At the end of the tango basic step pattern, the follower's right foot is free to repeat the basic step pattern.

Notice that the foot positions for both the leader and the follower start in a parallel first position, move to parallel fourth position (three walks), then to second position (side step), then back to parallel first position on the close.

From a promenade position, the tango basic step pattern may also be executed to the side (i.e., leader's left and follower's right). Just prior to moving into a promenade position, the leader snaps his head to look toward his left side (and the follower mirrors by snapping her head toward her right side). Then both partners take two "slow" walking steps to the side. The leader steps onto his left foot, then crosses his right foot over his left foot. The follower steps onto her right foot, then crosses her left foot over her right foot. Both partners take a short step toward the side onto the ball of their outside foot (leader's left foot and follower's right), then quickly shift weight back onto the opposite foot (leader's right foot and follower's left) and face each other (in closed position). Finish by slowly dragging the outside foot (leader's left foot and follower's right foot) to close your feet. This finish is much like a period at the end of a sentence.

The leader now has the option of traveling either forward (in closed position) or to his left side (in promenade position, then back to closed position again).

Figure 12.1 shows the various ways you might organize the counts and the footwork for the tango basic eight-count rhythm. Select those cues that most help you retain how to execute the tango basic step pattern.

FIGURE 12.1 KEYS TO SUCCESS: TANGO BASIC EIGHT-COUNT RHYTHM (SSQQS)

Footwork Cues

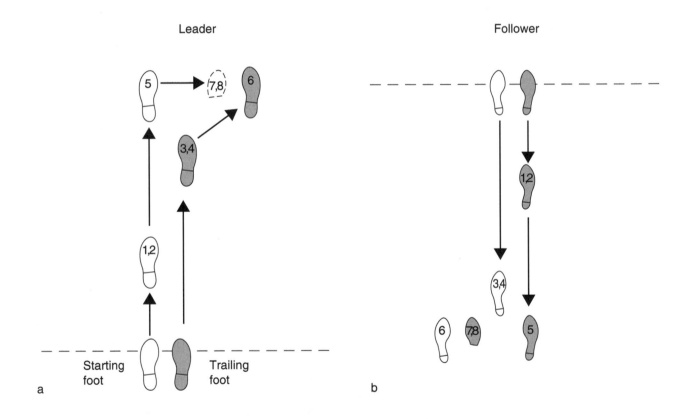

Closed Position
a. Leader: Forward, forward, forward-side-close
b. Follower: Backward, backward, backward-side-close

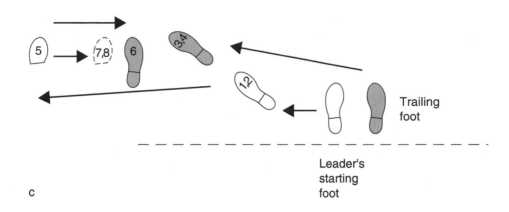

c

Trailing
foot

Leader's
starting
foot

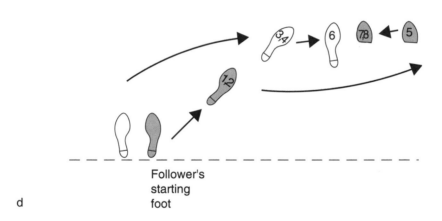

d

Follower's
starting
foot

Promenade Position

a. Leader: Side, cross, side, replace, close
b. Follower: Side, cross, side, replace, close

Timing Cues

4/4 time signature:	Four beats to a measure, each beat gets one count
Total counts:	Eight
Rhythmic counts:	1-2, 3-4, 5, 6, 7-8
Weight changes:	Four (in two measures, on counts 2, 4, 5, 6)
Duration of steps:	Slow, slow, quick, quick, slow
Length of steps:	Long, long, short, short, in place
Direction of steps:	a. Closed position: Forward, forward, forward, right side, in place (leader); or backward, backward, backward, left side, in place (follower) b. Promenade position: Left side, cross right, left side, replace right foot, in-place drag (leader); or right side, cross left, right side, replace left foot, in-place drag (follower)

TANGO BASIC STEP PATTERN AND TRANSITION

DRILLS

1. Forward Direction Execution Challenge

The eight beats in the tango basic step pattern are grouped into three parts: slow, slow; quick, quick; slow. Review Figure 12.1, a and b, for executing two walking steps, then a forward, side, close. Sometimes it is helpful to use the cue "tan-go close" to correspond to the "quick, quick, slow" finish. When you take the side step, the heel of your opposite foot (leader's left and follower's right) comes slightly off the floor. Slowly drag the inside edge of the toe of that foot along the floor to bring your feet together, or close your feet (without making a weight change). Try to make the timing changes distinctly different in each part of the tango basic step pattern.

Success Goal = Two consecutive minutes of executing the SSQQS rhythm (use track 18)___

Success Check
• Keep a narrow base (i.e., feet no more than two to three inches apart) on forward and backward steps___
• Each "slow" gets two beats or counts___
• Each "quick" gets one beat or count___
• Slowly drag the toe (inside edge) of your pointed foot inward to close your feet___

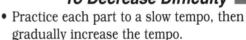

To Increase Difficulty
• Use a variety of slow tango music.
• Practice with different partners.

To Decrease Difficulty
• Practice each part to a slow tempo, then gradually increase the tempo.
• Practice traveling along an imaginary line on the floor, and check that you are stepping in the proper direction on each step.

2. Side Direction Execution Challenge

From a closed dance position with a partner, move into a basic promenade position by maintaining frame with your partner's arms and rotating your lower body to face your extended hands. Take two slow walking steps, first stepping with your outside foot, then crossing over with your inside foot on the next step. Continue by taking a small step with your outside foot, then shift (or replace) your weight onto your inside foot (review figure 12.1, c and d). Face your partner in closed position and slowly drag the inside edge of the toe of your outside foot along the floor to close your feet. After you are comfortable with the tango basic step pattern to the leader's left side, the leader can snap his head prior to rotating into the promenade position. The follower then snaps her head just prior to taking the two walking steps to the side.

Experiment with two tango basics in a forward direction, then two tango basics in a side direction. This alternating combination will allow you to make the transition from a closed to a promenade position, then back to closed again.

Success Goal =
a. Two consecutive minutes of executing the tango basic step pattern to the side___
b. 10 smoothly executed transitions from closed position to a promenade position and back to closed position___

Success Check
• The leader's outside foot is his left foot___
• The follower's outside foot is her right foot___
• Either prior to or on the first side step, snap your head (leader first, then follower) to add dramatic flair___
• Contrast slow and quick movements___

To Increase Difficulty

- Alternate the two directions, either forward or to the side, using any number of repetitions of the basic pattern in each direction. Can you do one repetition in each direction?

To Decrease Difficulty

- Practice alone until you can execute the basic without looking at your feet.
- Face a wall and place both hands on the wall approximately shoulder-width apart and in front of your shoulders. Without moving your hands, rotate your lower body to move from closed to promenade position, and practice the tango basic step pattern to the side (promenade position), then face the wall again (in closed position).
- The leader may start with his left shoulder toward the LOD so that multiple repetitions from promenade position will travel in the LOD.

TANGO VARIATIONS AND COMBINATIONS

DRILLS

1. Left Quarter Turn

An easy variation of the tango basic forward step is to add a left quarter turn lead just prior to the tango close. This variation may be added to both the forward and sideways directions, which gives the leader two options.

a. *From a closed position:* Both partners do the two walking steps in closed position (forward). The leader then rotates his upper torso and frame counterclockwise 45 degrees to make a left quarter turn. Finish with the regular tango close ending.

b. *From a promenade position:* Both partners do the two walking steps in promenade position (sideways). Prior to the tango close, the leader rotates his upper torso and frame counterclockwise 45 degrees. Both partners finish with their tango close ending.

Success Goal = Eight repetitions of the left quarter turn (a) from closed position and (b) from promenade position to slow tango music___

Success Check
- The left quarter turn is led after the second walking step___
- The leader's rotation facilitates an angled foot position (toe-out for the leader and toe-in for the follower)___

To Increase Difficulty

- Randomly alternate the forward basic with a left quarter turn and the basic promenade with a left quarter turn.

To Decrease Difficulty

- Use a set pattern; for example, do two repetitions of the forward basic with a left quarter turn or two repetitions of the basic promenade with a left quarter turn before leading another variation.

2. Corté and Recover

The corté is a popular tango variation when in a closed position. It is done in a small space and may be led after any tango close. To lead the corté, the leader keeps his frame and right hand firm as he steps back (see figure 12.2a) onto his left foot ("slow"). To recover, he then rocks his weight forward (see figure 12.2b) onto his right foot ("slow"). The follower does the opposite, shifting her weight forward onto her right foot, then backward onto her left foot. Then both partners do the normal tango close ending (quick, quick, slow or forward, side, close).

a   b

Figure 12.2   Corté and recover positions.

Success Goal = Eight repetitions of the corté and recover after any tango close ending to slow tango music___

Success Check

- The leader rocks or shifts his weight back onto his left foot on the first "slow," then forward onto his right foot on the second "slow"___
- Remain in closed position___
- Bend one knee (more like a lunge) during the corté___
- Finish with a tango close___

To Increase Difficulty

- Experiment with leading the corté and recover after either of the left quarter turn options.
- Use the corté as a final pose at the end of a song.
- Experiment with adding two more "slows" prior to the corté and recover so that the leader rocks forward, backward, then backward (corté) and forward (recover), then tango close.

To Decrease Difficulty

- Practice without a partner to a slow tempo.
- Repeat the corté and recover at least twice.
- Use as many basics as needed between leading the corté and recover.

3. Forward Basic With Rock Steps

The forward tango basic may be modified with syncopation steps (i.e., two triple steps) and additional counts (four more counts) to the regular tango basic step pattern. In this variation, two additional "quick, quick, slow" portions are inserted after the two forward walking steps.

Instead of going directly to the tango close, the leader signals forward-backward-forward rocks twice, corresponding to the "quick, quick, slow," by keeping his frame and right hand firm. Thus, the leader slightly twists his torso to his left side to initiate rocks with his left-right-left foot while the follower rocks with her right-left-right foot. The leader then slightly twists his torso to his right side to repeat these three rocks starting with the opposite foot (right-left-right for the leader and left-right-left for the follower) while still in a closed position (see figure 12.3). Keep your feet in a forward-backward stride (parallel fourth foot position) on the two forward triples. The leader's left foot is now free again to finish with the tango close ending.

■ **Figure 12.3** Syncopated rock steps (triple step) on the leader's right side and a 45 degree angle.

Success Goal = Eight repetitions of the forward basic with rock steps to slow tango music___

✔ **Success Check**
• Remain in closed dance position throughout___
• Insert two triple steps after the "slow, slow" forward walking steps, then finish with a tango close___
• Quickly shift weight three times to alternate the forward and backward directions, matching a weight change with each rhythm cue___

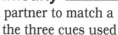
To Increase Difficulty
• Alternate the basic forward with rock steps with any other variation that you know so far.

To Decrease Difficulty
• Practice footwork without a partner to match a weight change with each of the three cues used for the rocks.
• Repeat this variation at least twice.

4. Open Position With Fans

This variation starts from a promenade position. The open position occurs when the leader releases his right hand to permit opening to an inside-hands-joined partner position. Both partners then execute two fans prior to a tango close ending. It takes two full basics to complete this variation.

a. *For the leader:* Start in promenade and do two walks. The leader releases his right hand and arcs his right arm across his midline (like a roll-out transition in the swing) as he takes two quick steps (left side, right side). With the follower on his left side in an open position (see figure 12.4a), the leader drags his left toe in to close his feet.

During the first "slow" of the next basic, the leader steps toward his left-front diagonal with his left foot (see figure 12.4b). Then, he swivels counterclockwise and closes his right foot. On the second "slow," the leader crosses his right foot to step toward his right-front diagonal onto his right foot (see figure 12.4c). The partners then resume a closed dance position during the finish with a left quarter turn on the tango close (see figure 12.4, d-f).

a Tango close   b Slow   c Slow

d Quick   e Quick   f Slow

Figure 12.4 Open position with fans for the tango.

b. *For the follower:* Do two walks in promenade. Step forward onto your right foot, then swivel counterclockwise a half turn to step to your left side onto your left foot. With the leader on your right side in open position, drag your right toe in to finish the close.

　　During the first "slow" of the next basic, the follower steps toward her right-front diagonal with her right foot, swivels 45 degrees clockwise, and extends or points her left foot (for the first fan). On the second "slow," the follower steps toward her left-front diagonal onto her left foot, swivels 45 degrees counterclockwise, and either extends her right foot (for the second fan) or brings it beside her left foot. Resume a closed dance position during the finish with a left quarter turn on the tango close (quick, quick, slow).

Success Goal = Eight repetitions of the open position with fans variation to slow tango music___

✔ **Success Check**
- Keep your extended hand in front of your shoulder and curved symmetrically with your partner's extended hand___
- Leaders and followers alternate either the left-front or right-front diagonals on the cross and point steps, respectively___

To Increase Difficulty
- Alternate the basic open variation with any other variation that you know so far.

To Decrease Difficulty
- Go through just the footwork without a partner, then add a partner, and then add the arms.
- Repeat the basic open at least twice before leading another variation.

5. Open Position With Figure-Eight Fans

The basic open variation may be extended to include at least two more fans (six total additional counts) prior to the drag to close. The leader initiates the figure-eight fans during the left quarter turn after the "quick, quick." Taking advantage of the CCW rotation, the leader overrotates the follower to place her on his right side. Then he does a rock step back onto his left foot, then forward onto his right foot, while the follower does two fans. The fans result from a crossover of one foot, then tracing the big toe of the other foot in an arc on the floor. Repeat this twice to create a figure-eight, or fanlike, motion. The fans are executed on the "slow, slow," then the partners finish with a tango close. During the figure-eight fans, the leader needs to pull with the fingers of his right hand, then press or push with the heel of his right hand, using a figure-eight motion with his right wrist to guide the follower on these two "slows."

Success Goal = Eight repetitions of the open position with figure-eight fans to slow tango music____

✔ **Success Check**
- The leader brings the follower to his right side for the fans, guiding her with a figure-eight wrist motion___
- To end the fans, the leader keeps the follower in front of him to finish in closed position with a tango close___
- The fans result from a cross and point while swiveling on one foot___

To Increase Difficulty
- Alternate the open position with figure-eight fans variation with the open position variation.
- Experiment with leading multiple repetitions of the fans (e.g., try two consecutive figure-eight fans). The leader needs to be quick to rotate on the two "quicks" prior to the two fans (on the "slows").

To Decrease Difficulty
- Practice the footwork and the hand position for leading the fans without a partner, then practice them with a partner using a very slow tempo.

6. Combine Three Variations

It is time to challenge yourself by linking at least three tango variations into longer combinations. For practice, try each of the following sample combinations:

- Basic promenade, forward basic, corté and recover
- Forward basic, forward basic with a left quarter turn, basic promenade
- Basic promenade, promenade with a left quarter turn, open position with fans
- Basic forward, basic forward with rock steps, corté and recover
- Basic forward with left quarter turn, basic forward with rock steps, open position with figure-eight fans

Now it is your turn to either modify the sample combinations or to create your own combinations of three or more variations. Use the following summary chart to reference the tango variations covered in this book.

Tango Variation Summary

1. Basic forward (closed position)
2. Basic promenade (transition option)
3. Basic forward with a left quarter turn
4. Basic promenade with a left quarter turn
5. Corté and recover
6. Basic forward with rock steps
7. Open position with fans
8. Open position with figure-eight fans

 **Success Goal =** Four repetitions of each of the practice combinations listed in drill 6, then four different combinations linking any three or more tango variations, each repeated for the length of one song___

 To Increase Difficulty
- Repeat with different partners.
- Use a variety of tempos.
- Link more than three variations together.

To Decrease Difficulty
- Repeat each variation as many times as needed to prepare for a new lead.
- Link variations in the order that you learned them, gradually adding another variation until you can link at least three together.

✔**Success Check**
- Smoothly link each variation___
- Practice proper partner etiquette___

TANGO SUCCESS SUMMARY

The tango has Latin origins that are exemplified in the characteristic smooth walks, then the dramatic tango close finish to each basic step pattern. The drama is a result of contrasting the quick and slow steps, which takes a lot of control. The basic step pattern uses eight counts in an SSQQS rhythm. Since the tango is mainly executed from closed position, the only transition used is with promenade position. The variations in the tango are also dramatic, using staccato foot movements and timing changes.

STEP 13 SALSA/MAMBO: ADDING FLAVOR

The word *salsa* refers to "sauce" or "hot" flavor, which is characteristic of this popular social dance. It is a Latin American dance that is similar to the mambo, but not as structured. The mambo, a spot dance with compact steps, was introduced in the United States near the end of the Second World War and imported from Cuba. The mambo basic is structured such that the break occurs on beat 2. In contrast, the salsa may break on beat 1 or 2, depending on the music. Salsa music is distinguished from other Latin American styles by the New York sound developed by Puerto Rican musicians in that city. Many mambo-type step variations are used in the salsa. The salsa will be described in detail in the following paragraphs; however, once you know the salsa, you only need to adjust the timing of the basic step to make it more structured for the mambo.

The salsa basic step pattern may be executed from either a shine position or a closed position. The eight-count rhythm repeats a quick, quick, slow (QQS) rhythm twice before the starting foot is free again. The salsa basic step pattern has a forward break and a backward break. The leader starts with the forward break while the follower starts with the backward break. Side breaks are also popular. A break is a quick change of direction such as forward, then backward, and vice versa, or left, then right, and vice versa.

For the leader: Step or break forward with your left foot by shifting weight forward onto your left foot. Then shift your weight back to your right foot; that is, replace your right foot in its original location. These two weight changes correspond to the "quick, quick." Step onto your left foot for the "slow." Your right foot is now free to execute the backward break (see the follower's directions).

For the follower: Step or break backward onto your right foot. Then shift your weight forward onto your left foot, keeping it in its original location. These two weight changes correspond to the "quick, quick." Step onto your right foot for the "slow." Your left foot is now free to execute the forward break (see the leader's directions).

Notice that the salsa basic step pattern uses the following foot positions: starting in first position parallel, break step (forward or backward) in either fourth position parallel or fifth position, then step and hold in first position parallel.

Figure 13.1 shows various ways you might use to organize the counts and footwork for the salsa. Select those cues that most help you retain how to execute the salsa basic step pattern.

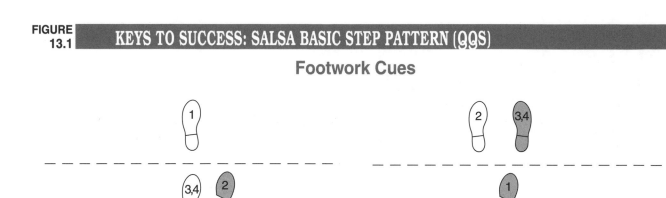

FIGURE 13.1 KEYS TO SUCCESS: SALSA BASIC STEP PATTERN (QQS)

Footwork Cues

Left foot forward
break and hold

Right foot backward
break and hold

Leader

Forward break, step and hold

Follower

Backward break, step and hold

Timing Cues

4/4 time signature:	Four beats to a measure, each beat gets one count
Total counts:	Eight (two measures)
Rhythmic counts:	1, 2, 3-4, 5, 6, 7-8; or mambo is 2, 3, 4-5, 6, 7, 8-1
Weight changes:	Six (on beats 1, 2, 3, 5, 6, 7; or mambo is cued per weight change as 2, 3, 4, 6, 7, 8
Duration of steps:	Quick, quick, slow; quick, quick, slow
Direction of steps:	a. Leader: Forward, backward, in place
	b. Follower: Backward, forward, in place

For variety, the salsa break steps may be executed to the side. These side breaks are sometimes called second-position breaks due to the second-position footwork used (see figure 13.2). When the leader's left foot is free, he may step sideways to his left, then shift weight back to his right foot during the "quick, quick" cues. The leader then steps in place with his left foot on the "slow." The follower steps with her right foot to the right side, shifts weight onto her left foot, and steps in place with her right foot. Each partner then repeats the basic QQS starting with the opposite foot.

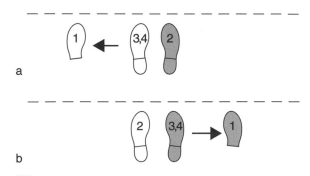

Figure 13.2 Salsa basic with side or second-position breaks.

SALSA/MAMBO BASIC STEP PATTERN

DRILLS

1. Basic Without a Partner

To start this drill, you and your partner stand facing the same wall. Both partners start with the left foot to execute the forward break-and-hold, then both start with the right foot to execute the backward break-and-hold. Keep alternating these directions. It helps to bend your knees slightly on the break steps and to keep your weight centered over both feet, rather than letting your upper torso move either forward or backward over the ball of the foot that initiates the break step.

After you feel comfortable with the basic timing (review figure 13.1), you might experiment with adding a bit more styling. One option is to execute a small heel dig, or kick, at the end of each hold, or on beats 4 and 8. These non-weight actions give you something to do on each beat of the two measures.

Success Goal = Two consecutive minutes of executing the salsa basic step pattern without a partner to salsa music (use track 19)___

Success Check
- Move in unison beside a partner___
- Left foot starts the forward break on the first "quick"___
- Right foot starts the backward break on the first "quick"___
- Reverse directions on the second "quick"___
- Either hold the "slow" for two beats or hold on beats 3 and 5 and add a heel dig on beats 4 and 8___

To Increase Difficulty
- Use a variety of salsa music.
- Increase the tempo.
- Face a different wall and repeat the drill.
- Repeat using the mambo basic step timing (either hold count 1 and break on counts 2, 3, or take a slow side step on counts 4-and-1, then break on counts 2, 3).

To Decrease Difficulty
- Use a slow count, then gradually increase tempo until it matches the tempo of slow salsa music.
- Mentally repeat "QQS" and make a weight change with each cue.

2. Basic With a Partner

Face a partner in shine position (without touching). Verbally cue your partner when to begin. The leader starts with his left foot and the forward break (see previous drill). The follower starts with her right foot and the backward break. After you can move in unison with a partner to slow salsa music in shine position, practice the basic with a partner in closed position. When in closed position, remember that the follower stands offset, or more on the leader's right side (versus facing toe-to-toe). This will help you avoid stepping on your partner's feet.

Success Goal = Two consecutive minutes of executing the salsa basic step pattern with a partner (a) in shine position, then (b) in closed position___

Success Check
- Take small steps___
- Leaders break forward with left foot to start___
- Followers break backward with right foot to start___
- Either continue to hold or add a heel dig on beats 4 and 8___

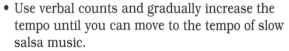

To Increase Difficulty
- Use a variety of salsa music.
- Practice with different partners.
- Experiment to find when it is easiest to make the transition from a shine to a closed position and then back to a shine position.
- Repeat using the mambo basic step timing.

To Decrease Difficulty
- Use verbal counts and gradually increase the tempo until you can move to the tempo of slow salsa music.
- Use only one partner position for the length of one song.

3. Side or Second-Position Breaks

Without a partner, practice the salsa basic step pattern with side or second-position breaks (review figure 13.2, a and b). The same basic rhythm is used. The leader steps left, right, left, then right, left, right. The follower steps right, left, right, then left, right, left. Make sure that you use a second foot position on the "quick, quick" and a parallel first foot position on the "slow." Once you are comfortable without a partner, practice in closed dance position with a partner.

Success Goal = Two consecutive minutes of side or second-position breaks___

Success Check
- Maintain a stationary position___
- Side step should be approximately shoulder width___

To Increase Difficulty
- Use a variety of salsa music.
- Practice with different partners.
- Repeat using the mambo basic step timing.

To Decrease Difficulty
- Use the shine position with a partner.
- Use slow salsa music.

4. Alternate Two Directions

Combine the direction changes used in the previous two drills to create a practice combination. Do four salsa basic step patterns (QQS) while breaking forward and backward, then do four salsa basic step patterns while breaking to each side. When you are comfortable with the order, start in a closed dance position with a partner and repeat the combination.

Success Goal = Two consecutive minutes of alternating four forward/backward breaks with four side or second-position breaks___

Success Check
- Make smooth transitions___
- Maintain the rhythm___

To Increase Difficulty
- Vary the number of repetitions of each part of the combination.
- Practice with different partners.
- Increase the tempo.

To Decrease Difficulty
- Start in shine position with a partner.
- Use the "rule of two" for the minimum number of repetitions to execute before changing to another move, especially as the salsa basic uses two measures of music (eight beats) before the starting foot is free again.

DRILLS

1. Leads From Closed to One-Hand-Joined Position and Back to Closed Position

The quicker timing of the salsa/mambo compared to the cha-cha makes this underarm turn transition challenging and fun. Start in a closed dance position with your partner and execute the basic salsa (quick, quick, slow). The break steps occur on the "quick, quick" when you rock or shift your weight either forward, then backward (left to right foot), or backward, then forward (right to left foot). The leader may signal an underarm turn for the follower prior to executing any backward break step by lifting his left hand and arm to form an arch. The follower needs to be ready to execute a pivot turn (180-degree turn) during her forward break steps, then continue her CW turn by spinning to face her partner again. The leader has the option of resuming a closed dance position immediately after the follower's underarm turn or of executing the basic step pattern from a one-hand-joined position. If the latter option is selected, then an easy way to change back to the closed position is to lead the underarm turn again on any of the leader's backward break steps.

Due to the faster timing of this underarm turn, there are two options for executing it. In the first option, the follower executes the pivot portion of the underarm turn in a forward-backward direction (similar to the half chase, except with an underarm turn; review figure 10.7, page 151). In the second option, the follower executes the pivot portion of the underarm turn in a side-to-side direction (see figure 10.4, page 147). The lead for the second option is initiated when the leader chooses to step sideways with his left foot as he makes the arch with his left hand, which signals the follower to step sideways with her right foot. No matter what direction the pivot turn is executed in, the follower needs to continue to spin to face her partner for the "slow" cue.

Success Goal = 10 smoothly executed transitions from a closed dance position to a one-hand-joined position and back to a closed position___

✔ Success Check
- Keep your free arm curved at approximately waist height and slightly in front of your body___
- Move through the underarm turn quickly, then recover on the slow portion of the basic step pattern___

To Increase Difficulty
- Randomly transition to either a one-hand-joined or a closed position.
- Use a variety of tempos.

To Decrease Difficulty
- Use a slow count or tempo.
- Execute transitions without a partner, then with a partner.

2. Leads From One-Hand- to Two-Hands-Joined Position and Back to One-Hand-Joined Position

The first portion of this drill helps you get into a two-hands-joined position. The second portion shows you how to alternately make the transition from a two-hands-joined to a one-hand-joined position while opening to each side.

a. *Grasp, then release:* Once in a one-hand-joined position, the leader has the option of moving closer and grasping the follower's left hand with his right hand. The basic step pattern may be executed in a two-hands-joined position. Then the leader may release his right hand grasp to resume a one-hand-joined position. Usually, these transitions are easier during the slow portion of the basic step pattern, although there is no hard-and-fast rule. Rather, it is a matter of smoothly grasping hands without reaching or releasing one hand at the end of any of the leader's backward break steps.

b. *Cross-body lead:* From a two-hands-joined position, the leader has the option of changing direction to execute a cross-body break to each side, rather than only forward and backward. A cross-body lead is used to signal the follower that a direction change is coming up. The leader actually brings either his right hand across his body (or midline) to open to his left side or his left hand across his body (or midline) to open to his right side. After the leader's forward break step, he needs to take his "slow" step to his left side (with his left foot). The leader then swivels on the ball of his left foot as he releases his left hand grasp in order to face his left side. Both partners execute a cross-body break with their inside foot (the one closest to their partner). At the end of the cross-body break, the partners swivel back to face each other on the next "slow." The transitions are repeated until the leader can join both hands again (review figure 10.6, and substitute one weight change, or step, for the triple steps used in the cha-cha).

Success Goal = 10 smoothly executed transitions moving from a one-hand-joined to a two-hands-joined position and back to a one-hand-joined position___

Success Check
• Wait until your bodies come close enough together that your hands can meet in the center between you and your partner before grasping___

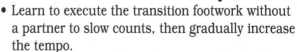**To Increase Difficulty**
• Transition from a forward-backward direction to a side-to-side direction on the "quick, quick" steps.
• Use a variety of tempos.

To Decrease Difficulty
• Learn to execute the transition footwork without a partner to slow counts, then gradually increase the tempo.
• Repeat the basic step pattern with a partner at least four times in a forward-backward direction before transitioning to a side-to-side direction.

3. Leads Into and From Shine Position

The transition into a shine, or apart, position is signaled by the leader releasing his hand grasp(s) after any backward break. The transition back to either a one-hand- or a two-hands-joined position is to move closer and regrasp hands. The timing for this lead occurs after any backward break for the leader.

Success Goal = 10 smoothly executed transitions into and from a shine position___

✔ **Success Check**
• Avoid reaching for your partner's hand(s). Wait until your bodies come closer together naturally while executing the basic step pattern___

To Increase Difficulty
• Randomly alternate from and into a shine position.
• Repeat the basic step pattern at least two times before changing direction or hand positions.

To Decrease Difficulty
• Practice to a slow tempo.
• Repeat the basic step pattern at least four times before changing direction or hand positions.

SALSA/MAMBO VARIATIONS AND COMBINATIONS

DRILLS

1. Alternating Underarm Turns

Alternating underarm turns are a composite variation of the underarm turn transition from closed position (and executed to the side) and the figure-eight turns executed in the cha-cha. In this variation, the follower does an underarm turn to her right side, then the leader does an underarm turn to his right side. The leader initiates the follower's turn with a left-hand arch for the follower to turn under. The leader then rotates his right hand counterclockwise with his thumb down and palm facing the follower to signal for her to place her left hand in his right hand. The leader does a pivot turn (like the push-away turn in the cha-cha) to turn under his own right arm. The leader may continue to alternate "she, then he" turns until he no longer lifts one hand for an arch. In the salsa/mambo, the timing of the lead for an underarm turn by the follower occurs on any second half basic (or the leader's backward break). Between the pivot turns, the leader steps to the side.

Success Goal = 10 random repetitions grouping at least three alternating underarm turns: for the follower, for the leader, then for the follower___

✔ **Success Check**
• Both partners alternately execute right underarm turns on each half basic___
• The leader steps to the side on each "slow" rhythm cue to presignal the turn___

To Increase Difficulty
• Execute more than three consecutive underarm right turns.
• Randomly combine the alternating underarm turns with a right underarm turn.

To Decrease Difficulty
• Practice the pivot without a partner.
• Execute the basic multiple times between leading the alternating right turns.

2. Full Chase

From a shine position, the full chase variation from the cha-cha also works in salsa/mambo. Both include a full turn during the forward half basic, first with the leader executing the turn, then with the follower executing the turn. Whenever the leader's left foot is free, he may initiate the full chase. Place the left foot forward ("quick"), pivot 180 degrees clockwise, step onto your right foot ("quick"), then continue your CW turn another 180 degrees to face your partner again and step onto your left foot ("slow"). Then it is the follower's turn to do the same execution for a full chase while the leader does his backward half basic. The full chase ends when the leader remains facing his partner and executes the basic step.

Success Goal = 10 random repetitions of the full chase___

Success Check
- Alternately, the leader turns, then the follower turns___
- The leader may start the turn whenever his left foot is free___

To Increase Difficulty
- Randomly execute more than one full chase (for each partner).
- Combine any number of repetitions of the alternating turns with the full chase.

To Decrease Difficulty
- Practice without a partner.

3. Push-Away Turns

The push-away turns are variations from the cha-cha. During any side or cross-body break, the leader may signal a full turn for both partners. The leader extends his left hand toward his right side, then releases his grasp with a gentle push to signal a CW turn for the leader (and a CCW turn for the follower). Square up by facing your partner with shoulders parallel and grasping two hands. Then, repeat on the opposite side to do a cross-body break to the leader's left side.

Success Goal = 10 random repetitions of any number of consecutive push-away turns___

Success Check
- Keep your elbows bent approximately 90 degrees with your forearms extended___
- Match your inside arms on the pivot, then face your partner___

To Increase Difficulty
- Randomly add push-away turns during the cross-body breaks (e.g., try two consecutive push-away turns, then four consecutive push-away turns).
- Combine the push-away turns with the full chase.

To Decrease Difficulty
- Use a set pattern for practice (e.g., execute three cross-body breaks with a push-away turn only on every fourth cross-body break).

4. Fifth-Position Breaks

The fifth-position breaks from the rumba are used in the salsa/mambo with two modifications. One modification is called "waist-to-waist." The outside arms may open to each side (as done with the weave step in the waltz). Although this variation is called "waist-to-waist," the leader's hand position actually alternates from the follower's left to right shoulder blades or upper back (see figure 13.3). The second modification is called "hand-to-hand" (see figure 13.4). The leader grasps the follower's inside hand on each side. Both partners execute the fifth-position breaks while the leader uses either a waist-to-waist or a hand-to-hand position.

a. *Waist-to-waist:* At the end of any backward half basic, the leader may step to his right side with his right foot and release his left hand grasp. Both partners open arms in a semicircle toward the leader's left side as they do a fifth-position break (with his left foot and her right foot stepping back). Face your partner on the "slow" step.

   To repeat on the other side, the leader releases his right hand from the follower's left shoulder blade. He then places his left hand on the follower's right shoulder blade and extends his right hand and arm (her left hand and arm) in a semicircle toward his right side. Both do a fifth-position break and continue alternating from side to side. Whenever the leader's left foot is free, he may resume a closed dance position and execute the basic forward and backward step pattern.

b. *Hand-to-hand:* Another option for the leader is to open up the space between him and his partner by moving apart until he can grasp her inside hand on each fifth-position break. Repeat at least four times before resuming a closed dance position again.

a   b   c

Figure 13.3   Waist-to-waist option during fifth-position breaks.

Figure 13.4 Hand-to-hand option during fifth-position breaks.

Success Goal = Eight consecutive fifth-position breaks alternating four repetitions each using (a) a waist-to-waist, then (b) a hand-to-hand position___

Success Check
- Keep arms curved and in frame (held in position versus letting gravity take over)___
- Open shoulders approximately 45 degrees on each fifth-position break___

To Increase Difficulty
- Experiment with any even number of repetitions using a waist-to-waist, a hand-to-hand, then a waist-to-waist position during the fifth-position breaks.

To Decrease Difficulty
- Practice each part separately, then in some set combination.

5. Side Cross Basic

The side cross basic, or cumbia, is a versatile variation that may be used from a variety of partner positions: closed, two-hands-joined, or shine position. Notice that the side cross basic (cumbia) must be repeated twice until your starting foot is free again. The leader starts with his left foot while the follower starts with her right foot. The footwork is the same for both the leader and the follower, yet is the mirror reverse when facing each other.

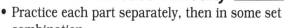

a. *Left-side cross basic:* To travel to your left side, your left foot must be free. Slide your left foot diagonally backward and step onto your left foot ("quick"). Bring your right foot toward your left side to cross it over your left foot, then step onto your right foot ("quick"). Step again to your left side on the "slow" and leave your right toe on the floor. During the second-count hold of the "slow," you may either point your right toe (without a weight change) or dig the heel of your right foot (without a weight change) toward your right side.

b. *Right-side cross basic:* To travel to your right side, your right foot must be free. Slide your right foot diagonally backward and step onto your right foot ("quick"). Bring your left foot toward your right side to cross it over your right foot, then step onto your left foot ("quick"). Step again to your right side with your right foot and hold the fourth count (with either a left toe point or a left heel dig (toward your left side). Figure 13.5, c-e (on page 194) shows the side cross (cumbia) basic footwork from a one-hand-joined position.

Mirror your partner's actions when in a shine position. When in a two-hands-joined position, the leader gently guides both hands to the appropriate side. When in a closed position, both partners need to take small steps and open their shoulder slightly toward the direction of travel; for example, open your left shoulder when traveling to your left.

Success Goal = Eight repetitions of the side cross basic (cumbia) in each of three partner positions: (a) shine, (b) two-hands-joined, and (c) closed___

Success Check
- The first side step is diagonally back to make room to cross your opposite foot___
- Four counts to each side___
- Leave your nonweighted foot in the center on the fourth count (during the hold)___

To Increase Difficulty
- Combine the side cross basic (cumbia) with fifth-position breaks using any even number of repetitions of each.

To Decrease Difficulty
- Practice in shine position, then from a two-hands-joined position.

6. Open Left Underarm Turn

An open left underarm turn is a variation that combines both a backward break and a side cross basic (cumbia). What is interesting about multiple repetitions of this variation is that you'll end up making a quarter turn to face a new wall each time. The open left underarm turn is led from a one-hand-joined partner position.

a. *For the leader:* Instead of breaking forward with your left foot, break backward with your left foot (see figure 13.5a). This action creates a rubber-band effect on the "quick, quick" such that both partners move apart, then toward each other. The leader then needs to take advantage of directing the follower's forward motion toward his right side to lead the left underarm turn during the "slow" step. To start the turn, bring your left hand toward your right shoulder, lift it up to make an arch, then loop it counterclockwise over the follower's head (see figure 13.5b). As you step forward with your left foot, rotate clockwise a quarter turn to face your partner. To end the turn, bring your hand down. Finish with a side cross basic (step right, cross left, step right) to your right side (see figure 13.5, c-e).

b. *For the follower:* Break backward as usual, then step diagonally left during your forward step onto your right foot on the "slow" (review figure 13.5, a and b). Turn counterclockwise approximately three-quarters of a turn to face your partner. Square up your shoulders with your partner (review figure 13.5c) as you execute your side cross basic to your left side (review figure 13.5, c-e).

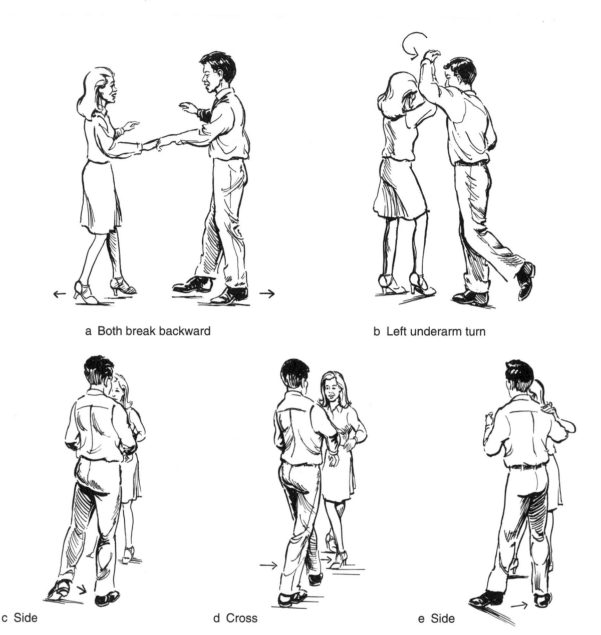

a Both break backward

b Left underarm turn

c Side

d Cross

e Side

Figure 13.5 Open left underarm turn for the salsa/mambo, followed by a cumbia (side, cross, side).

Success Goal = Eight repetitions of the open left underarm turn with any even number of basics between turns___

✔**Success Check**
• Two measures of 4/4 time music, or a total of eight counts for each open left underarm turn___
• Both partners square up (with shoulders parallel) prior to executing the side cross basic in unison___

To Increase Difficulty
• Lead consecutive open left underarm turns (e.g., two, three, then four times) to get back to where you started.
• Lead a right underarm turn after any number of open left underarm turns.

To Decrease Difficulty
• On the turn, isolate the "slow" rhythm cue into two parts: left underarm turn, then square up with your partner, giving each action one count.

7. Combine Four Variations

It is time to challenge yourself by linking at least four salsa/mambo variations into longer combinations. For practice, try each of the following sample combinations using any number of repetitions of each:

- Basic forward and backward in shine position, full chase, side cross basic (cumbia), basic forward and backward in a one-hand-joined position, right underarm turn
- Basic forward and backward in a one-hand-joined position, right underarm turn, alternating underarm turns, and open left underarm turn
- Basic forward and backward in closed position, second-position breaks, basic forward and backward, fifth-position breaks (with waist-to-waist, then hand-to-hand leads)
- Basic forward and backward in closed position, cross-body lead to cross-body breaks, push-away turns, full chase

Now it is your turn to either modify the sample combinations or create your own combinations of three or more variations. Use the following summary chart to reference the salsa/mambo variations covered in this book.

Salsa/Mambo Variation Summary

A. Variation Options
   1. Basic forward and backward
   2. Second-position breaks
   3. Right underarm turn
   4. Alternating underarm turns
   5. Full chase
   6. Cross-body breaks
   7. Push-away turns
   8. Fifth-position breaks
   9. Side cross basic (cumbia)
   10. Open left underarm turn
B. Transitions
   1. Underarm turn
   2. Grasp, then release
   3. Cross-body lead

Success Goal = Four repetitions of each of the practice combinations, then four different combinations linking any three or more salsa/ mambo variations, each repeated for the length of one song___

Success Check
- Smoothly link each variation___
- Practice proper partner etiquette___

To Increase Difficulty
- Repeat with different partners.
- Use a variety of tempos.

To Decrease Difficulty
- Repeat each variation as many times as needed to prepare for a new lead. Due to the fast tempo of the music, start with four repetitions of each variation.
- Link variations in the order that you learned them, gradually adding another variation until you can link at least three together.

SALSA/MAMBO SUCCESS SUMMARY

The salsa is a Latin dance that is similar to the mambo. Both are done to a fast tempo. The main difference is that the salsa may break on either the downbeat or the upbeat—i.e., count 1 or 2—whereas the mambo breaks on count 2. The salsa timing is dependent on the music and on one's preference. Many of the same transitions and variations from the other Latin dances, especially the cha-cha, can be done in the salsa and mambo. The variations are fun and exciting due to the characteristic Latin styling.

STEP 14

RULES OF THE ROAD: DEMONSTRATING GOOD FLOOR CRAFT

In a practice setting, many couples are executing the same set combination at the same time. However, once you are ready for an evening of dancing, you'll soon find that a set combination does not necessarily work when the other couples on the dance floor are doing different combinations at different times—the flow of traffic is random and unpredictable. For example, if one of your favorite combinations includes variations that facilitate travel in the LOD and another couple moves immediately in front of you, blocking your forward motion, what should you do? Or, when given a choice, where should you stand on the social dance floor to start your combination? In the social dance setting, the type of dance dictates both where couples may locate on the dance floor and what types of movements to select. There are two basic categories of dances: progressive and spot dances. You are now ready to make the transition from a practice to a social setting, including how to modify your dancing to prevent collisions, use the floor space effectively, and practice good floor etiquette.

Why Are Rules of the Road Important?

Dance floor etiquette entails certain "rules of the road" that make social dancing more enjoyable for all couples. Once you know these rules, you can become a better social dancer by either following the rules or modifying them to fit the situation. But the rules don't work if you are the only one who knows them. Thus, at times it is beneficial to bend the rules a bit to prevent any accidents on the dance floor. In these cases, you must become a defensive "driver"

and watch out for the unexpected. However, when the rules are known and followed, social dancing becomes a more enjoyable experience for all involved.

The ability to avoid collisions or bumping into other couples on the dance floor is known as demonstrating good floor craft. To avoid collisions, the leader needs to focus externally to be aware of others, use peripheral vision to survey the field (observe other couples' locations on the dance floor), and make spontaneous decisions as to which moves to execute for the particular situation (or configuration of couples) encountered. The follower needs to recognize the various leads, to trust the leader to make the correct decisions, and to respond to the leads (without anticipating or initiating them). Both partners need to dance with control, including being aware of when the floor is too crowded to travel very fast or to extend their arms too far out into another couple's space.

Demonstrating good floor craft is part of the etiquette expected on the social dance floor. Typically, the outside lane is for progressive dances that travel in the LOD, such as the foxtrot, waltz, and polka. The inside lane is for slower dances that travel in the LOD and include some stationary as well as LOD traveling movements. If you are in the fast lane, avoid moving in a reverse line of dance; rather, move to the slower, inside lane. The center of the floor is for spot dances such as various forms of swing and line dances. You may dance anywhere on the floor within your own small area for dances such as the cha-cha, rumba, tango, and salsa/mambo. These dances are sometimes called spot dances because a spot is staked out on the dance floor, as in the swing. However, in contrast, it is your option whether to do a swing or a foxtrot, particularly with fast foxtrot tempos. Thus, the swing dance forms need to be executed in the center of the floor, particularly when other couples are executing the foxtrot in the progressive lanes. Figure 14.1 shows a diagram of the locations for executing various dance styles on the social dance floor. Following these etiquette "rules of the road" will make it more enjoyable for all dancers.

Progressive Dance Strategies

The ultimate goal for progressive dances that travel in the LOD is to travel—whenever there is space to do so! However, when another couple suddenly blocks your progression, you need to slow down and mark time or remain relatively stationary until the path is open again. You may pass other couples, but avoid cutting across the center of the room. Thus, one strategy for selecting the appropriate variation for the situation encountered is to separate the variations that you know so far according to whether they progress you forward in the LOD or keep you relatively stationary. As a review, the following strategies may be used when progressing in the LOD:

- When another couple abruptly moves into your path, select any of the stationary variations to execute. Continue with stationary variations until your path opens up again.

- When no other couple is immediately in your path, select any of the traveling variations to execute. Continue with traveling variations until your path is blocked or the traffic has slowed down.

- Avoid getting too close to other couples. Regulate the pace of your moves to adjust to the speed of the other couples. If they are moving slowly, select more stationary variations and avoid showy moves with extended arms and hands. If they are moving quickly, select more traveling variations to execute. If you happen to bump into another couple, excuse yourself and apologize at a convenient time.

Spot Dance Strategies

One of the characteristics of spot dances is that they are executed within a small space. For spot dances, when selecting a variation to execute with a partner, the leader may use the following strategies:

- Select variations that help you remain within (or return to) your small circular area.
- Adjust the size of your small area depending on the number of other couples on the floor at the same time.
- Avoid getting too close to others. If an unavoidable bump occurs, excuse yourself and apologize at a convenient time.

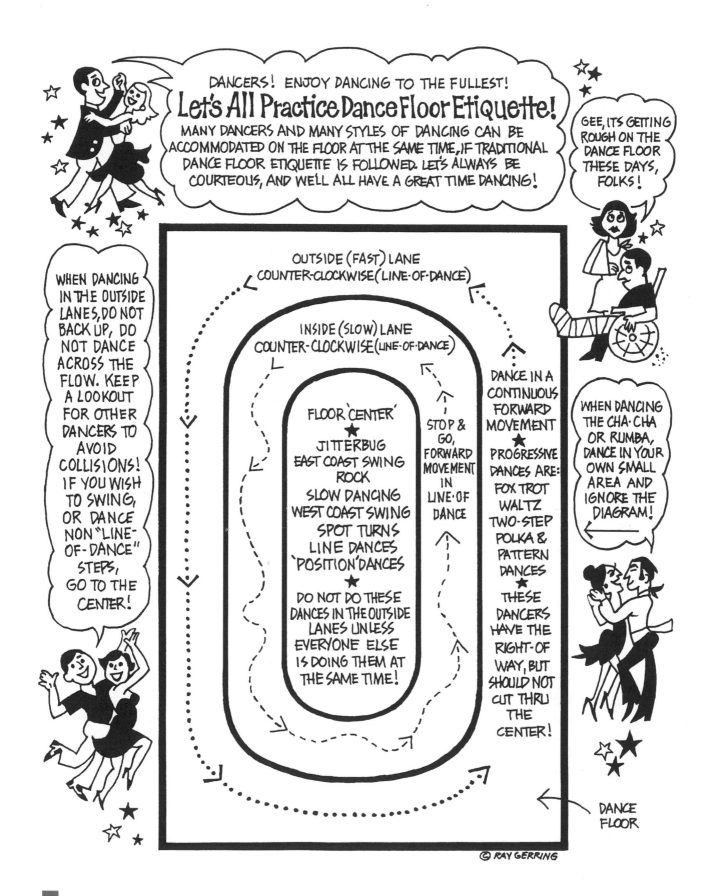

Figure 14.1 Good floor etiquette is a must.

©1995 by Ray H. Gerring. All rights reserved. Reprinted with permission.

PROGRESSIVE DANCE RULES OF THE ROAD

DRILLS

1. No Room to Travel

If the dance floor is very crowded and you cannot travel, or progress, forward, you can opt to do any of the stationary variations you know so far. In this situation, the leader's task is to select from those variations that can be executed in place so as to maintain a stationary position.

    a. *Foxtrot:* Here, you have seven choices:
- Box step
- Left box turn
- Basic rock step
- Rock turn
- Side rock step
- Cross step
- Weave step

    b. *Waltz:* Here, you have five choices:
- Box step
- Box turn (left or right)
- Cross step
- Balance (forward and backward, side to side, or promenade)
- Weave

    c. *Polka:* Here, you have three choices:
- Basic in place
- Around-the-world
- Reverse around-the-world

    Politely ask a partner to dance, and create at least four different sequences that combine any three stationary variations. You may vary both the order and the number of repetitions of each.

Success Goal = Four different sequences (combining any three or more stationary variations) to music for each of the following progressive dances: (a) foxtrot, (b) waltz, and (c) polka___

Success Check
- Write down at least four different combinations using only stationary variations___
- Circle the number of the combination that flows most easily for you___

To Increase Difficulty
- Experiment with a variety of combinations to find those that link most naturally.
- Where possible, combine more than four stationary variations.

To Decrease Difficulty
- One combination strategy is to use the order of stationary variations as listed.
- For foxtrot and waltz, combine the last four stationary variations as listed.

2. Room to Travel

If the dance floor is not crowded, the ultimate goal for progressive dances is to travel in the LOD. In this situation, the leader's task is to select from any of the variations that permit travel in the LOD.

a. *Foxtrot:* You now have eight traveling variations to select from:
- Half-box progressions forward
- Two left quarter turns followed by two right quarter turns
- Basic forward step (six-count basic)
- Conversation step
- Basic forward and backward combination
   a. Using a zigzag floor path
   b. Using right and left parallel partner positions
- Rollovers
- Sandwich option (two left quarter turns, any even number of half-box progressions backward, two right quarter turns)

b. *Waltz:* You now have three choices:
- Half-box progressions (forward and backward)
- Rollovers
- Scissors

c. *Polka:* You now have five choices:
- Underarm turns
- Partner turns
- Gallop combination
- Twist combination
- Front-to-front and back-to-back

Politely ask a partner to dance, and create at least four different sequences that combine at least three traveling variations. You may vary both the order and the number of repetitions of each.

Success Goal = Four different sequences (combining three or more traveling variations) to music for each of the following progressive dances: (a) foxtrot, (b) waltz, and (c) polka___

Success Check
- Write down at least four different combinations of any three or more traveling variations___
- Circle the number of your favorite combination___

To Increase Difficulty
- Experiment with a variety of combinations.
- Link more than three traveling variations together.

To Decrease Difficulty
- Use as many basics between each variation as needed to prepare for the next lead.

3. Spontaneous Adjustments to the Traffic Encountered

Rarely will you be able to do either all stationary or all traveling variations on the dance floor. Therefore, you need to be able to spontaneously select the most appropriate variations for the flow of traffic encountered. Each time that you dance will be different. Thus, the ability to create spontaneous combinations is the ultimate achievement on the social dance floor. In this situation, the leader's task is to spontaneously intermix both stationary and traveling variations, as needed.

Politely ask a partner to dance. Randomly select variations as they best fit the flow of traffic encountered, depending on whether or not there is room to progress, for the length of any one song. Notice what works best for particular situations. Are there certain combinations that you tend to repeat over and over?

Success Goal = Six different songs intermixing stationary and traveling variations as appropriate to the situation for each of the following progressive dances: (a) foxtrot, (b) waltz, and (c) polka___

Success Check
• Use any order and any number of repetitions of each variation___
• Create fluid, spontaneous combinations as appropriate to the flow of traffic encountered___

To Increase Difficulty
• Repeat this drill with a different partner for each song.
• Use a variety of variations.

To Decrease Difficulty
• Use only selected variations.
• Use slow tempos.

SPOT DANCE RULES OF THE ROAD

DRILLS

1. Find a Spot

Be aware of how you enter and exit the dance floor so as to avoid bumping into other dancers. Find an open space, or spot, on the floor that you can temporarily stake a claim to for the length of any one song. Remember that for some foxtrot music selections, either a swing or a foxtrot may be executed. In this case, the swing dancers need to move to the center of the floor so that the foxtrot couples may progress in the LOD. With other music selections, social dancers typically execute the same basic step pattern, for example, for the cha-cha, rumba, tango, and salsa/mambo. Identify the appropriate music being played, then find your spot on the dance floor without touching any other couples.

Success Goal = Six different songs for each of the following spot dances: (a) swing, (b) cha-cha, (c) rumba, (d) tango, and (e) salsa/mambo___

Success Check
• Practice avoiding collisions each time you're on the dance floor___
• Select an appropriate open space on the dance floor___

To Increase Difficulty
• Practice with a variety of partners.
• Use a variety of tempos and variations.

To Decrease Difficulty
• Select any one dance at a time.
• Gradually increase your repertoire.

2. Practice Good Floor Etiquette

Good floor etiquette involves sharing the dance floor with other dancers without interfering with their dancing. Once you have found your spot on the dance floor, the leader's task is to use peripheral vision to notice how the surrounding space changes as other dancers do their own moves. The leader may need to adjust the direction within the spontaneous combinations to accommodate the shifting floor locations of other dancers. For example, in the swing, if the leader is preparing to lead a single under, but another couple suddenly moves into the space where he and his partner intended to move, what might the leader do? One option is to repeat the basic step pattern and rotate in either direction until enough space is open for a single under to be executed. Another option might be to do the single under without getting very far apart so as to reduce the amount of space used. Practice selecting the appropriate variations and direction changes for the length of one song.

Other common courtesies are to avoid eating, drinking, or standing and talking with other dancers on the dance floor when other couples are trying to dance. If you want to talk with other dancers, just move off the dance floor.

Success Goal = Spontaneous combinations during six different songs for each of the following spot dances: (a) swing, (b) cha-cha, (c) rumba, (d) tango, and (e) salsa/mambo___

Success Check

- Practice good floor etiquette each time you are on the dance floor___
- Excuse yourself if you happen to bump into or collide with another dancer___
- The leader needs to create smooth and fluid combinations that fit the dynamic situations encountered___
- Avoid impeding the flow of traffic in any way___

To Increase Difficulty

- Practice with different partners.
- Use different tempos and variations.

To Decrease Difficulty

- Problem solve how you might handle a particular situation. What options do you have?
- Use a slow tempo.

RULES OF THE ROAD SUCCESS SUMMARY

Whenever you move from a structured practice setting to a social setting, it is important to be aware of certain dance floor etiquette "rules of the road" that will make everyone's experience more enjoyable. The ability to avoid collisions or bumping into other couples on the dance floor requires the leader to demonstrate good floor craft. This means knowing the basic steps and variations so well that the leader can focus more on the traffic encountered, which is constantly changing.

As a general rule, progressive dances that travel in the LOD should use the outside lane. Stop-and-start dances that travel in the LOD should use the inside lane. The center of the floor is for spot dances that remain more stationary or within a restricted area, especially if other dancers are traveling in the LOD. For some spot dances, especially when other dancers are not traveling in the LOD, the dancers may use the entire floor as long as they don't bump into other couples.

Last, be ready to modify the rules in order to blend with other dancers' interpretation or unawareness of the rules. Use the appropriate social etiquette needed to prevent collisions on the dance floor. Be ready to be a defensive "driver"!

STEP 15

TURN TECHNIQUE AND STYLING: LOOKING GOOD ON THE DANCE FLOOR

At some point in the search for new variations and combinations to do on the dance floor, you'll soon realize that it is more important to do a few moves well versus a lot of moves with poor execution or poor styling. In particular, how you execute turns and how precisely you project the characteristic styling of each dance will make you stand out on the dance floor. An obvious indicator of poor turn execution is when something goes wrong, such as loss of balance on turns (dizziness) or lack of control with timing (being late or out of sync with your partner or the music, or both). An indicator of poor styling is when it is difficult to identify the dance style being performed. For example, even though the same basic step pattern is used in different dances, such as the box step in the waltz, foxtrot, and rumba, each dance style should look qualitatively different.

When you find that you have a large enough repertoire of moves to dance comfortably on the social dance floor, then it is time to hone both your technique on turns and your projection of characteristic styling. You can improve your balance and control once you know how to initiate, execute, and end turns effectively—both without and with a partner. You can more accurately demonstrate the styling traditionally associated with different dance styles by becoming more aware of the unique characteristics of each style.

Why Are Turn Technique and Styling Important?

A popular variation in most dances is some sort of turn (rotating 360 degrees). Once you understand a few turn technique tips, you can not only improve your confidence and timing, but also avoid getting dizzy on turns. It helps to know where to place your feet, how to position your body, where to focus your eyes (or spot), how fast to turn, when to turn, and how to grasp hands with your partner. Once you know how to execute a single turn, the next challenge is to execute a double turn. With practice, you'll be able to do multiple consecutive turns without difficulty.

During the early stages of learning to dance, you need to break down moves into parts and to memorize what to do on each move. During the middle to later stages of learning, the basic step patterns become more automatic. Once you have fewer things to think about, it is important to make sure that you demonstrate the flavor and essence of each dance versus dancing each dance qualitatively the same. This contrast reflects the transition between practice (more mechanical) and performance (more expressive) situations. Once you get on the social dance floor, you are performing. Wouldn't you like to hear compliments about your dancing?

Turn Technique Tips

Using a foot-to-head order, there are at least four areas that contribute to your ability to execute a turn with finesse: foot placement, body torque, spotting, and timing. Don't expect to be able to tackle these areas all at once. Start with your footwork, then gradually focus on another aspect. If your footwork is not balanced, everything else will be off too. After focusing on your personal techniques, it is important to work with your partner too. Hand grips can often be too tight, especially with underarm turns. Thus, your hand positions with your partner will affect your ease of execution.

Foot Placement

When the leader signals a turn, it is a cue for the follower to position her feet in preparation for the turn. Angling the foot approximately 45 degrees sets up the turn so as to overcome inertia and gain momentum. An angled foot is also a more stable foot, as it widens your base of support. Typically, turns are set up from either an extended third or an extended fifth foot position to improve balance and control.

Generally, three types of turns are popular in social dance: pivot turns, three-step turns, or spins. A pivot turn is a half turn, as you've seen in a number of variations so far (e.g., in the half chase or the push-away turns used in the cha-cha). As you practice the push-away turns, place your feet in a heel-to-toe or fifth foot position. Start with your left foot angled outward (45 degrees to your left-front diagonal). Transfer your weight from your left foot to your right foot during the CW pivot turn. End the pivot with your right foot angled outward (45 degrees to your right-front diagonal).

The three-step turn is sometimes called a chainé turn. Keep your weight on the balls of your feet throughout. The amount of turn on each step is quarter, half, half. You may use either a first or second foot position in the middle. If speed is important and you need to remain in a stationary position, use a first foot position and the cues "step, together, step." Or, if using a second foot position, avoid stepping beyond the width of your shoulders. You have been using this turn without knowing its name, for example, in the underarm turn variation of the foxtrot's conversation step. In comparison, a three-step turn is executed faster than a pivot turn.

The most difficult turn is a spin, or a 360-degree turn on the ball of one foot. A new variation, a tuck and spin for the swing, will be described in the drills.

Body Torque

Your shoulders provide body torque to facilitate your turn execution, especially on spins. As you step with your foot angled outward to set up the turn, notice that your opposite shoulder also rotates in the direction of the angled foot. This opposition is called contra-body positioning, or CBP (see figure 15.1). You use CBP each time that you walk, as opposite arms and legs move together. Just as when ice skaters twist or rotate their upper torso one way, then unwind in the opposite direction prior to a turn, your shoulders provide momentum, or torque, for the turn.

Think of either your right shoulder rotating back on right, or CW, turns or your left shoulder rotating back on left, or CCW, turns.

Another technique tip is to commit your weight onto your angled foot such that your center of gravity is above the ball of that foot. If you don't shift your weight onto your angled foot, you will not be able to complete the turn. The combination of CBP and weight over the angled foot will create momentum to either prepare for a pivot turn or a chainé turn or to spin at least 360 degrees on one foot!

Figure 15.1 Contra-body positioning is used to set up turns. In this example, the right shoulder is rotated toward the angled left foot to set up a left turn.

Spotting

Typically, you need to look in the direction that you are going to turn. Once you know the direction of the turn, it helps if you focus your eyes on one spot throughout the turn, rather than letting your eyes wander so that you become dizzy from seeing everything in the room. This focusing technique is called spotting. Spotting technique is the same whether you want to execute a single or multiple turns. It involves the ability to isolate your head from the rest of your body—which sounds more difficult than it is! Without worrying about any footwork, select a spot at approximately eye level in the direction you want to turn (see figure 15.2a). Keep watching that spot as you turn your body counterclockwise (shoulders rotate in the direction of the turn) until you are at the point where you might not be able to watch your spot if you go any farther (see figure 15.2b). Then quickly snap your head around (faster than your body) to visually locate your spot again (see figure 15.2c). Let your body and shoulders continue the turn as you continue to watch your spot. Spotting permits you to watch one spot throughout the turn, or one point that you are traveling toward, which helps you avoid getting dizzy. Try this without a partner. Practice spotting while turning clockwise, too.

On the dance floor and with a partner, you have several choices as to where to spot. In progressive dances, either the LOD or the RLOD are useful spots. In spot dances, either your partner or the general direction of the turn may be used.

Timing

The speed of your turn will affect your balance and overall execution. On spins, practice moving quickly through the spin as you spot. Since a spin is executed on the ball of one foot, the less time you balance on one foot, the less likely it is that you will lose

your balance. It is helpful to use the cue "spot through" as a reminder to move quickly through each turn. On other turns, you can coordinate the timing of the turn with your point of focus. For example, on the half chase in the cha-cha, focus forward, backward, then forward again (or partner, back wall, partner). Or on push-away turns in the cha-cha (or other Latin dances), focus wall, wall, partner (or side wall, side wall, partner).

To stop the momentum created to set up and turn, slightly lower your center of gravity by bending your knees or widen your base of support. For example, to avoid losing your balance at the end of your turn, you might let your weight shift from the ball of one foot onto the heel of that foot or take a more flat-footed step onto the other foot, or you might step with your feet slightly apart (either sideways, forward, or backward).

Hand Positions on Underarm Turns

If you grip your partner's hand too tightly, it will be difficult to do an underarm turn. Start with an arch (leader raises his left arm). Let the follower do a CW or right underarm turn. Figure 15.3 shows the leader's palm facing downward while the follower's palm faces upward. There needs to be enough downward or upward pressure so that your hands stay

a   b   c

Figure 15.2 Head and shoulder positions while spotting on a turn.

Figure 15.3 Hand positions on underarm turn.

connected. Notice how the fingertips are able to rotate freely on the underarm turn. You need to stay connected with your partner throughout the turn. Avoid straightening your elbow on the turn; both partners need to keep their elbows slightly rounded. Try this and see how it works with your partner!

Characteristic Styling

Once you know the basic step patterns and can execute a few variations, you need to remember that each dance has its own unique styling. The challenge now is learning how to demonstrate the characteristic stylings for each dance so that your dances don't all look alike. Any knowledgeable observer should be able to recognize which dance you and your partner are executing. If you execute every dance with the same quality, for example, everything is smooth, then you will be less expressive on the dance floor than dancers who "play" with the timing to contrast fast and slow movements and demonstrate the characteristic styling.

TURN TECHNIQUE AND STYLING

DRILLS

1. Three-Step Turn

One underarm turn variation for the follower that uses the three-step turn may be added during the conversation step (or promenade to the side) in the foxtrot. The three-step turn is completed within three weight changes. To execute a three-step turn clockwise, angle your right foot toward the right side (or LOD) and step onto that foot ("slow"). Spin on the ball of your right foot to face the outside wall ("and"). Step in the LOD either in a second foot position or bring your feet together as you transfer weight onto your left foot ("slow"), then continue your CW spin on your left foot to face your partner ("and"). Note that the different foot positions in the middle depend on how much you and your partner travel during the turn. Both partners face to execute the "side, together" steps.

   To lead the underarm turn, the leader forms an arch by lifting his left hand on the first "slow." This sets up the turn for the follower to position her feet in either an extended fifth or third foot position (and to use CBP for torque on the turn). In addition, the leader indicates the direction of turn (LOD) by gently pressing with the heel of his right hand on the follower's left shoulder blade. The follower then completes the turn and finishes the basic step facing her partner.

Success Goal = Two consecutive repetitions of the three-step turn as an option when executing the conversation step in the foxtrot___

✓ Success Check
- Feet in either extended third or fifth foot position to set up the turn (first weight change)___
- Spot in the direction of the turn (i.e., LOD)___
- Use either a first or second foot position on the second weight change (facing away from your partner)___
- Use either a first or second foot position on the third weight change (facing toward your partner)___

To Increase Difficulty
- Lead two consecutive underarm turns during any one conversation step.
- Identify and experiment with other variations where the three-step turn might be useful (either in the foxtrot or in any other dance style that you know so far). For example, add a three-step turn during the "quick, quick, slow" of a cumbia (side cross basic) to either side in the salsa/mambo.

To Decrease Difficulty
- Maintain the rhythmic timing and tempo regardless of foot positions during the turns.
- Foxtrot turn timing is on the "slow, slow" then side together is on the "quick, quick."
- Salsa turn timing is on the "quick, quick" then side is on the "slow."

2. Spin Turn

One variation in the swing that uses a 360-degree turn is called a tuck and spin. From a one-hand-joined position, during any basic, the leader may transfer the follower's right hand from his left to his right hand. Either during the same basic or on the next basic, the leader rotates his right wrist with palm up to alter his normal right-to-right hand grasp. This signals the follower to expect a tuck and spin. On the first slow, the leader draws his right hand and elbow slightly backward and close to his right side in a 90-degree angle. The follower steps toward the leader's right side with her elbow positioned at 90 degrees as well. At the end of the first "slow," the follower presses into the leader's hand and arm to gain momentum to spin 360 degrees clockwise on the ball of her right foot. The leader firmly maintains his right arm at a 90-degree angle until the follower pushes. Then he can push forward to help the follower complete her spin. At the end of the spin, the leader catches the follower's right hand with his left hand as both take their second "slow" step. Both do the ball-change steps together.

Success Goal = 10 random repetitions of the tuck and spin to swing music___

✓ Success Check
- The leader's arm position must be solid as a rock on the tuck___
- Keep the forearms level (or parallel to the floor) on the tuck___
- Elbows are bent 90 degrees and close to your sides___
- The leader's palm is facing up during the tuck___

To Increase Difficulty
- Both partners may spin at the same time (clockwise on follower's right foot and counterclockwise on leader's left foot).

To Decrease Difficulty
- Use the single-time swing basic step pattern for this variation.
- Practice the tuck portion against a wall (i.e., lean in and push off the wall to gain momentum for the spin).

3. Double Turn

A fun variation in many dances is a double turn. It is the leader's job to initate and end turns, and for a double turn, he will need to keep his left hand high longer. Generally, as long as the leader keeps his hand above the follower's head, the turn is to be continued. This can be a problem for the follower, however, especially if she doesn't spot. Once the leader lowers his hand below his partner's head, the turn is over. The challenge in this drill is to lead two consecutive turns, or a double turn. Examples from three different dance styles follow.

a. *Swing:* With slow music and the triple-swing basic step pattern, a CCW double turn may be led from a one-hand-joined position. After any ball-change, the leader may release his right hand, rotate clockwise to face the follower, and bring his left hand across his midline toward his right shoulder. The leader starts the follower's CCW turns with a small circle above the partner's head during the first triple step, and without lowering his hand, he can continue making another small circle above the partner's head during the second triple step. The leader lowers his left hand to end the turn so both partners can do their ball-change step. The leader needs to continue rotating clockwise to face the follower during his execution of the two triple steps.

b. *Cha-cha:* From a shine position, a double turn may be used as a variation of the chase. Start with a regular half chase (or half turn), then add another 1 1/2 turns on the cha-cha-cha steps in order to face your partner again. As in the regular chase variations, the leader executes a double-turn chase, then the follower executes a double-turn chase. This alternation continues until the leader remains facing his partner to execute his forward break. Spotting can break this double turn into parts for easier execution. On the first half turn focus forward, then to the back wall. Do a full turn while spotting on the back wall. Then, finish the last half turn and spot forward again (on your partner)

c. *Polka:* From a closed position, execute the polka basic step pattern on both sides of your body (i.e., four counts). To signal a double turn, the leader lifts his left hand to form an arch and gently presses with the heel of his right hand on the follower's left shoulder blade to indicate the direction of the turn (clockwise under the arch and toward the LOD). As long as the leader keeps his left hand high, the follower knows to continue turning on each half-basic step. After two turns (or when the leader's left foot is free again), the leader may lower his left hand and resume a closed position with his partner.

Success Goal = Eight repetitions of each of the double turn variations described___

Success Check
- Maintain the tempo throughout your turn___
- Keep your free arm extended from your center___
- Select a specific spot or focus during the turns (e.g., on the LOD, the RLOD, or your partner)___
- Prep your foot in the direction of the turn (i.e., left foot angles on left turns, right foot angles on right turns)___

To Increase Difficulty
- Alternate any of the double turn variations with another variation within that dance style.
- Create a combination of any four to six variations that includes at least one double turn variation (as appropriate to the selected dance style).

To Decrease Difficulty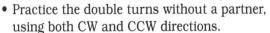
- Practice the double turns without a partner, using both CW and CCW directions.

4. Characteristic Styling

How you move on the dance floor can make your dancing more dramatic and engaging for you, your partner, and spectators. The flair with which you execute both the basics and the variations in each dance style will bring your dancing to life and make it more exciting to watch and to perform. As the footwork becomes more automatic, you can shift your concentration to expressing characteristic styling for each dance style.

Two ways to add more excitement and styling to your performance are to (a) vary the timing or speed of execution of certain variations, as appropriate to the selected dance style; and (b) reflect the appropriate images for each dance style selected. Following is a summary of selected descriptions to support the desired images that are characteristic of the eight dance styles covered in this book.

- Foxtrot—smooth, gliding, and regal
- Swing—torso leans, jazzy, and syncopated
- Waltz—stately posture, wavelike rise-and-fall motions, and an accent on the downbeat
- Polka—lively, fun, and springing
- Cha-cha—staccato, Latin, and flirtatious
- Rumba—sultry, romantic, and the "dance of love"
- Tango—dramatic moves, slow catlike walks, and staccato foot movements
- Salsa/mambo—"hot," Latin, expressive, and compact

Success Goal = Demonstrate characteristic styling and timing for each dance style listed, using the appropriate music___

Success Check
- Match styling with your partner___
- Position your free arms___
- You, your partner, and the music should connect___

To Increase Difficulty
- Vary the tempo.
- Dance with different partners.
- Randomly demonstrate characteristic styling for a variety of dance styles (equivalent to an evening of social dance). For example, can you make the box step used in the waltz, foxtrot, and rumba look different by styling each one differently?

To Decrease Difficulty
- Select only one dance style to work on at a time.

TURN TECHNIQUE AND STYLING SUCCESS SUMMARY

The fun begins when you are able to execute both single and double turns as variations within a variety of dance styles. It is also the time to hone your turn technique to maintain balance and control. Specific turn technique tips address four typical concerns: where to place your feet to initate turns, how to create body torque to get more speed on turns, where to focus your attention during the turn to avoid getting dizzy, and how fast or slow to execute the turn (as well as when to turn). New variations were introduced for using at least three types of turns: three-step turns, spin turns, and double turns.

Now that you are more comfortable with the basics and selected variations within a variety of dance styles, it is important to review and concentrate on how well you are projecting the characteristic styling associated with each style. The selected descriptions provided will give you a sense of the flavor or image to achieve with each of the eight dance styles covered in this book.

STEP 16

MORE DANCE OPTIONS: ADJUSTING TO NEW SITUATIONS

The goal in social dancing is to dance with a variety of partners and treat each other with respect as you are having fun on the dance floor. This means you need to find out where you can go dancing in your community. Look in the newspaper and ask around about clubs or studios or sponsored dances that you might be able to attend. Sometimes this means being creative at using the resources available to practice your dancing and get to know other people.

You'll soon find that some modifications and adaptations are necessary to "go with the flow" of other dancers when you are in certain situations. Besides having to know the "rules of the road" and the proper etiquette, you might encounter additional situations such as the following: dancing to unfamiliar music, needing to adjust the timing to better fit the tempo of the music being played, moving within a restricted space during LOD dances, and creating or modifying basic step patterns, variations, and combinations to fit the specific situations encountered. These creative challenges require problem solving, which takes time.

So don't expect to have an immediate idea or to have an immediately polished sequence or routine. However, you can use certain guidelines reflecting the decision-making stages built into this book to inspire your creativity. Selected strategies, guidelines, typical "problems" to solve, and sample solutions will be presented in the drills.

Why Is It Important to Expand Your Dance Options?

If you can increase your opportunities to dance, you can increase your rehearsal time and have a better chance of polishing your skills. So as you survey your community to locate places where you can practice or perform, you may need to be flexible so as to adapt to a variety of dance settings. Many basic rhythmic step patterns may be executed either exactly the same or slightly modified to match the music. The most important goal is to work in unison with your partner to create fluid movements that fit the music.

DRILLS

1. Finding a Basic Step That Fits the Music

During an evening of social dance, rarely will anyone announce the type of dance appropriate to the song being played. You'll need to be able to quickly assess which basic step best fits the music. Obviously, some types of dances, such as the waltz or the polka, are easier to identify than others. However, when in doubt, especially with contemporary, country-western, Latin, or folk-dance music, you may need to experiment with different basic step patterns that you think might work. Try out each basic step pattern that might be a solution until you find one that fits. For example, the six-count basic step patterns used in the foxtrot and in the swing are very versatile basic step patterns that may work with a variety of music styles.

Sometimes the same basic step pattern, such as the waltz, polka, or cha-cha, may be executed for any waltz, polka, or cha-cha song, as these are recognizable across a variety of music styles. For example, with German, Polish, or country-western polkas, the same basic polka step may be used and/or modified slightly to reflect different music styling. The German polka uses stomps, the Polish polka uses dainty, light steps, while the country-western polka may eliminate the hop and only use the triple steps, which are called shuffle steps.

Success Goal = Experiment with different basic step patterns until you find one that fits the music being played___

✔ Success Check

• Move in unison with your partner and the music___
• Change to another basic step pattern if one doesn't work___

To Increase Difficulty

• Listen to unfamiliar music and test yourself on which basic step pattern would best fit that music.
• Once you've found an acceptable match with the music, include the appropriate variations associated with the selected basic step.

To Decrease Difficulty

• Listen to contemporary music on the radio or ask a partner to play random selections of songs for you to identify which basic step pattern would best fit the music.

2. Dancing to Very Slow (or Very Fast) Music

Whenever you find that the music is either too slow or too fast to execute your regular basic step patterns, you need to make some timing adjustments. In the foxtrot, for example, if the tempo is too slow for you and your partner, then make all of your steps "quick" steps. Or if the tempo is too fast, make all of your steps "slow" steps. Remember that "quicks" and "slows" are relative to each other and are not absolutes.

If the dance style has more than one basic step pattern to choose from, then one of them will usually fit the tempo of the music better than the other(s), especially with extreme tempos. This option is possible with both the foxtrot and the swing dance styles.

Success Goal = Make appropriate adjustments to the timing of your basic step patterns to best fit the tempo played___

Success Check
- Faster tempos require shorter or more stationary steps, or both___
- Faster tempos in the foxtrot may be altered to all slow rhythm steps___
- Slower tempos permit longer or additional traveling steps, or both___
- Slower tempos in the foxtrot may be altered to all quick rhythm steps___

To Increase Difficulty
- Adjust the timing of appropriate variations to also fit the tempo.
- Attend a variety of dances and be willing to learn from your mistakes.

To Decrease Difficulty
- In the foxtrot, if the tempo is too fast, select primarily six-count basic step variations to execute, such as the rock step in place or with quarter turns. The faster tempo may require more repetitions of any one variation to give both you and your partner time to react.
- In the swing, as you know, there are three basic step patterns to choose from based on the tempo of the music. If you have a tendency to do only one of these basic step patterns for all swing tempos, then now is the time to hone both your listening and execution skills to select the appropriate basic step pattern for the tempo, whether slow, moderate, or fast.

3. No Room to Travel in the LOD

Sometimes at weddings or other events that include dancing, you may be unable to travel in the LOD. Usually this occurs when the majority of the guests are unaware of the rules to follow on the dance floor. In Step 14, you practiced selecting the appropriate variation for the flow of traffic—either a stationary or a traveling variation. Another option in this situation is to execute additional variations that can be done without traveling in the LOD. Thus, several new nontraveling or stationary foxtrot and polka variations follow.

a. *Sway (slow dance) variation:* When the floor is very crowded, you might try a sway variation, which may be used when slow dancing. To execute the sway, the leader steps onto his left foot toward his left side, then rocks his weight onto his right foot toward his right foot. The follower does the reverse. Each side step is equivalent to a "slow," or two counts per weight change. Additional styling options include swaying or leaning in rhythm with your upper body in the direction of each side step or bringing your free foot beside the instep of your weight-bearing foot to briefly touch on counts 2 and 4.

Another nontraveling variation when slow dancing is to rotate either clockwise or counterclockwise while doing the sway variation. Just as you rotated with the basic swing step pattern, gradually turn your shoulders prior to each step in the intended direction. Take your time completing the turn. These are useful stationary variations to add to your repertoire.

b. *Jessie Polka (stationary variation):* When there is limited space to travel in the LOD, the Jessie Polka is a fun variation that can be done with a partner or with any three or more people. Line up in a single row (of two, three, or more people). Facing the LOD, stand side by side with your partner(s), hook inside elbows, and place outside hands on hips. Everyone starts with the left foot and executes the following actions:

Part A

Counts 1 and 2: Left heel dig forward and step in place (see figure 16.1, a and b)
Counts 3 and 4: Right toe touch backward and tap in place (see figure 16.1, c and d)
Counts 5 and 6: Right heel dig forward and step in place (see figure 16.1, e and f)
Counts 7 and 8: Left heel dig forward and cross in the air (see figure 16.1, g and h)

Counts 1, 2

a Left heel forward   b Together

Figure 16.1   Jessie Polka footwork positions for part A.

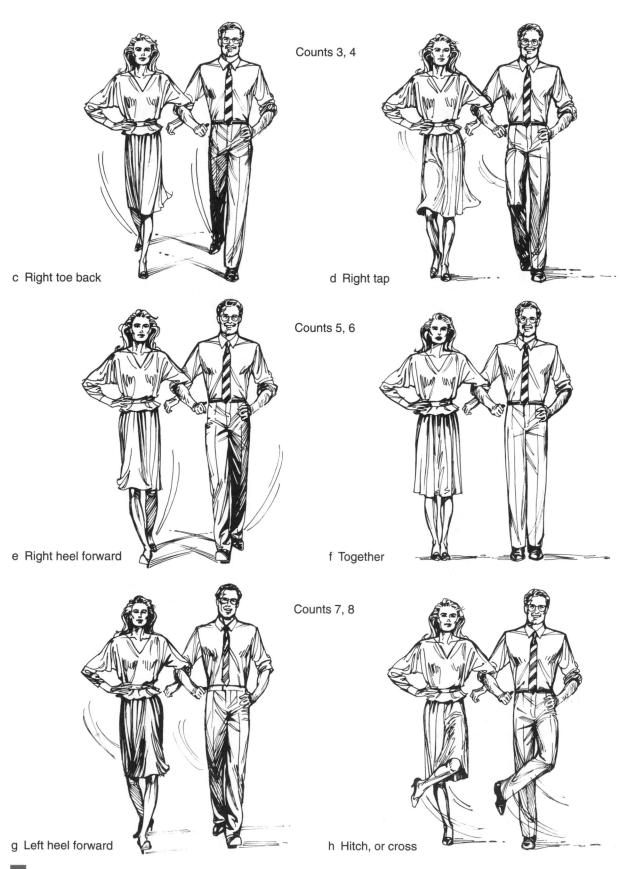

Counts 3, 4

c Right toe back

d Right tap

Counts 5, 6

e Right heel forward

f Together

Counts 7, 8

g Left heel forward

h Hitch, or cross

Figure 16.1 *(continued).*

Part B

Counts 1 to 8: Four polka basics (executed in place, as if marking time; or travel in the LOD, if space permits)

c. *Heel-and-toe polka:* If you have approximately 5 to 10 feet of space in which to move to either side, you might try a heel-and-toe variation with your partner. Start in a semi-open dance position with outside feet (leader's left, follower's right) and do the following: heel (see figure 16.2a), toe (see figure 16.2b), heel, toe, slide, slide, slide, and change weight to your outside foot on the fourth slide (eight counts). Then repeat to the opposite side (eight counts).

a   b

■ **Figure 16.2** Heel-and-toe polka positions.

Success Goal = Execute both foxtrot and polka nontraveling variations when appropriate both for the music and for the floor traffic encountered___

✔ Success Check
- Maintain a constant tempo that fits the tempo of the music played___
- Move in unison with your partner and the music___

To Increase Difficulty

a. Foxtrot or slow dance
- Experiment with the foxtrot's side rock and the side rock quarter turns during slow dances.
- Create a rhythm with the sway variation; for example, two slow sways, then four quick sways to each side (for a total of eight counts).

b. Polka
- In each row of the Jessie Polka, all lean backward approximately 45 degrees on the forward heel digs, then lean forward approximately 45 degrees on the backward toe touches.
- Another stationary option when in trios for the Jessie Polka is to hold hands throughout and to modify part B by adding another set of eight counts (for a total of 16 counts) as follows: For the first eight counts, the dancers in the center and on the right side lift their hands to form an arch for the dancer on the left side to walk under (the center person must follow under the arch to unwind). Repeat on the other side for the dancer on the right side to walk under the arch (again, the center person must follow under the arch to unwind).
- If you have an announcer, enough space to travel in the LOD, and willing participants, the Jessie Polka may be modified to be a mixer. At the end of either version of part B, the announcer may call out one of three people to move forward to join the next row; for example, center person, left side person, or right side person (group more than three people together to represent a center and left and right sides). The mixer option adds eight counts to part B.

To Decrease Difficulty

- Execute your steps in place.

4. Creating a Demonstration Routine

When performing in front of an audience, it is important to consider the impact of the music, the costumes (colors), and the choreography (at minimum, you'll need a strong introduction and ending). Experiment with the following challenge situation, and decide what works best for you and your partner.

Challenge

a. Consider the audience appeal of your music selection. Then decide on a specific beginning that fits the music.

b. Decide on a middle that fits the music. You might consider two different approaches to creating combinations appropriate for a demonstration routine. Some dancers prefer to plan a set sequence that never varies. Other dancers prefer to cluster some favorite combinations, vary the order of the clustered combinations with basics, and use transitions between each cluster. The latter approach introduces the element of surprise, because both dancers have to be ready for any possible combination.

c. Decide on an ending that fits the music. If the music trails off, then let your movements trail off or wind down (perhaps as you exit the floor or as you move slowly into a pose). If the music has a definite ending, make your ending obvious by holding your final pose at least two to five seconds or by somehow bringing your dance to a conclusion (e.g., with a bow).

Sample Solution

a. Select cha-cha music that is motivating for you, your partner, and your audience. Stand apart from your partner in a pose (perhaps with hands on hips and one shoulder forward). Select arm and body movements that reflect the quality of the music (e.g., sustained, staccato, percussive). Mirror your partner as follows: sharply turn only your head (and/or extend an arm) to one side either on the downbeat or on an accent in the music. Repeat to the other side.

   Touch one foot to the side, then step cross your other foot (or you might syncopate these side touch and cross steps). Repeat with the opposite foot. Continue your jazzy touch and cross moves until you meet your partner (ideally keeping your introduction in sets of eight counts).

b. Start your cha-cha basic step pattern in shine position and do your favorite variations that best fit the music. Remember to relate to your partner as much as you can with arm, head, and eye movements.

c. End with a spin into a dip, or use a corté for a final pose, if there is a strong note ending the music. For other ideas on ending poses, consider using different levels (with one partner lower than the other). Another alternative is to contrast different tempos at the end, especially if the music fades out (in which case it is effective to move from fast to slow turns or arm movements—as if winding down).

In addition, two sample solutions for a foxtrot demonstration routine follow:

a. If you have trouble getting your routine started, experiment with using a theme to give you inspiration and help you remember what comes next. For example, one of my students imagined himself as Fred Astaire walking casually down the street, tipping his hat to his dance partner, inviting her to dance, sharing her company (spinning, rotating), and thanking her for the dance.

b. Alternatively, the leader might start apart from his partner and extend his left hand for her grasp. Then he would extend his right hand to connect with his partner, and both would assume a closed position in time to start doing the foxtrot basic step pattern together. The partners would move in the LOD to execute selected variations and combinations. To end the routine, the leader might release his right hand, spin the follower, then both would move apart to bow with free arms extended.

Success Goal = Create and present to an audience a demonstration routine that has a definite beginning, middle, and ending that appropriately matches the music___

Success Check

• If you have strong memorization skills, consider creating a set routine that is preplanned___
• If you are able to react spontaneously, consider creating clusters of different combinations that can be put in any order and bridged using a random number of repetitions of appropriate basics and transitions___

To Increase Difficulty

• Create a demonstration routine for a variety of dance styles.

To Decrease Difficulty

• Start with short routines, perhaps no longer than a minute and a half in length.
• Practice only one dance style at a time.

DANCE OPTIONS SUCCESS SUMMARY

Whenever you get the opportunity to go to a dance, take advantage of it. Go to as many dances as you can and practice your social dancing skills. Accept the fact that it is normal for mistakes to occur on the dance floor. Even advanced dancers make mistakes, but they cover them so well that most people do not notice anything went wrong. So try to learn from your mistakes, including how not to "telegraph" or make them stand out. Try to do at least one thing better each time you dance. Remember to demonstrate good partner and floor etiquette, including thanking your host(s) for the evening. Social dancing is more than just executing dance steps. Have fun and enjoy your journey—it can last a lifetime!

Rating Your Progress

Y ou have covered a lot of material in this book. In particular, you have explored rhythm and timing elements, and you have learned basic steps, how to communicate with your partner verbally and nonverbally, and how to use your new dance skills in various situations. Take time to evaluate your progress by completing the following charts.

Technique and Execution

	Very good	Good	Fair	Poor
1. Move with good posture	❏	❏	❏	❏
2. Center weight over base of support	❏	❏	❏	❏
3. Position arms to create a frame	❏	❏	❏	❏
4. Hear and walk to an underlying beat	❏	❏	❏	❏
5. Signal leads prior to the downbeat	❏	❏	❏	❏
6. Practice and demonstrate proper etiquette	❏	❏	❏	❏
7. Execute the basic step patterns to music without a partner, then move in unison with a partner to music	❏	❏	❏	❏
8. Make smooth transitions between the appropriate partner dance positions per dance style	❏	❏	❏	❏
9. Execute and combine appropriate variations per dance style	❏	❏	❏	❏
10. Select variations to best fit the floor traffic and other situations encountered on the dance floor	❏	❏	❏	❏
11. Add appropriate style per dance style	❏	❏	❏	❏
12. Dance with fluidity and confidence per dance style	❏	❏	❏	❏

Overall Success

In general, how do you feel about your overall progress at this point?

_____Very successful

_____Somewhat successful

_____Fairly successful

_____Unsuccessful

Now look over all of your previous ratings and identify not only your strong points, but also those points that may need a little more practice. Place a star beside your three strongest points, and circle your three weakest points. Decide how you can improve any weak areas. Start by reviewing the appropriate section(s) in this book. Then, go out and dance!

GLOSSARY

accents—Selected beat(s) within a measure of music that are emphasized, or made to stand out, e.g., are stronger.

alignment—Correct body posture while standing stationary. From a side view, visualize an imaginary plumb line aligning with the ear, shoulder, hips, knees, and ankles.

ball-change—Two weight changes in a backward, then forward direction. Step onto only the ball of one foot (leader's left foot and follower's right foot), then replace (step onto the other foot while keeping it in the same location (leader's right foot and follower's left foot).

ballroom dance—A partner dance typically done in a ballroom.

broken rhythm—A combination of slow and/or quick beats that takes more than one measure, such as the swing basic step pattern (which takes one and a half measures, or six-counts).

basic step pattern—The traditional footwork utilizing a recurring rhythmic pattern that is associated with a particular dance style.

centering—Keeping your body's weight above your base of support. The exact center of your body weight is sometimes called the "center of gravity," or the "center point of balance" (CPB). Both terms refer to a three-dimensional point near the center of your body (however, the CPB is a bit higher, just below your ribcage).

carriage—Correct alignment of body parts while moving.

close—To bring the free foot beside the supporting foot without a weight transfer onto that foot.

clockwise (CW)—A right turn, or direction.

closed position—A partner dance position with right sides facing and with the following points of contact: leader's left (and follower's right) hand; leader's right hand on follower's left shoulder blade; leader's right (and follower's left) elbow, and the follower's left hand on the leader's right upper arm.

contra-body positioning (CBP)—Using the position of your shoulders to create torque to facilitate turns and spins, such that the opposite shoulder rotates in the direction of the turn. For example, the right shoulder rotates counterclockwise on left turns, while the left shoulder rotates clockwise on right turns.

counterclockwise (CCW)—A left turn, or direction.

downbeat—The first count of any measure.

even rhythm—Steady, or consistent steps, or weight changes, each getting an equal time value.

frame—The curved position that arms are held in relative to your own body when in a partner dance position.

free foot—The foot without any weight on it, or not touching the floor.

inside foot—The foot closest to your partner.

inside-hands joined—A partner dance position with the leader on the left side and the follower on the right side and his right hand holding her left hand or vice versa.

leading foot—The foot in front, or ahead of, the other foot.

line of dance (LOD)—An imaginary line that refers to the flow of traffic, which is counterclockwise around the perimeter of the room.

locomotor movements—Actions that transport you from one location to another, such as walk, run, leap, jump, hop, skip, gallop, slide, and so forth.

measure—The number of beats grouped together according to the time signature.

outside foot—The foot farthest away from your partner.

phrase—Two or more measures grouped together.

progressive dance—A dance that travels in the LOD, such as the waltz, foxtrot, or polka.

promenade, or semiopen position—A variation of the closed partner dance position with a 45-degree hip rotation towards the extended hands and arms.

quick—The rhythmic length of a step, or weight change. It is usually one count, or beat, but not always. Basically, it is relative to the slow rhythmic cue.

reverse line of dance (RLOD)—An imaginary line that refers to the flow of traffic, which is clockwise around the perimeter of the room.

rhythmic pattern—A recurring series of counts and/or actions.

replace—After lifting one foot, put it down in the same location, or place, and transfer weight onto that foot.

shine position—A partner dance position that is facing, yet partners are standing apart without touching and shoulders parallel.

slow—The rhythmic length of a step, or weight change. It is usually one weight change within two beats, but it can be slower relative to other beats. This is also called single-time rhythm.

social dance—A partner dance done for recreational purposes.

spot dance—A dance done within a small area on the floor (as opposed to traveling in the LOD).

spotting—A focusing technique used to facilitate turn execution by keeping your eyes focused on one point, or spot, throughout the turn and by isolating your head and shoulders.

step—A transfer of weight from one foot to the other.

starting foot—Typically, the leader starts with the left foot, while the follower starts with the right foot.

supporting foot—The foot with weight on it.

sweetheart position—A side-by-side partner dance position with the leader on the left side and the follower on the right side. The follower's hands are placed palms-out in front of her shoulders. The leader's fingers lightly connect with the follower's fingers.

tempo—The speed of the music.

time signature—The number and duration of beats in a measure.

together—To bring the free foot beside the supporting foot and transfer weight onto it.

trailing foot—The foot behind, or following, the other foot.

triple step—Three steps, or weight changes, taken within two beats of music (an example of uneven rhythm and of a syncopation).

underlying beat—The number of beats per measure, usually apparent in the drumbeat in the music.

uneven rhythm—A combination of both whole and half steps or counts (i.e., slow and quick beats) in a recurring pattern without an equal time value to each step, or weight change.

upbeat—The second and fourth beat within a four-beat measure.

About the Author

Judy Patterson Wright, PhD, is an accomplished dancer who has taught social dance at the junior high, high school, and college levels since 1971. Dr. Wright's dance experience includes a wide variety of styles: ballroom and social dance, tap dance, jazz, modern dance, ballet, folk dance, square dance, country western dance, line dance, and aerobic dancercise.

She has been recognized as one of the Outstanding Young Women of America (1982) and repeatedly as an Excellent Teacher at the University of Illinois at Urbana-Champaign. She has judged and competed in dance competitions, and she specializes in progressive teaching workshops both for social and competitive dancers. Judy and her husband, Sam, placed second overall in the Silver Advanced Showcase Division at the World finals in 1996 and 1997. They are the 1997 World Silver Advanced Showcase Cha-Cha Champions.

Dr. Wright, currently an acquisitions editor, is the creator of the format for the Steps to Success Activity Series. This series evolved out of her dissertation research on the stages that learners go through when learning sequential movements and how the teacher can facilitate the learning process. She is the author of the companion title *Social Dance Instruction: Steps to Success*, which highlights the instructor's steps to successful class teaching. She resides in Mahomet, Illinois.